# REAL

# 진짜 영어 실력을 위한 초등 VOCA 800

# ENGLISH

정승익 지음

NEVER
GIVE UP

KB027636

# EBS영어강사가

## 초등 아들딸을 직접 가르치기 위해서 만든 영단어 교재

### 1. 교육부 선정 초등 필수 영단어 800개를 수록

- 교육부에서 선정한 초등학생이라면 알아야 할 영단어 800개를 빠짐없이 수록

### 2. 듣기, 읽기, 말하기, 쓰기를 이용한 암기 방식

- 단어, 표현을 듣는 1단계
- 단어가 활용된 문장을 읽는 2단계
- 단어가 활용된 대화문을 말해보는 3단계
- 단어가 활용된 일기를 읽고 써보는 4단계

### 3. 초등 고학년, 영단어로 승부하라

- 영어에 어려움을 느끼는 초등 고학년이라면 영단어를 챙기자.
- 초등 고학년에서 800개의 단어를 제대로 공부하면 역전은 언제나 가능하다.
- 영단어 암기를 시작으로 진짜 영어 공부를 시작하자.

# STUDY PLANNER

단어를 외우기 위한 계획을 세우는 단계입니다. 각각의 DAY를 언제 공부할지 기록하세요. DAY 1 2024. 07. 01. 이런 식으로 연도, 월, 일을 기록하세요.

| | |
|---|---|
| DAY 1 | DAY 2 |
| . . . | . . . |
| DAY 3 | DAY 4 |
| . . . | . . . |
| DAY 5 | DAY 6 |
| . . . | . . . |
| DAY 7 | DAY 8 |
| . . . | . . . |
| DAY 9 | DAY 10 |
| . . . | . . . |
| DAY 11 | DAY 12 |
| . . . | . . . |
| DAY 13 | DAY 14 |
| . . . | . . . |
| DAY 15 | DAY 16 |
| . . . | . . . |

# STUDY PLANNER

DAY 17

DAY 18

DAY 19

DAY 20

DAY 21

DAY 22

DAY 23

DAY 24

DAY 25

DAY 26

DAY 27

DAY 28

DAY 29

DAY 30

DAY 31

DAY 32

# STUDY PLANNER

| | |
|---|---|
| DAY 33 | DAY 34 |
| . . . | . . . |
| DAY 35 | DAY 36 |
| . . . | . . . |
| DAY 37 | DAY 38 |
| . . . | . . . |
| DAY 39 | DAY 40 |
| . . . | . . . |
| DAY 41 | DAY 42 |
| . . . | . . . |
| DAY 43 | DAY 44 |
| . . . | . . . |
| DAY 45 | DAY 46 |
| . . . | . . . |
| DAY 47 | DAY 48 |
| . . . | . . . |

# STUDY PLANNER

DAY 49

DAY 50

DAY 51

DAY 52

DAY 53

DAY 54

DAY 55

DAY 56

DAY 57

DAY 58

DAY 59

DAY 60

DAY 61

DAY 62

DAY 63

DAY 64

# STUDY PLANNER

DAY 65

. . .

DAY 66

. . .

DAY 67

. . .

DAY 68

. . .

DAY 69

. . .

DAY 70

. . .

DAY 71

. . .

DAY 72

. . .

DAY 73

. . .

DAY 74

. . .

DAY 75

. . .

DAY 76

. . .

DAY 77

. . .

DAY 78

. . .

DAY 79

. . .

DAY 80

. . .

# STUDY PLANNER

DAY 81

DAY 82

DAY 83

DAY 84

DAY 85

DAY 86

DAY 87

DAY 88

DAY 89

DAY 90

DAY 91

DAY 92

DAY 93

DAY 94

DAY 95

DAY 96

# STUDY PLANNER

DAY 97

. . .

DAY 99

. . .

DAY 101

. . .

DAY 103

. . .

DAY 105

. . .

DAY 107

. . .

DAY 109

. . .

DAY 111

. . .

DAY 98

. . .

DAY 100

. . .

DAY 102

. . .

DAY 104

. . .

DAY 106

. . .

DAY 108

. . .

DAY 110

. . .

DAY 112

. . .

# STUDY PLANNER

DAY 113

DAY 114

DAY 115

DAY 116

DAY 117

DAY 118

DAY 119

DAY 120

DAY 121

DAY 122

DAY 123

DAY 124

DAY 125

DAY 126

DAY 127

DAY 128

# STUDY PLANNER

| | |
|---|---|
| DAY 129 | DAY 130 |
| . . . | . . . |
| DAY 131 | DAY 132 |
| . . . | . . . |
| DAY 133 | DAY 134 |
| . . . | . . . |
| DAY 135 | DAY 136 |
| . . . | . . . |
| DAY 137 | DAY 138 |
| . . . | . . . |
| DAY 139 | DAY 140 |
| . . . | . . . |
| DAY 141 | DAY 142 |
| . . . | . . . |
| DAY 143 | DAY 144 |
| . . . | . . . |

# STUDY PLANNER

DAY 145

DAY 146

DAY 147

DAY 148

DAY 149

DAY 150

DAY 151

DAY 152

DAY 153

DAY 154

DAY 155

DAY 156

DAY 157

DAY 158

DAY 159

DAY 160

DATE . . . .

DAY 1

**Step1** 단어를 익히세요.

| heat | go | different | glass | catch |
|---|---|---|---|---|
| 열 | 가다 | 다른 | 유리 | 잡다 |

**Step2** 단어가 사용된 문장을 해석해 보세요.

The heat is very strong today. ____________________

Let's go to the park. ____________________

This dress is different from mine. ____________________

The glass broke into pieces. ____________________

Can you catch the ball? ____________________

**Step3** 다음 대화를 말해 보세요.

A: The heat is very strong today.
B: Yes, it is. Where should we go?
A: Let's go to a different place today.
B: Okay. How about the park with the glass house?
A: That sounds good. Can we catch the bus from here?
B: Yes, if we hurry, we can catch it.

**Challenge** 오늘 배운 단어가 활용된 영어 일기를 해석한 후, 따라서 써 보세요.

It was very hot, so I went to a different room. I saw a glass of water and caught it. Drinking the water made me feel better.

<따라 쓰기>

____________________

____________________

**QUIZ** 오늘 배운 단어로 빈칸을 채워 문장을 완성하세요.

The ____________ is very strong today.

Let's ____________ to the park.

This dress is ____________ from mine.

The ____________ broke into pieces.

Can you ____________ the ball?

DATE . . . .

DAY 2

**Step1** **단어를 익히세요.**

| down | north | joy | bread | giant |
|---|---|---|---|---|
| 아래로 | 북쪽 | 기쁨 | 빵 | 거인, 거대한 |

**Step2** **단어가 사용된 문장을 해석해 보세요.**

The cat is climbing down the tree. ________________

We are traveling north for the vacation. ________________

She felt a great joy. ________________

I bought some fresh bread. ________________

The giant tower is very tall. ________________

**Step3** **다음 대화를 말해 보세요.**

A: Look down there! What is that?

B: It looks like a giant statue.

A: Wow, it's so big. Let's go north to see it.

B: Sure. We can bring some bread for a picnic.

A: Yes, that would be a joy!

B: I'm excited. Let's go now!

**Challenge** **오늘 배운 단어가 활용된 영어 일기를 해석한 후, 따라서 써 보세요.**

Today, I went north. I felt joy when I bought a giant bread. I walked down the street to go home.

<따라 쓰기>

________________

________________

**QUIZ** **오늘 배운 단어로 빈칸을 채워 문장을 완성하세요.**

The cat is climbing ________________ the tree.

We are traveling ________________ for the vacation.

She felt a great ________________.

I bought some fresh ________________.

The ________________ tower is very tall.

DATE . . . .

DAY 3

**Step1** 단어를 익히세요.

| guide | happy | water | puppy | bottom |
|---|---|---|---|---|
| 가이드, 안내하다 | 행복한 | 물 | 강아지 | 바닥 |

**Step2** 단어가 사용된 문장을 해석해 보세요.

A guide showed us the way to the hospital. ____________________

She is always happy in the morning. ____________________

Drink a lot of water every day. ____________________

The puppy is very cute. ____________________

There is a treasure at the bottom of the sea. ____________________

**Step3** 다음 대화를 말해 보세요.

A: Look at that puppy by the water!

B: It's so cute! It's playing at the bottom of the hill.

A: Do you want to go see it? I can guide you there.

B: Yes, I would be happy to see the puppy up close.

A: Let's go! It will be a happy day.

B: I agree. Let's go now!

**Challenge** 오늘 배운 단어가 활용된 영어 일기를 해석한 후, 따라서 써 보세요.

I guided my puppy to the park, and we played near the water. The puppy was very happy as it splashed around. Seeing my puppy's joy made me feel happy, too.

<따라 쓰기>

____________________

____________________

**QUIZ** 오늘 배운 단어로 빈칸을 채워 문장을 완성하세요.

The tour ____________ was very helpful.

She is always ____________ in the morning.

Drink a lot of ____________ every day.

The ____________ is very cute.

There is a treasure at the ____________ of the sea.

DATE . . . .

DAY 4

**Step1** 단어를 익히세요.

| fat | worry | taste | listen | fool |
|---|---|---|---|---|
| 뚱뚱한 | 걱정하다 | 맛보다 | 듣다 | 바보 |

**Step2** 단어가 사용된 문장을 해석해 보세요.

The cat is a bit fat. ✎ ______

Don't worry about the test. ✎ ______

Can I taste your cake? ✎ ______

Listen to the music. ✎ ______

He acted like a fool. ✎ ______

**Step3** 다음 대화를 말해 보세요.

A: Do you think this dog is fat?

B: No, don't worry about it.

A: Have you tasted this cookie?

B: Yes, I did. It tastes delicious!

A: Let's listen to some music while we eat.

B: Great idea! We don't want to look like fools just by sitting here.

**Challenge** 오늘 배운 단어가 활용된 영어 일기를 해석한 후, 따라서 써 보세요.

I tasted the new dish and didn't worry about getting fat. My friend called me a fool, but I listened and enjoyed the meal. The taste made me very happy.

<따라 쓰기>

______

______

**QUIZ** 오늘 배운 단어로 빈칸을 채워 문장을 완성하세요.

The cat is a bit ______.

Don't ______ about the test.

Can I ______ your cake?

______ to the music.

He acted like a ______.

DATE . . . .

DAY 5

## Step1 단어를 익히세요.

| big | sound | football | already | hurry |
| --- | --- | --- | --- | --- |
| 큰 | 소리 | 축구 | 이미 | 서두르다 |

## Step2 단어가 사용된 문장을 해석해 보세요.

That is a big house. ______________________

I heard a strange sound. ______________________

We play football every weekend. ______________________

She has already left. ______________________

Hurry up, we are late! ______________________

## Step3 다음 대화를 말해 보세요.

A: Did you hear that loud sound?

B: Yes, I did. What was it?

A: It was from the football game.

B: Oh, I see. The big game has already started?

A: Yes, it started a few minutes ago.

B: Let's hurry! We don't want to miss it.

## Challenge 오늘 배운 단어가 활용된 영어 일기를 해석한 후, 따라서 써 보세요.

I heard a big sound from the stadium and hurried over. The football game had already started. The cheers from the crowd were very exciting.

<따라 쓰기>

______________________

______________________

## QUIZ 오늘 배운 단어로 빈칸을 채워 문장을 완성하세요.

That is a ____________ house.

I heard a strange ____________.

We play ____________ every weekend.

She has ____________ left.

____________ up, we are late!

DATE . . . .

DAY 6

## Step1 단어를 익히세요.

| hope | the | say | head | lady |
|---|---|---|---|---|
| 희망하다 | 그 | 말하다 | 머리 | 숙녀 |

## Step2 단어가 사용된 문장을 해석해 보세요.

I hope you feel better soon. ______

The cat is sleeping. ______

What did you say? ______

He hurt his head. ______

The lady is very kind. ______

## Step3 다음 대화를 말해 보세요.

A: I hope the lady is okay.
B: What happened to her?
A: She hit her head.
B: Oh no! What did the doctor say?
A: The doctor said she will be fine.
B: That's good to hear. I hope she recovers soon.

## Challenge 오늘 배운 단어가 활용된 영어 일기를 해석한 후, 따라서 써 보세요.

I hope I did well on the test today. The teacher said I was very focused. A nice lady patted my head and said I did a great job.

<따라 쓰기>

______

______

## QUIZ 오늘 배운 단어로 빈칸을 채워 문장을 완성하세요.

I ______ you feel better soon.

______ cat is sleeping.

What did you ______?

He hurt his ______.

The ______ is very kind.

DATE . . . .

DAY 7

## Step1 단어를 익히세요.

| design | run | collect | handsome | I |
|---|---|---|---|---|
| 디자인 | 달리다 | 수집하다 | 잘생긴 | 나 |

## Step2 단어가 사용된 문장을 해석해 보세요.

She likes to design clothes. ______________________

We run every morning. ______________________

He collects stamps. ______________________

He is very handsome. ______________________

I am happy today. ______________________

## Step3 다음 대화를 말해 보세요.

A: Did you design this poster?
B: Yes, I did. Do you like it?
A: It's very nice! By the way, do you like to run?
B: Yes, I run every morning. What about you?
A: I collect stamps. It's my hobby.
B: That's interesting. You're also very handsome, by the way.
A: Thank you! I appreciate that.

## Challenge 오늘 배운 단어가 활용된 영어 일기를 해석한 후, 따라서 써 보세요.

I designed a new poster and then went for a run. On the way, I collected some beautiful flowers. A handsome man smiled at me, and I felt happy.

<따라 쓰기>

______________________

______________________

## QUIZ 오늘 배운 단어로 빈칸을 채워 문장을 완성하세요.

She likes to ______________ clothes.

We ______________ every morning.

He ______________ stamps.

He is very ______________.

______________ am happy today.

DATE . . . .

DAY 8

## Step1 단어를 익히세요.

| gate | sorry | basic | cost | print |
|---|---|---|---|---|
| 문 | 미안한 | 기본적인 | 비용 | 인쇄하다 |

## Step2 단어가 사용된 문장을 해석해 보세요.

The gate is open. ______________________

I am sorry for being late. ______________________

This is a basic recipe. ______________________

What is the cost of this book? ______________________

Can you print this document? ______________________

## Step3 다음 대화를 말해 보세요.

A: Can you open the gate for me?

B: Sure, no problem. Here you go.

A: Thank you! I'm sorry for asking.

B: It's okay. It's a basic thing to do.

A: By the way, do you know the cost to print this document?

B: Yes, it's very cheap. Don't worry about it.

## Challenge 오늘 배운 단어가 활용된 영어 일기를 해석한 후, 따라서 써 보세요.

I printed a basic flyer about the event and posted it on the gate. Someone pointed out a mistake, and I felt sorry. I promised to reprint it despite the extra cost.

<따라 쓰기>

______________________

______________________

## QUIZ 오늘 배운 단어로 빈칸을 채워 문장을 완성하세요.

The ______________ is open.

I am ______________ for being late.

This is a ______________ recipe.

What is the ______________ of this book?

Can you ______________ this document?

DATE . . . .

DAY 9

**Step1** 단어를 익히세요.

| forget | under | cap | check | horse |
| --- | --- | --- | --- | --- |
| 잊다 | 아래에 | 모자 | 확인하다 | 말 |

**Step2** 단어가 사용된 문장을 해석해 보세요.

Don't forget your homework. ______________________

The cat is under the table. ______________________

He wore a red cap. ______________________

Can you check my answer? ______________________

The horse is very fast. ______________________

**Step3** 다음 대화를 말해 보세요.

A: Did you forget your cap?
B: Oh no, I think I did. It must be under the table.
A: Let me check for you.
B: Thanks. By the way, did you see the horse in the field?
A: Yes, I did. It's a beautiful horse.
B: I agree. Let's go see it after you find my cap.
A: Sure, I'll find it quickly.

**Challenge** 오늘 배운 단어가 활용된 영어 일기를 해석한 후, 따라서 써 보세요.

I forgot my cap under the tree and went to check on my horse. The horse was fine, but I still needed to find my cap. Eventually, I found it and put it on.

<따라 쓰기>

______________________

______________________

**QUIZ** 오늘 배운 단어로 빈칸을 채워 문장을 완성하세요.

Don't ______________ your homework.

The cat is ______________ the table.

He wore a red ______________.

Can you ______________ my answer?

The ______________ is very fast.

DATE . . . .

DAY 10

**Step1** **단어를 익히세요.**

| future | death | rich | customer | ago |
|---|---|---|---|---|
| 미래 | 죽음 | 부유한 | 고객 | 전에 |

**Step2** **단어가 사용된 문장을 해석해 보세요.**

The future looks bright. ______________________

The death of the hero was sad. ______________________

He is very rich. ______________________

The customer is always right. ______________________

I met him two years ago. ______________________

**Step3** **다음 대화를 말해 보세요.**

A: What do you think about the future?
B: The future looks bright.
A: Did you hear about the hero's death?
B: Yes, it was very sad.
A: He was very rich, you know.
B: Really? I didn't know that.

**Challenge** **오늘 배운 단어가 활용된 영어 일기를 해석한 후, 따라서 써 보세요.**

I want to be rich in the future and have many customers. I learned about someone who died a long time ago in history class. It was fun to see how they changed the future.

<따라 쓰기>

______________________

______________________

**QUIZ** **오늘 배운 단어로 빈칸을 채워 문장을 완성하세요.**

The ____________ looks bright.

The ____________ of the hero was sad.

He is very ____________.

The ____________ is always right.

I met him two years ____________.

DATE . . . .

DAY 11

## Step1 단어를 익히세요.

| honey | triangle | P.M. | understand | cold |
|---|---|---|---|---|
| 꿀 | 삼각형 | 오후 | 이해하다 | 추운 |

## Step2 단어가 사용된 문장을 해석해 보세요.

Bees make honey. ______________________________

A triangle has three sides. ______________________________

The meeting is at 2 P.M. ______________________________

I understand what you mean. ______________________________

It's very cold outside. ______________________________

## Step3 다음 대화를 말해 보세요.

A: Do you like honey in your tea?
B: Yes, especially when it's cold.
A: Did you learn about the triangle?
B: Yes, I did it in math class at 3 P.M.
A: Did you understand its meaning?
B: Not really, it was a bit confusing.

## Challenge 오늘 배운 단어가 활용된 영어 일기를 해석한 후, 따라서 써 보세요.

In the cold afternoon, I enjoyed some honey. I looked at a triangle puzzle and tried to understand it. By 3 P.M., I finally figured it out and felt accomplished.

<따라 쓰기>

______________________________

______________________________

## QUIZ 오늘 배운 단어로 빈칸을 채워 문장을 완성하세요.

Bees make ____________________.

A ____________________ has three sides.

The meeting is at 2 ____________________.

I ____________________ what you mean.

It's very ____________________ outside.

DATE . . . .

DAY 12

**Step1** 단어를 익히세요.

| often | umbrella | guy | copy | pink |
|---|---|---|---|---|
| 자주 | 우산 | 남자 | 복사하다 | 분홍색 |

**Step2** 단어가 사용된 문장을 해석해 보세요.

I often go to the park. ____________________

Don't forget your umbrella. ____________________

That guy is my friend. ____________________

Can you copy this paper for me? ____________________

She wore a pink dress. ____________________

**Step3** 다음 대화를 말해 보세요.

A: Do you often need an umbrella?
B: Yes, especially in this weather.
A: Did you see the guy with the pink umbrella?
B: Yes, he stood out a lot.
A: He was trying to copy my style, I think.
B: Really? That's funny!

**Challenge** 오늘 배운 단어가 활용된 영어 일기를 해석한 후, 따라서 써 보세요.

I often see a guy with a pink umbrella. He uses it to stand out in the crowd. One day, I decided to copy his idea and bought a bright pink umbrella too.

<따라 쓰기>

____________________

____________________

**QUIZ** 오늘 배운 단어로 빈칸을 채워 문장을 완성하세요.

I ____________ go to the park.

Don't forget your ____________.

That ____________ is my friend.

Can you ____________ this paper for me?

She wore a ____________ dress.

DATE . . . .

DAY 13

**Step1** 단어를 익히세요.

| zoo | noon | boy | daughter | wood |
|---|---|---|---|---|
| 동물원 | 정오 | 소년 | 딸 | 나무 |

**Step2** 단어가 사용된 문장을 해석해 보세요.

We went to the zoo yesterday. ✎ ______________________________

Let's meet at noon. ✎ ______________________________

The boy is playing soccer. ✎ ______________________________

My daughter loves to read. ✎ ______________________________

The chair is made of wood. ✎ ______________________________

**Step3** 다음 대화를 말해 보세요.

A: Are we going to the zoo today?
B: Yes, let's go at noon.
A: Did you meet the boy at the park?
B: Yes, I did. Tom's daughter was playing nearby.
A: They were playing near the wood.
B: It looked like they were having so much fun.

**Challenge** 오늘 배운 단어가 활용된 영어 일기를 해석한 후, 따라서 써 보세요.

I went to the zoo at noon with my family. A boy was showing his daughter a big animal made of wood. We had so much fun looking at all the animals.

<따라 쓰기>

______________________________

______________________________

**QUIZ** 오늘 배운 단어로 빈칸을 채워 문장을 완성하세요.

We went to the ____________ yesterday.

Let's meet at ____________.

The ____________ is playing soccer.

My ____________ loves to read.

The chair is made of ____________.

DATE . . . .

DAY 14

## Step1 단어를 익히세요.

| feel | open | sale | garden | rainbow |
|---|---|---|---|---|
| 느끼다 | 열다 | 판매 | 정원 | 무지개 |

## Step2 단어가 사용된 문장을 해석해 보세요.

I feel happy today. ______________________

Can you open the door? ______________________

It's not for sale. ______________________

The garden is full of flowers. ______________________

Look at the beautiful rainbow. ______________________

## Step3 다음 대화를 말해 보세요.

A: How do you feel today?
B: I feel great! The garden is open now.
A: I heard there is a sale on plants.
B: Yes, I bought some flowers.
A: Did you see the rainbow over the garden?
B: Yes, it was beautiful!

## Challenge 오늘 배운 단어가 활용된 영어 일기를 해석한 후, 따라서 써 보세요.

I felt happy when I saw a rainbow in the garden. I decided to open a small sale stand there. Many people came to buy items, enjoying the colorful view.

<따라 쓰기>

______________________

______________________

## QUIZ 오늘 배운 단어로 빈칸을 채워 문장을 완성하세요.

I ______________ happy today.

Can you ______________ the door?

There is a ______________ at the store.

The ______________ is full of flowers.

Look at the beautiful ______________.

DATE . . . .

DAY 15

**Step1** 단어를 익히세요.

| police | up | what | gold | fantastic |
|---|---|---|---|---|
| 경찰 | 위로 | 무엇 | 금 | 환상적인 |

**Step2** 단어가 사용된 문장을 해석해 보세요.

The police are here to help. ______________________

Look up at the sky. ______________________

What are you doing? ______________________

She wore a gold necklace. ______________________

The movie was fantastic. ______________________

**Step3** 다음 대화를 말해 보세요.

A: Did you see the police car?
B: Yes, it went up the hill.
A: What did they find?
B: I heard they found gold there.
A: Really? That's fantastic!
B: Yes, it's all over the news.

**Challenge** 오늘 배운 단어가 활용된 영어 일기를 해석한 후, 따라서 써 보세요.

I saw a police car drive up the street today. The officer asked us, "What are you doing?" and showed us his gold badge. It was fantastic!

<따라 쓰기>

______________________

______________________

**QUIZ** 오늘 배운 단어로 빈칸을 채워 문장을 완성하세요.

The ______________ are here to help.

Look ______________ at the sky.

______________ are you doing?

She wore a ______________ necklace.

The movie was ______________.

DATE . . . .

DAY 16

## Step1 단어를 익히세요.

| turn | finish | college | hard | afternoon |
|---|---|---|---|---|
| 돌다 | 끝내다 | 대학 | 어려운 | 오후 |

## Step2 단어가 사용된 문장을 해석해 보세요.

Turn left at the corner. ____________________

I need to finish my homework. ____________________

She goes to college. ____________________

This problem is very hard. ____________________

Let's meet in the afternoon. ____________________

## Step3 다음 대화를 말해 보세요.

A: Did you finish your work?

B: Yes, I finished it this afternoon.

A: How was college today?

B: It was hard, but I managed.

A: Can you turn fast?

B: Sure, I can.

## Challenge 오늘 배운 단어가 활용된 영어 일기를 해석한 후, 따라서 써 보세요.

I turned in my homework and finished my tasks. My brother in college says it's hard work. In the afternoon, I played outside.

<따라 쓰기>

____________________

____________________

## QUIZ 오늘 배운 단어로 빈칸을 채워 문장을 완성하세요.

__________ left at the corner.

I need to __________ my homework.

She goes to __________.

This problem is very __________.

Let's meet in the __________.

DATE . . . .

DAY 17

## Step1 단어를 익히세요.

| blood | today | nature | friend | candy |
|---|---|---|---|---|
| 피 | 오늘 | 자연 | 친구 | 사탕 |

## Step2 단어가 사용된 문장을 해석해 보세요.

Blood is red. ____________________

What are you doing today? ____________________

I love spending time in nature. ____________________

He is my best friend. ____________________

I like to eat candy. ____________________

## Step3 다음 대화를 말해 보세요.

A: Did you see the blood on my knee?

B: Yes, what happened?

A: I fell while hiking today.

B: Oh no! Nature can be tough sometimes.

A: My friend gave me some candy to make me feel better.

B: That's nice of your friend.

## Challenge 오늘 배운 단어가 활용된 영어 일기를 해석한 후, 따라서 써 보세요.

Today, I learned about blood in science class. My friend and I talked about how amazing nature is. After school, we shared some candy.

<따라 쓰기>

____________________

____________________

## QUIZ 오늘 배운 단어로 빈칸을 채워 문장을 완성하세요.

____________ is red.

What are you doing ____________?

I love spending time in ____________.

He is my best ____________.

I like to eat ____________.

DATE . . . .

DAY 18

**Step1** 단어를 익히세요.

| chair | where | help | queen | A.M. |
| --- | --- | --- | --- | --- |
| 의자 | 어디 | 도움 | 여왕 | 오전 |

**Step2** 단어가 사용된 문장을 해석해 보세요.

Please sit on the chair. ____________________

Where are you going? ____________________

Can you help me? ____________________

The queen lives in a palace. ____________________

I wake up at 7 A.M. ____________________

**Step3** 다음 대화를 말해 보세요.

A: Where is the new chair that you bought?
B: It's in the dining room.
A: Can you help me move it?
B: Sure. Did you see the queen on TV this morning?
A: Yes, I saw her at 10 A.M.
B: She looked very elegant.

**Challenge** 오늘 배운 단어가 활용된 영어 일기를 해석한 후, 따라서 써 보세요.

I saw a fancy chair today and wondered where it came from. My teacher said it looked like a chair for a queen. In the A.M., I asked for help with my homework.

<따라 쓰기>

____________________

____________________

**QUIZ** 오늘 배운 단어로 빈칸을 채워 문장을 완성하세요.

Please sit on the ____________________.

____________________ are you going?

Can you ____________________ me?

The ____________________ lives in a palace.

I wake up at 7 ____________________.

DATE . . . .

DAY 19

## Step1 단어를 익히세요.

| see | bill | for | note | month |
|---|---|---|---|---|
| 보다 | 청구서 | 위해 | 메모 | 월 |

## Step2 단어가 사용된 문장을 해석해 보세요.

I can see you. ______________________

I received the bill. ______________________

This is for you. ______________________

Leave a note for me. ______________________

It's the first month of the year. ______________________

## Step3 다음 대화를 말해 보세요.

A: Did you see the bill for this month?

B: Yes, it's on the table.

A: Can you write a note for me?

B: Sure, what should it say?

A: Just remind me to pay the bill.

B: Okay, I will write it now.

## Challenge 오늘 배운 단어가 활용된 영어 일기를 해석한 후, 따라서 써 보세요.

I saw a bill on the table today. It was a note for my mom to pay next month. I reminded her so she wouldn't forget.

<따라 쓰기>

______________________

______________________

## QUIZ 오늘 배운 단어로 빈칸을 채워 문장을 완성하세요.

I can ______________ you.

I received the ______________.

This is ______________ you.

Leave a ______________ for me.

It's the first ______________ of the year.

DATE . . . .

DAY 20

**Step1** 단어를 익히세요.

| restaurant | enough | neck | newspaper | anger |
|---|---|---|---|---|
| 식당 | 충분한 | 목 | 신문 | 화 |

**Step2** 단어가 사용된 문장을 해석해 보세요.

We ate at a nice restaurant. ______________________

Do you have enough money? ______________________

He wore a scarf around his neck. ______________________

She reads the newspaper every morning. ______________________

He couldn't hide his anger. ______________________

**Step3** 다음 대화를 말해 보세요.

A: Did you like the restaurant we visited?

B: Yes, but the food wasn't enough.

A: I saw the manager's neck turn red with anger.

B: Yes, he was very angry. Did you read the newspaper today?

A: Yes, it talked about the restaurant.

B: I hope they get better soon.

**Challenge** 오늘 배운 단어가 활용된 영어 일기를 해석한 후, 따라서 써 보세요.

I went to a restaurant today. The food was delicious and there was enough for everyone. I saw a man reading a newspaper and rubbing his neck, as if he was trying to control his anger.

<따라 쓰기>

______________________

______________________

**QUIZ** 오늘 배운 단어로 빈칸을 채워 문장을 완성하세요.

We ate at a nice ____________.

Do you have ____________ money?

He wore a scarf around his ____________.

She reads the ____________ every morning.

He couldn't hide his ____________.

DATE . . . .

DAY 21

## Step1 단어를 익히세요.

| mother | by | dog | afraid | name |
|---|---|---|---|---|
| 어머니 | 옆에 | 개 | 두려운 | 이름 |

## Step2 단어가 사용된 문장을 해석해 보세요.

My mother is very kind. ______________________

He stood by the door. ______________________

The dog is barking. ______________________

She is afraid of spiders. ______________________

What is your name? ______________________

## Step3 다음 대화를 말해 보세요.

A: What is your dog's name?

B: His name is Max.

A: Is he by your mother?

B: Yes, he is. She loves him.

A: Are you afraid of big dogs?

B: No, I'm not. I like big dogs a lot.

## Challenge 오늘 배운 단어가 활용된 영어 일기를 해석한 후, 따라서 써 보세요.

I was with my mother by the park today. We saw a dog named Max. I was afraid at first, but he was very friendly.

<따라 쓰기>

______________________

______________________

## QUIZ 오늘 배운 단어로 빈칸을 채워 문장을 완성하세요.

My ______________ is very kind.

He stood ______________ the door.

The ______________ is barking.

She is ______________ of spiders.

What is your ______________?

DATE . . . .

DAY 22

## Step1 단어를 익히세요.

| group | bat | base | bell | dentist |
|---|---|---|---|---|
| 그룹 | 박쥐 | 기초, 맨 아래 부분 | 종 | 치과 의사 |

## Step2 단어가 사용된 문장을 해석해 보세요.

We are in the same group. ________________

I saw a bat in the cave. ________________

He stood at the base of the mountain. ________________

The bell rang loudly. ________________

I have an appointment with the dentist. ________________

## Step3 다음 대화를 말해 보세요.

A: Did you see the group of bats?

B: Yes, they were flying around the bell.

A: They made a loud sound when they flew by.

B: Yes, they did. Do you have a dentist appointment today?

A: Yes, I do. I need to check the base of my tooth.

B: I hope it goes well!

## Challenge 오늘 배운 단어가 활용된 영어 일기를 해석한 후, 따라서 써 보세요.

I went to the zoo with my group today. We saw a bat hanging upside down. At school, we learned the base facts about animals. The bell rang, and I remembered I had a dentist appointment.

<따라 쓰기>

________________

________________

## QUIZ 오늘 배운 단어로 빈칸을 채워 문장을 완성하세요.

We are in the same ________________.

I saw a ________________ in the cave.

He stood at the ________________ of the mountain.

The ________________ rang loudly.

I have an appointment with the ________________.

DATE . . . .

DAY 23

## Step1 단어를 익히세요.

| man | speed | library | yellow | bake |
|---|---|---|---|---|
| 남자 | 속도 | 도서관 | 노란색 | 굽다 |

## Step2 단어가 사용된 문장을 해석해 보세요.

The man is very tall. ______________________

The car is going at a high speed. ______________________

She borrowed a book from the library. ______________________

He is wearing a yellow shirt. ______________________

I like to bake cookies. ______________________

## Step3 다음 대화를 말해 보세요.

A: Did you see the man running at high speed?

B: Yes, he ran past the library.

A: He was wearing a yellow shirt.

B: I saw that too. Are you going to the library?

A: Yes, but I need to bake some cookies first.

B: That sounds delicious!

## Challenge 오늘 배운 단어가 활용된 영어 일기를 해석한 후, 따라서 써 보세요.

I saw a man running at high speed today. He was heading to the library. He wore a yellow shirt. After school, my mom and I baked cookies.

<따라 쓰기>

______________________

______________________

## QUIZ 오늘 배운 단어로 빈칸을 채워 문장을 완성하세요.

The ______________ is very tall.

The car is going at a high ______________.

She borrowed a book from the ______________.

He is wearing a ______________ shirt.

I like to ______________ cookies.

DATE . . . .

DAY 24

## Step1 단어를 익히세요.

| keep | shock | free | boat | pay |
| --- | --- | --- | --- | --- |
| 유지하다 | 충격 | 무료의 | 배 | 지불하다 |

## Step2 단어가 사용된 문장을 해석해 보세요.

Keep your room clean. ____________________

The news was a shock to everyone. ____________________

The tickets are free. ____________________

We sailed on a boat. ____________________

I need to pay the bill. ____________________

## Step3 다음 대화를 말해 보세요.

A: How do you keep your boat in good condition?

B: I clean it every week.

A: Did you hear about the free boat rides?

B: Yes, it was a shock to me.

A: Usually, you have to pay a lot for that.

B: I know! It's such a great offer.

## Challenge 오늘 배운 단어가 활용된 영어 일기를 해석한 후, 따라서 써 보세요.

I saw a free boat ride sign today. It was a shock because we usually have to pay.

I hope they keep it free for a long time.

<따라 쓰기>

____________________

____________________

## QUIZ 오늘 배운 단어로 빈칸을 채워 문장을 완성하세요.

__________ your room clean.

The news was a __________ to everyone.

The tickets are __________.

We sailed on a __________.

I need to __________ the bill.

DATE . . . .

DAY 25

## Step1 단어를 익히세요.

| who | field | boss | habit | when |
|---|---|---|---|---|
| 누구 | 들판 | 상사 | 습관 | 언제 |

## Step2 단어가 사용된 문장을 해석해 보세요.

Who is your favorite teacher? ______________________

The field is full of flowers. ______________________

My boss is very kind. ______________________

Brushing your teeth is a good habit. ______________________

When is your birthday? ______________________

## Step3 다음 대화를 말해 보세요.

A: Who is that in the field?

B: That's my boss.

A: What is he doing there?

B: He has a habit of walking there.

A: When does he usually go?

B: He goes every morning.

## Challenge 오늘 배운 단어가 활용된 영어 일기를 해석한 후, 따라서 써 보세요.

I went to the field today with my class. Our teacher asked us, "Who knows the names of these plants?" It's his habit to quiz us when we go on trips.

<따라 쓰기>

______________________

______________________

## QUIZ 오늘 배운 단어로 빈칸을 채워 문장을 완성하세요.

__________ is your favorite teacher?

The __________ is full of flowers.

My __________ is very kind.

Brushing your teeth is a good __________.

__________ is your birthday?

DATE . . . .

DAY 26

**Step1** 단어를 익히세요.

| music | rabbit | comedy | difficult | hobby |
|---|---|---|---|---|
| 음악 | 토끼 | 코미디 | 어려운 | 취미 |

**Step2** 단어가 사용된 문장을 해석해 보세요.

I love listening to music. ____________________

The rabbit is hopping around. ____________________

That movie is a comedy. ____________________

This math problem is difficult. ____________________

My hobby is painting. ____________________

**Step3** 다음 대화를 말해 보세요.

A: What is your favorite hobby?
B: I love listening to music.
A: Do you have any pets?
B: Yes, I have a rabbit.
A: Do you enjoy watching comedy shows?
B: Yes, but some jokes are difficult to understand.

**Challenge** 오늘 배운 단어가 활용된 영어 일기를 해석한 후, 따라서 써 보세요.

I shared my hobby with the class today. I like music, watching comedy shows, and taking care of my pet rabbit. It was difficult to choose just one to talk about!

<따라 쓰기>

____________________

____________________

**QUIZ** 오늘 배운 단어로 빈칸을 채워 문장을 완성하세요.

I love listening to ____________.

The ____________ is hopping around.

That movie is a ____________.

This math problem is ____________.

My ____________ is painting.

DATE . . . .

DAY 27

**Step1** 단어를 익히세요.

| boot | one | child | kick | around |
| --- | --- | --- | --- | --- |
| 부츠 | 하나 | 아이 | 차다 | 주변에 |

**Step2** 단어가 사용된 문장을 해석해 보세요.

She bought a new pair of boots. ____________________

I have one apple left. ____________________

The child is playing. ____________________

He can kick the ball far. ____________________

Look around for clues. ____________________

**Step3** 다음 대화를 말해 보세요.

A: Whose boot is this?

B: It belongs to one of the children.

A: Did the child lose it?

B: Yes, they were playing around here.

A: Did you see them kick the ball?

B: Yes, that's when they lost the boot.

**Challenge** 오늘 배운 단어가 활용된 영어 일기를 해석한 후, 따라서 써 보세요.

I lost one of my boots at recess today. A child found it and kicked it around the playground. We all laughed as we ran to get it back.

<따라 쓰기>

____________________

____________________

**QUIZ** 오늘 배운 단어로 빈칸을 채워 문장을 완성하세요.

She bought a new pair of ____________________.

I have ____________________ apple left.

The ____________________ is playing.

He can ____________________ the ball far.

Look ____________________ for clues.

DATE . . . .

DAY 28

**Step1** 단어를 익히세요.

| ghost | tiger | hat | about | weight |
|---|---|---|---|---|
| 유령 | 호랑이 | 모자 | 대하여 | 무게 |

**Step2** 단어가 사용된 문장을 해석해 보세요.

Some people believe in ghosts. ✎ ______________________________

The tiger is a strong animal. ✎ ______________________________

He wore a funny hat. ✎ ______________________________

Tell me about your day. ✎ ______________________________

What is the weight of this box? ✎ ______________________________

**Step3** 다음 대화를 말해 보세요.

A: Did you hear about the ghost in the old house?
B: Yes, and the story about the tiger too.
A: That's scary. Did you see my hat?
B: Yes, it's over there by the door.
A: Do you know anything about its weight?
B: It's very light, like a feather.

**Challenge** 오늘 배운 단어가 활용된 영어 일기를 해석한 후, 따라서 써 보세요.

I read a book about a ghost and a tiger today. The ghost wore a funny hat, and the tiger talked about its weight. It was a very interesting story!

<따라 쓰기>

______________________________

______________________________

**QUIZ** 오늘 배운 단어로 빈칸을 채워 문장을 완성하세요.

Some people believe in __________.

The __________ is a strong animal.

He wore a funny __________.

Tell me __________ your day.

What is the __________ of this box?

DATE . . . .

DAY 29

## Step1 단어를 익히세요.

| brake | chain | no | key | hill |
|---|---|---|---|---|
| 브레이크 | 사슬 | 아니 | 열쇠 | 언덕 |

## Step2 단어가 사용된 문장을 해석해 보세요.

The car's brakes are very strong. ________________

The dog is tied with a chain. ________________

No, I don't want it. ________________

I lost my key. ________________

They climbed the hill. ________________

## Step3 다음 대화를 말해 보세요.

A: Did you check the brakes on your bike?
B: No, not yet.
A: You should, especially on this hill.
B: Yes, and the chain looks loose too.
A: Do you have the key to the lock?
B: Yes, it's in my pocket.

## Challenge 오늘 배운 단어가 활용된 영어 일기를 해석한 후, 따라서 써 보세요.

The brakes didn't work, so I had to stop with my feet. I used a chain to lock my bike because I didn't have the key.

<따라 쓰기>

________________

________________

## QUIZ 오늘 배운 단어로 빈칸을 채워 문장을 완성하세요.

The car's ________________ is very strong.

The dog is tied with a ________________.

________________, I don't want it.

I lost my ________________.

They climbed the ________________.

DATE . . . .

DAY 30

## Step1 단어를 익히세요.

| academy | calm | idea | try | east |
| --- | --- | --- | --- | --- |
| 학원 | 침착한 | 아이디어 | 시도하다 | 동쪽 |

## Step2 단어가 사용된 문장을 해석해 보세요.

He studies at an academy. ______________________________

Stay calm in an emergency. ______________________________

That's a great idea. ______________________________

Let's try this new game. ______________________________

The sun rises in the east. ______________________________

## Step3 다음 대화를 말해 보세요.

A: Hey, there's a new academy in the east.

B: Really? That sounds fun. I want to go.

A: Yeah, it's a good idea. You can learn new things there.

B: That sounds nice. Should I try it?

A: Yes, try it. It's very calm and nice.

B: Great! I'll tell my mom.

## Challenge 오늘 배운 단어가 활용된 영어 일기를 해석한 후, 따라서 써 보세요.

I went to my new academy in the east part of town today. I had an idea to try and stay calm during my first class. It helped me learn a lot!

<따라 쓰기>

______________________________

______________________________

## QUIZ 오늘 배운 단어로 빈칸을 채워 문장을 완성하세요.

He studies at the ______________.

Stay ______________ in an emergency.

That's a great ______________.

Let's ______________ this new game.

The sun rises in the ______________.

DATE . . . .

DAY 31

## Step1 단어를 익히세요.

| bowl | lion | mathematics | need | certain |
|---|---|---|---|---|
| 그릇 | 사자 | 수학 | 필요하다 | 확실한 |

## Step2 단어가 사용된 문장을 해석해 보세요.

I ate a bowl of soup. ______________________

The lion is the king of the jungle. ______________________

Mathematics is my favorite subject. ______________________

I need some help. ______________________

Are you certain about that? ______________________

## Step3 다음 대화를 말해 보세요.

A: Do you need a bowl for the soup?
B: Yes, I do. Thanks.
A: Have you seen the lion at the zoo?
B: Yes, it was amazing.
A: Are you good at mathematics?
B: I'm not certain, but I try my best.

## Challenge 오늘 배운 단어가 활용된 영어 일기를 해석한 후, 따라서 써 보세요.

I need help with my mathematics homework. My teacher said I should be certain of my answers. After school, I saw a lion in a picture on my cereal bowl.

<따라 쓰기>

______________________

______________________

## QUIZ 오늘 배운 단어로 빈칸을 채워 문장을 완성하세요.

I ate a ______________ of soup.

The ______________ is the king of the jungle.

______________ is my favorite subject.

I ______________ some help.

Are you ______________ about that?

DATE . . . .

DAY 32

**Step1** 단어를 익히세요.

| from | earth | frog | fire | hate |
|---|---|---|---|---|
| ~에서 | 지구 | 개구리 | 불 | 싫어하다 |

**Step2** 단어가 사용된 문장을 해석해 보세요.

I got this gift from my friend. ____________________

We live on Earth. ____________________

The frog is green. ____________________

Do not play with fire. ____________________

I hate getting up early. ____________________

**Step3** 다음 대화를 말해 보세요.

A: Where is this frog from?
B: It's from the earth's wetlands.
A: Do you think frogs hate fire?
B: Yes, they do. Fire is dangerous for them.
A: Did you see the fire in the forest?
B: Yes, it was scary.

**Challenge** 오늘 배운 단어가 활용된 영어 일기를 해석한 후, 따라서 써 보세요.

I learned about frogs in science class today. They need water from the earth to live. I also learned they hate fire and stay far away from it.

<따라 쓰기>

____________________

____________________

**QUIZ** 오늘 배운 단어로 빈칸을 채워 문장을 완성하세요.

I got this gift ____________ my friend.

We live on ____________.

The ____________ is green.

Do not play with ____________.

I ____________ getting up early.

DATE . . . .

DAY 33

## Step1 단어를 익히세요.

| diary | pear | couple | wife | yes |
|---|---|---|---|---|
| 일기 | 배 | 커플 | 아내 | 예 |

## Step2 단어가 사용된 문장을 해석해 보세요.

I write in my diary every night. ______________________________

She ate a sweet pear. ______________________________

The couple is very happy. ______________________________

His wife is a doctor. ______________________________

Yes, I can help you. ______________________________

## Step3 다음 대화를 말해 보세요.

A: Do you keep a diary?
B: Yes, I write in it every night.
A: Did you see the couple with the pears?
B: Yes, they were sharing them.
A: Is the woman his wife?
B: Yes, she is. They seem very happy.

## Challenge 오늘 배운 단어가 활용된 영어 일기를 해석한 후, 따라서 써 보세요.

I wrote in my diary about my day at school. I saw a couple sharing a pear during lunch. The boy asked, "Is this for your wife?" and the girl laughed and said, "Yes, it's for you!"

<따라 쓰기>

______________________________

______________________________

## QUIZ 오늘 배운 단어로 빈칸을 채워 문장을 완성하세요.

I write in my ______________ every night.

She ate a sweet ______________.

The ______________ is very happy.

His ______________ is a doctor.

______________, I can help you.

DATE . . . .

DAY 34

**Step1** 단어를 익히세요.

| any | smell | another | baseball | during |
|---|---|---|---|---|
| 어떤 | 냄새, 냄새가 나다 | 다른 | 야구 | ~동안 |

**Step2** 단어가 사용된 문장을 해석해 보세요.

Do you have any questions? ________________

I love the smell of flowers. ________________

Can I have another piece? ________________

Baseball is my favorite sport. ________________

He fell asleep during the movie. ________________

**Step3** 다음 대화를 말해 보세요.

A: Do you smell something strange?
B: Yes, I do. It's coming from the kitchen.
A: Do you have any idea what it is?
B: Maybe it's the food. Let's check.
A: Do you want to watch another baseball game?
B: Sure, during the next break.

**Challenge** 오늘 배운 단어가 활용된 영어 일기를 해석한 후, 따라서 써 보세요.

I played baseball during recess today. I didn't like any of the snacks they had. Another kid shared his chips with me, and they had a weird smell.

<따라 쓰기>

________________

________________

**QUIZ** 오늘 배운 단어로 빈칸을 채워 문장을 완성하세요.

Do you have ________ questions?

I love the ________ of flowers.

Can I have ________ piece?

________ is my favorite sport.

He fell asleep ________ the movie.

DATE . . . .

DAY 35

**Step1** 단어를 익히세요.

| potato | dirty | bubble | mountain | brown |
|---|---|---|---|---|
| 감자 | 더러운 | 거품 | 산 | 갈색 |

**Step2** 단어가 사용된 문장을 해석해 보세요.

I like to eat potatoes. ______________________

My shoes are dirty. ______________________

She blew a big bubble. ______________________

We climbed the mountain. ______________________

The dog is brown. ______________________

**Step3** 다음 대화를 말해 보세요.

A: Did you see the brown potato chips on the table?

B: Yes, they look delicious, but my hands are dirty.

A: Do you need some soap to wash them?

B: Yes, please. Do you have the soap that makes big bubbles?

A: Have you been to the mountain nearby?

B: Yes, it's beautiful there.

**Challenge** 오늘 배운 단어가 활용된 영어 일기를 해석한 후, 따라서 써 보세요.

I helped plant potatoes in the school garden today. My hands got dirty with the brown soil. Later, I blew bubbles and watched them float towards the mountain.

<따라 쓰기>

______________________

______________________

**QUIZ** 오늘 배운 단어로 빈칸을 채워 문장을 완성하세요.

I like to eat ______________.

My shoes are ______________.

She blew a big ______________.

We climbed the ______________.

The dog is ______________.

DATE . . . .

DAY 36

**Step1** 단어를 익히세요.

| quiet | advise | nurse | castle | sky |
|---|---|---|---|---|
| 조용한 | 조언하다 | 간호사 | 성 | 하늘 |

**Step2** 단어가 사용된 문장을 해석해 보세요.

The library is very quiet. ______

Can you advise me on this? ______

The nurse was very kind. ______

We visited an old castle. ______

The sky is clear today. ______

**Step3** 다음 대화를 말해 보세요.

A: The castle looks beautiful against the sky.
B: Yes, it's so quiet here.
A: I need some advice. Can you help?
B: Sure, what do you need?
A: Should I become a nurse?
B: Yes, I think you would be great at it.

**Challenge** 오늘 배운 단어가 활용된 영어 일기를 해석한 후, 따라서 써 보세요.

I went to a quiet place to read today. A nurse came by and advised me to rest more. I imagined living in a castle under the bright blue sky.

<따라 쓰기>

______

______

**QUIZ** 오늘 배운 단어로 빈칸을 채워 문장을 완성하세요.

The library is very ______.

Can you ______ me on this?

The ______ was very kind.

We visited an old ______.

The ______ is clear today.

DATE . . . .

DAY 37

**Step1** 단어를 익히세요.

| swim | knife | think | thing | nose |
|---|---|---|---|---|
| 수영하다 | 칼 | 생각하다 | ~것 | 코 |

**Step2** 단어가 사용된 문장을 해석해 보세요.

I love to swim in the pool. ______________________

Be careful with the knife. ______________________

I think it's a good idea. ______________________

What is that thing? ______________________

I broke my nose in the fight. ______________________

**Step3** 다음 대화를 말해 보세요.

A: Do you like to swim?
B: Yes, I love it.
A: What do you think of this knife?
B: It's sharp. Be careful!
A: What's your favorite thing to do?
B: I think it's reading.

**Challenge** 오늘 배운 단어가 활용된 영어 일기를 해석한 후, 따라서 써 보세요.

I went to the pool to swim today. I saw a shiny thing in the water and thought it was a knife. When I looked closer, it was just a toy near my nose.

<따라 쓰기>

______________________

______________________

**QUIZ** 오늘 배운 단어로 빈칸을 채워 문장을 완성하세요.

I love to ______________ in the pool.

Be careful with the ______________.

I ______________ it's a good idea.

What is that ______________?

I broke my ______________ in the fight.

DATE . . . .

DAY 38

## Step1 단어를 익히세요.

| clean | nice | bee | marry | score |
|---|---|---|---|---|
| 깨끗한 | 좋은 | 벌 | 결혼하다 | 점수 |

## Step2 단어가 사용된 문장을 해석해 보세요.

The room is very clean. ____________________

She is a nice person. ____________________

A bee stung me on my neck. ____________________

They will marry next year. ____________________

He got a high score on the test. ____________________

## Step3 다음 대화를 말해 보세요.

A: Look, I cleaned my room!
B: It looks so nice and clean.
A: Do you think we can marry our dolls now?
B: Yes, let's have a wedding. My doll can be the bride.
A: And my doll can be the groom. Oh no, there's a bee!
B: Don't worry, the bee will go away. Let's play and score points in our game.

## Challenge 오늘 배운 단어가 활용된 영어 일기를 해석한 후, 따라서 써 보세요.

I helped clean the classroom today. My teacher said I did a nice job and gave me a good score.
At recess, we saw a bee and talked about how bees help flowers "marry" to make seeds.

<따라 쓰기>

____________________

____________________

## QUIZ 오늘 배운 단어로 빈칸을 채워 문장을 완성하세요.

The room is very ____________________.

She is a ____________________ person.

A ____________________ stung me on my neck.

They will ____________________ next year.

He got a high ____________________ on the test.

DATE . . . .

DAY 39

**Step1** 단어를 익히세요.

| slow | sing | stop | chance | space |
|---|---|---|---|---|
| 느린 | 노래하다 | 멈추다 | 기회 | 공간 |

**Step2** 단어가 사용된 문장을 해석해 보세요.

The turtle is slow. ________________

She loves to sing. ________________

Please stop talking. ________________

This is my chance to shine. ________________

There is a lot of space here. ________________

**Step3** 다음 대화를 말해 보세요.

A: Do you think bees are slow?
B: No, they move very fast.
A: Have you ever heard them sing?
B: No, they never stop working.
A: Do you think we have a chance to see them up close?
B: Yes, if we find a safe space to watch.

**Challenge** 오늘 배운 단어가 활용된 영어 일기를 해석한 후, 따라서 써 보세요.

I sang a slow song in music class today. The teacher asked me to stop and then gave me another chance. I felt happy because I had space to improve.

<따라 쓰기>

________________

________________

**QUIZ** 오늘 배운 단어로 빈칸을 채워 문장을 완성하세요.

The turtle is ________________.

She loves to ________________.

Please ________________ talking.

This is my ________________ to shine.

There is a lot of ________________ here.

DATE . . . .

DAY 40

## Step1 단어를 익히세요.

| form | toy | color | soccer | wash |
| --- | --- | --- | --- | --- |
| 형태 | 장난감 | 색깔 | 축구 | 씻다 |

## Step2 단어가 사용된 문장을 해석해 보세요.

We need to fill out a form. ______________________

The toy is broken. ______________________

My favorite color is blue. ______________________

We play soccer every Saturday. ______________________

She washes her clothes every Sunday. ______________________

## Step3 다음 대화를 말해 보세요.

A: What form does this toy take?

B: It's in the shape of a car.

A: I like its color. It's bright red.

B: Yes, it's very nice. Do you play soccer?

A: Yes, I do. It's my favorite sport.

B: Make sure to wash your hands after playing!

## Challenge 오늘 배운 단어가 활용된 영어 일기를 해석한 후, 따라서 써 보세요.

I played with a toy that was in the form of a car today. It changed color when I washed it. Afterward, I played soccer with my friends.

<따라 쓰기>

______________________

______________________

## QUIZ 오늘 배운 단어로 빈칸을 채워 문장을 완성하세요.

We need to fill out a ______________.

The ______________ is broken.

My favorite ______________ is blue.

We play ______________ every Saturday.

She ______________es her clothes every Sunday.

DATE . . . .

DAY 41

## Step1 단어를 익히세요.

| clock | long | cheap | old | remember |
|---|---|---|---|---|
| 시계 | 긴 | 싼 | 오래된 | 기억하다 |

## Step2 단어가 사용된 문장을 해석해 보세요.

The clock is ticking. ______

She has long hair. ______

The shirt was cheap. ______

This is an old book. ______

Do you remember my name? ______

## Step3 다음 대화를 말해 보세요.

A: Do you see that old clock on the wall?
B: Yes, it's been there for a long time.
A: I remember when we bought it.
B: Was it cheap?
A: Yes, it was very cheap back then.
B: I can't believe it still works!

## Challenge 오늘 배운 단어가 활용된 영어 일기를 해석한 후, 따라서 써 보세요.

I saw an old clock in the attic today. It had a long pendulum and still worked. I remember my grandma saying it was very cheap when she bought it.

<따라 쓰기>

## QUIZ 오늘 배운 단어로 빈칸을 채워 문장을 완성하세요.

The ______ is ticking.

She has ______ hair.

The shirt was ______.

This is an ______ book.

Do you ______ my name?

DATE . . . .

DAY 42

## Step1 단어를 익히세요.

| between | inside | visit | culture | plan |
|---|---|---|---|---|
| 사이 | 안에 | 방문하다 | 문화 | 계획 |

## Step2 단어가 사용된 문장을 해석해 보세요.

The park is between the school and the store. ✎ ______

The cat is inside the house. ✎ ______

We will visit our grandparents this weekend. ✎ ______

I love learning about different cultures. ✎ ______

Do you have a plan? ✎ ______

## Step3 다음 대화를 말해 보세요.

A: Do you plan to visit any new places soon?

B: Yes, I'm planning to visit Japan.

A: That's exciting! What's your plan?

B: I want to explore the culture and visit museums.

A: Will you travel between cities?

B: Yes, and I also want to see the inside of old temples.

## Challenge 오늘 배운 단어가 활용된 영어 일기를 해석한 후, 따라서 써 보세요.

I have a plan to visit the museum this weekend. It's interesting to see the culture inside. I'll walk between the exhibits to learn more.

<따라 쓰기>

______

______

## QUIZ 오늘 배운 단어로 빈칸을 채워 문장을 완성하세요.

The park is ______ the school and the store.

The cat is ______ the house.

We will ______ our grandparents this weekend.

I love learning about different ______.

Do you have a ______?

DATE . . . .

DAY 43

## Step1 단어를 익히세요.

| eraser | beach | background | aloud | like |
|---|---|---|---|---|
| 지우개 | 해변 | 배경 | 소리 내어 | 좋아하다 |

## Step2 단어가 사용된 문장을 해석해 보세요.

Use an eraser to fix your mistake. ____________________

We are going to the beach tomorrow. ____________________

The background of the picture is beautiful. ____________________

Please read aloud. ____________________

I like ice cream. ____________________

## Step3 다음 대화를 말해 보세요.

A: Do you have an eraser I can use?

B: Yes, it's right here.

A: Do you like the beach?

B: Yes, I love it, especially with the sunset in the background.

A: Can you read this aloud?

B: Sure, I like reading out loud.

## Challenge 오늘 배운 단어가 활용된 영어 일기를 해석한 후, 따라서 써 보세요.

I found an eraser shaped like a star today. I took it to the beach and drew pictures in the sand. The waves in the background sounded nice as I said aloud, "I like the beach!"

<따라 쓰기>

____________________

____________________

## QUIZ 오늘 배운 단어로 빈칸을 채워 문장을 완성하세요.

Use an ____________________ to fix your mistake.

We are going to the ____________________ tomorrow.

The ____________________ of the picture is beautiful.

Please read ____________________.

I ____________________ ice cream.

DATE . . . .

DAY 44

## Step1 단어를 익히세요.

| ship | week | bite | flower | look |
|---|---|---|---|---|
| 배 | 주 | 물다 | 꽃 | 보다 |

## Step2 단어가 사용된 문장을 해석해 보세요.

The ship is sailing on the sea. ______________________

I will see you next week. ______________________

The dog tried to bite me. ______________________

The flower is blooming. ______________________

Look at the stars. ______________________

## Step3 다음 대화를 말해 보세요.

A: Did you see the big ship in the harbor?

B: Yes, it arrived last week.

A: Look at those beautiful flowers on the deck.

B: They are lovely. Did you get a bite to eat?

A: Yes, I did. The food on the ship was great.

B: I would love to go on a trip like that.

## Challenge 오늘 배운 단어가 활용된 영어 일기를 해석한 후, 따라서 써 보세요.

I saw a big ship at the harbor this week. While I was there, a bug tried to bite me. I looked at a pretty flower to distract myself.

<따라 쓰기>

______________________

______________________

## QUIZ 오늘 배운 단어로 빈칸을 채워 문장을 완성하세요.

The ______________ is sailing on the sea.

I will see you next ______________.

The dog tried to ______________ me.

The ______________ is blooming.

______________ at the stars.

DATE . . . .

DAY 45

**Step1** 단어를 익히세요.

| bring | textbook | sock | cloth | tooth |
|---|---|---|---|---|
| 가져오다 | 교과서 | 양말 | 천 | 이 |

**Step2** 단어가 사용된 문장을 해석해 보세요.

Please bring your book. ______________________

I need my math textbook. ______________________

My sock has a hole in it. ______________________

This cloth is very soft. ______________________

My tooth hurts. ______________________

**Step3** 다음 대화를 말해 보세요.

A: Can you bring my textbook to me?

B: Sure, where is it?

A: It's next to the blue cloth on the table.

B: Okay, I see it. Do you need anything else?

A: Yes, my sock and toothbrush, please.

B: Got it. I'll bring everything to you.

**Challenge** 오늘 배운 단어가 활용된 영어 일기를 해석한 후, 따라서 써 보세요.

I forgot to bring my textbook to school today. My friend helped me clean my desk with a cloth. I also found a lost sock and a tooth inside my drawer!

<따라 쓰기>

______________________

______________________

**QUIZ** 오늘 배운 단어로 빈칸을 채워 문장을 완성하세요.

Please ______________ your book.

I need my math ______________.

My ______________ has a hole in it.

This ______________ is very soft.

My ______________ hurts.

DATE . . . .

DAY 46

**Step1** 단어를 익히세요.

| luck | well | error | picnic | too |
|---|---|---|---|---|
| 운 | 잘 | 오류 | 소풍 | 너무 |

**Step2** 단어가 사용된 문장을 해석해 보세요.

Good luck on your test. ______

She did well on her exam. ______

There was an error in the report. ______

We had a picnic in the park. ______

It's too hot today. ______

**Step3** 다음 대화를 말해 보세요.

A: Are we going on a picnic today?
B: Yes, if the weather is good.
A: I hope we have good luck.
B: Me too. I hope everything goes well.
A: Did you check for any errors in the plan?
B: Yes, everything is ready. Let's go!

**Challenge** 오늘 배운 단어가 활용된 영어 일기를 해석한 후, 따라서 써 보세요.

I had good luck at the picnic today. Everything went well and there were no errors. We had fun, but I ate too much!

<따라 쓰기>

______

______

**QUIZ** 오늘 배운 단어로 빈칸을 채워 문장을 완성하세요.

Good ______ on your test.

She did ______ on her exam.

There was an ______ in the report.

We had a ______ in the park.

It's ______ hot today.

DATE . . . .

DAY 47

**Step1** 단어를 익히세요.

| brush | branch | light | with | call |
|---|---|---|---|---|
| 솔 | 나뭇가지 | 빛 | 함께 | 전화하다 |

**Step2** 단어가 사용된 문장을 해석해 보세요.

I need a new brush for painting. ______

The branch broke in the wind. ______

Turn off the light. ______

I will go with you. ______

I will call you later. ______

**Step3** 다음 대화를 말해 보세요.

A: Can you hand me the brush?
B: Sure, here it is.
A: Look at that branch with the bird.
B: It's beautiful in the morning light.
A: Do you want to call Sarah to join us?
B: Yes, I'll call her right now.

**Challenge** 오늘 배운 단어가 활용된 영어 일기를 해석한 후, 따라서 써 보세요.

I saw a bird on a branch today. The sunlight made the leaves look bright and pretty. I used a brush to paint the scene and called my friend to share it with him.

<따라 쓰기>

______

______

**QUIZ** 오늘 배운 단어로 빈칸을 채워 문장을 완성하세요.

I need a new ______ for painting.

The ______ broke in the wind.

Turn off the ______.

I will go ______ you.

I will ______ you later.

DATE . . . .

DAY 48

**Step1** 단어를 익히세요.

| soft | climb | invite | gesture | captain |
|---|---|---|---|---|
| 부드러운 | 오르다 | 초대하다 | 제스처 | 캡틴 |

**Step2** 단어가 사용된 문장을 해석해 보세요.

This pillow is very soft. ____________________

We will climb the mountain tomorrow. ____________________

I will invite you to my party. ____________________

He made a friendly gesture. ____________________

The captain led the team. ____________________

**Step3** 다음 대화를 말해 보세요.

A: The blanket is so soft.
B: Yes, it feels nice. Did you see the captain?
A: Yes, he waved to us to climb aboard.
B: Should we invite him to join us?
A: Yes, let's invite him.
B: I'll go ask him now.

**Challenge** 오늘 배운 단어가 활용된 영어 일기를 해석한 후, 따라서 써 보세요.

I climbed a tree and felt the soft leaves today. My friend invited me to play a game, and I accepted with a big gesture. I became the captain of our team.

<따라 쓰기>

____________________

____________________

**QUIZ** 오늘 배운 단어로 빈칸을 채워 문장을 완성하세요.

This pillow is very ____________.

We will ____________ the mountain tomorrow.

I will ____________ you to my party.

He made a friendly ____________.

The ____________ led the team.

DATE . . . .

DAY 49

## Step1 단어를 익히세요.

| leg | away | believe | watermelon | dream |
|---|---|---|---|---|
| 다리 | 멀리 | 믿다 | 수박 | 꿈 |

## Step2 단어가 사용된 문장을 해석해 보세요.

My leg hurts. ______________________

The bird flew away. ______________________

I believe in you. ______________________

The watermelon is sweet. ______________________

I had a strange dream. ______________________

## Step3 다음 대화를 말해 보세요.

A: My leg hurts from walking so much.
B: Let's rest for a while. Look at that watermelon.
A: It looks delicious. I can't believe how big it is.
B: Yes, it's huge. Do you ever dream about flying?
A: Sometimes. I dream of flying away to a new place.
B: That sounds amazing. I believe you can do anything in your dreams.

## Challenge 오늘 배운 단어가 활용된 영어 일기를 해석한 후, 따라서 써 보세요.

I had a dream last night about a giant watermelon. I tried to carry it, but my legs felt too weak. I believe it rolled away down the hill!

<따라 쓰기>

______________________

______________________

## QUIZ 오늘 배운 단어로 빈칸을 채워 문장을 완성하세요.

My ______________ hurts.

The bird flew ______________.

I ______________ in you.

The ______________ is sweet.

I had a strange ______________.

DATE . . . .

DAY 50

**Step1** 단어를 익히세요.

| travel | bear | book | vegetable | watch |
|---|---|---|---|---|
| 여행하다 | 곰 | 책 | 채소 | 보다 |

**Step2** 단어가 사용된 문장을 해석해 보세요.

I love to travel. ________________

The bear is sleeping. ________________

This book is very interesting. ________________

I eat a lot of vegetables. ________________

Let's watch a movie. ________________

**Step3** 다음 대화를 말해 보세요.

A: Do you like to travel?

B: Yes, I love it. Have you read this book about bears?

A: No, but it sounds interesting. Do you like vegetables?

B: Yes, I eat them every day. Do you want to watch a movie?

A: Sure, let's watch one about nature.

B: Great idea!

**Challenge** 오늘 배운 단어가 활용된 영어 일기를 해석한 후, 따라서 써 보세요.

I love to travel and see new places. On my last trip, I saw a bear in the forest. I brought a book with me to read while eating vegetables and watching the sunset.

<따라 쓰기>

________________

________________

**QUIZ** 오늘 배운 단어로 빈칸을 채워 문장을 완성하세요.

I love to ________________.

The ________________ is sleeping.

This ________________ is very interesting.

I eat a lot of ________________.

Let's ________________ a movie.

DATE . . . .

DAY 51

**Step1** 단어를 익히세요.

| bottle | clerk | why | town | young |
|---|---|---|---|---|
| 병 | 직원 | 왜 | 마을 | 젊은 |

**Step2** 단어가 사용된 문장을 해석해 보세요.

The bottle is full of water. ______

The clerk helped me find a book. ______

Why are you late? ______

This town is very quiet. ______

She is young and energetic. ______

**Step3** 다음 대화를 말해 보세요.

A: Hi! Can you help me find a bottle?

B: Sure! What kind of bottle?

A: A water bottle, please.

B: Here are some water bottles. Do you like this one?

A: Yes, I do! Why do you have so many?

B: Many young kids in town need them for school.

**Challenge** 오늘 배운 단어가 활용된 영어 일기를 해석한 후, 따라서 써 보세요.

I went to the store in town and talked to a young clerk. I asked, "Why are there so many bottles here?" He smiled and said, "People in this town love to recycle."

<따라 쓰기>

______

______

**QUIZ** 오늘 배운 단어로 빈칸을 채워 문장을 완성하세요.

The ______ is full of water.

The ______ helped me find a book.

______ are you late?

This ______ is very quiet.

She is ______ and energetic.

DATE . . . .

DAY 52

## Step1 단어를 익히세요.

| battle | will | brave | put | bad |
|---|---|---|---|---|
| 전투 | 의지 | 용감한 | 놓다 | 나쁜 |

## Step2 단어가 사용된 문장을 해석해 보세요.

The battle was intense. ______________________

He has a strong will. ______________________

The soldier is very brave. ______________________

Please put your books here. ______________________

He got a bad grade on his test. ______________________

## Step3 다음 대화를 말해 보세요.

A: Look, there is a battle in the storybook!

B: Yes, the brave knight will fight.

A: Why will he fight?

B: He wants to stop the bad dragon.

A: He is so brave!

B: Yes, he is! He will put an end to the battle.

## Challenge 오늘 배운 단어가 활용된 영어 일기를 해석한 후, 따라서 써 보세요.

I read a story about a brave knight today. He showed his will to win the battle against the bad dragon. He put his shield down only when the dragon was defeated.

<따라 쓰기>

______________________

______________________

## QUIZ 오늘 배운 단어로 빈칸을 채워 문장을 완성하세요.

The ______________ was intense.

He has a strong ______________.

The soldier is very ______________.

Please ______________ your books here.

That was a ______________ decision.

DATE . . . .

DAY 53

**Step1** 단어를 익히세요.

| take | hit | white | bean | dead |
|---|---|---|---|---|
| 가지다 | 때리다 | 흰색 | 콩 | 죽은 |

**Step2** 단어가 사용된 문장을 해석해 보세요.

Take an umbrella with you. ________________

Don't hit your brother. ________________

She wore a white dress. ________________

I like to eat beans. ________________

The plant is dead. ________________

**Step3** 다음 대화를 말해 보세요.

A: What are you going to take?
B: I will take a white bean.
A: Why do you need a white bean?
B: I want to plant it in my garden.
A: Be careful not to hit the plants!
B: I will. Look, there is a dead leaf.
A: Yes, let's pick it up.

**Challenge** 오늘 배운 단어가 활용된 영어 일기를 해석한 후, 따라서 써 보세요.

I saw a white bean on the ground today. I tried to take it, but it hit my foot. Then, I noticed a dead leaf beside it.

<따라 쓰기>

________________

________________

**QUIZ** 오늘 배운 단어로 빈칸을 채워 문장을 완성하세요.

________________ an umbrella with you.

Don't ________________ your brother.

She wore a ________________ dress.

I like to eat ________________.

The plant is ________________.

DATE . . . .

DAY 54

**Step1** 단어를 익히세요.

| rock | job | mail | dinner | join |
|---|---|---|---|---|
| 바위 | 일 | 우편 | 저녁 | 참여하다 |

**Step2** 단어가 사용된 문장을 해석해 보세요.

The rock is heavy. ✎ ______________________

He got a new job. ✎ ______________________

I received a mail today. ✎ ______________________

We had pasta for dinner. ✎ ______________________

Will you join us? ✎ ______________________

**Step3** 다음 대화를 말해 보세요.

A: What is that big rock?
B: It's part of my job to move it.
A: Wow! That sounds hard.
B: Yes, but I enjoy it.
A: Did you get the mail?
B: Yes, I did. It came after dinner.

**Challenge** 오늘 배운 단어가 활용된 영어 일기를 해석한 후, 따라서 써 보세요.

I climbed a big rock after school. My job was to check the mail before dinner. After that, I joined my family for a nice meal.

<따라 쓰기>

______________________

______________________

**QUIZ** 오늘 배운 단어로 빈칸을 채워 문장을 완성하세요.

The ______________ is heavy.

He got a new ______________.

I received a ______________ today.

We had pasta for ______________.

Will you ______________ us?

DATE . . . .

DAY 55

## Step1 단어를 익히세요.

| brain | add | we | control | heaven |
|---|---|---|---|---|
| 뇌 | 더하다 | 우리 | 통제하다 | 천국 |

## Step2 단어가 사용된 문장을 해석해 보세요.

The brain is a complex organ. ______________________

Add some sugar to the tea. ______________________

We are friends. ______________________

You need to control your emotions. ______________________

They believe in heaven. ______________________

## Step3 다음 대화를 말해 보세요.

A: What does the brain do?
B: It helps us think and control our body.
A: Can we add more knowledge to our brain?
B: Yes, we can learn new things every day.
A: Is it true that some people believe in heaven?
B: Yes, many people believe in heaven.

## Challenge 오늘 배운 단어가 활용된 영어 일기를 해석한 후, 따라서 써 보세요.

I learned that our brain helps us think and control our body. When we add new information, we get smarter. My teacher said that learning new things is like adding a little bit of heaven to our minds.

<따라 쓰기>

______________________

______________________

## QUIZ 오늘 배운 단어로 빈칸을 채워 문장을 완성하세요.

The ______________ is a complex organ.

______________ some sugar to the tea.

______________ are friends.

You need to ______________ your emotions.

They believe in ______________.

DATE . . . .

DAY 56

**Step1** 단어를 익히세요.

| father | same | size | welcome | beef |
|---|---|---|---|---|
| 아버지 | 같은 | 크기 | 환영하다 | 소고기 |

**Step2** 단어가 사용된 문장을 해석해 보세요.

My father is very tall. ______

We have the same shoes. ______

What is your shoe size? ______

Welcome to my house. ______

I like beef steak. ______

**Step3** 다음 대화를 말해 보세요.

A: Is your father coming to dinner?
B: Yes, he is. We will welcome him.
A: Do you like beef for dinner?
B: Yes, we both like the same food.
A: Do you want the same size steak?
B: Yes, the same size would be perfect!

**Challenge** 오늘 배운 단어가 활용된 영어 일기를 해석한 후, 따라서 써 보세요.

I had dinner with my father today. We both had the same size steak because we love beef. He said, "Welcome home," and we enjoyed our meal together.

<따라 쓰기>

______

______

**QUIZ** 오늘 배운 단어로 빈칸을 채워 문장을 완성하세요.

My ______ is very tall.

We have the ______ shoes.

What is your shoe ______?

______ to my house.

I like ______ steak.

DATE . . . .

DAY 57

**Step1** 단어를 익히세요.

| so | ball | large | grape | forever |
|---|---|---|---|---|
| 그래서 | 공 | 큰 | 포도 | 영원히 |

**Step2** 단어가 사용된 문장을 해석해 보세요.

I forgot my keys, so I went back. ______________________

The ball is round. ______________________

They live in a large house. ______________________

I like eating grapes. ______________________

I will love you forever. ______________________

**Step3** 다음 대화를 말해 보세요.

A: Look at this ball!

B: Wow, it's very large!

A: Yes, it's bigger than a grape.

B: Do you want to play with it?

A: Yes, let's play forever!

B: Okay, so let's go outside!

**Challenge** 오늘 배운 단어가 활용된 영어 일기를 해석한 후, 따라서 써 보세요.

I found a large ball in the yard today. It was as big as a bunch of grapes, so we played with it for hours. We had so much fun, and I wished we could play forever.

<따라 쓰기>

______________________

______________________

**QUIZ** 오늘 배운 단어로 빈칸을 채워 문장을 완성하세요.

I forgot my keys, ____________ I went back.

The ____________ is round.

They live in a ____________ house.

I like eating ____________.

I will love you ____________.

DATE . . . .

DAY 58

**Step1** 단어를 익히세요.

| goal | morning | mad | god | story |
|---|---|---|---|---|
| 목표 | 아침 | 화난 | 신 | 이야기 |

**Step2** 단어가 사용된 문장을 해석해 보세요.

My goal is to become a doctor. ______________________

Good morning! ______________________

She was mad at him. ______________________

They believe in one god. ______________________

He told an interesting story. ______________________

**Step3** 다음 대화를 말해 보세요.

A: What is your goal for today?
B: My goal is to finish my story.
A: Did you start writing it this morning?
B: Yes, I did. But I got mad because my pen broke.
A: Oh no! Maybe it's a sign from god to take a break.
B: Maybe! I'll finish it later.

**Challenge** 오늘 배운 단어가 활용된 영어 일기를 해석한 후, 따라서 써 보세요.

My goal this morning was to read a story. I got mad when I couldn't find the book. Then, my mom said, "Don't worry, even the gods lose things sometimes."

<따라 쓰기>

______________________

______________________

**QUIZ** 오늘 배운 단어로 빈칸을 채워 문장을 완성하세요.

My __________ is to become a doctor.

Good __________!

She was __________ at him.

They believe in one __________.

He told an interesting __________.

DATE . . . .

DAY 59

## Step1 단어를 익히세요.

| tower | black | ocean | example | small |
|---|---|---|---|---|
| 탑 | 검정색 | 대양 | 예 | 작은 |

## Step2 단어가 사용된 문장을 해석해 보세요.

The tower is very tall. ______________________

She wore a black dress. ______________________

The ocean is vast. ______________________

This is an example of good work. ______________________

The kitten is small. ______________________

## Step3 다음 대화를 말해 보세요.

A: Look at that tall tower!

B: Yes, it looks so big next to the ocean.

A: The tower is black.

B: It's a good example of a tall building.

A: I see a small boat near it.

B: Yes, the boat looks tiny next to the tower.

## Challenge 오늘 배운 단어가 활용된 영어 일기를 해석한 후, 따라서 써 보세요.

I saw a tall tower by the ocean today. It was black and stood out against the blue water. It was a great example of how a small thing can look big in the right place.

<따라 쓰기>

______________________

______________________

## QUIZ 오늘 배운 단어로 빈칸을 채워 문장을 완성하세요.

The ______________ is very tall.

She wore a ______________ dress.

The ______________ is vast.

This is an ______________ of good work.

The kitten is ______________.

DATE . . . .

DAY 60

**Step1** 단어를 익히세요.

| agree | road | floor | monkey | far |
|---|---|---|---|---|
| 동의하다 | 길 | 바닥 | 원숭이 | 멀리 |

**Step2** 단어가 사용된 문장을 해석해 보세요.

I agree with your idea. ____________________

The road is long and winding. ____________________

The floor is clean. ____________________

The monkey is eating a banana. ____________________

How far is the station? ____________________

**Step3** 다음 대화를 말해 보세요.

A: Do you agree with this plan?
B: Yes, I agree. Let's take that road.
A: Look, there's a monkey on the road!
B: Oh wow, it's sitting on the floor.
A: How did it get so far from the forest?
B: I don't know, but it looks happy.

**Challenge** 오늘 배운 단어가 활용된 영어 일기를 해석한 후, 따라서 써 보세요.

I saw a monkey at school today. It was sitting on the floor near the road. I agree with my friend that it must have come from far away.

<따라 쓰기>

____________________

____________________

**QUIZ** 오늘 배운 단어로 빈칸을 채워 문장을 완성하세요.

I ____________________ with your idea.

The ____________________ is long and winding.

The ____________________ is clean.

The ____________________ is eating a banana.

How ____________________ is the station?

DATE . . . .

DAY 61

## Step1 단어를 익히세요.

| return | address | become | zebra | lunch |
|---|---|---|---|---|
| 돌아오다 | 주소 | 되다 | 얼룩말 | 점심 |

## Step2 단어가 사용된 문장을 해석해 보세요.

Please return the book to the library. ______________________

What is your home address? ______________________

She wants to become a teacher. ______________________

The zebra has black and white stripes. ______________________

What's for lunch? ______________________

## Step3 다음 대화를 말해 보세요.

A: When will you return home?
B: I will return after lunch.
A: Do you need my address?
B: Yes, please. I will write it down.
A: Look, there's a zebra in the book!
B: It has become my favorite animal!

## Challenge 오늘 배운 단어가 활용된 영어 일기를 해석한 후, 따라서 써 보세요.

I returned home after lunch today. I wrote my address and sent a letter to a zoo to learn how zebras become striped. It was fun to learn new things.

<따라 쓰기>

______________________

______________________

## QUIZ 오늘 배운 단어로 빈칸을 채워 문장을 완성하세요.

Please ______________ the book to the library.

What is your home ______________?

She wants to ______________ a teacher.

The ______________ has black and white stripes.

What's for ______________?

DATE . . . .

DAY 62

## Step1 단어를 익히세요.

| wind | top | sick | wear | give |
| --- | --- | --- | --- | --- |
| 바람 | 위 | 아픈 | 입다 | 주다 |

## Step2 단어가 사용된 문장을 해석해 보세요.

The wind is blowing hard. ________________

The cat is sitting on top of the shelf. ________________

I feel sick today. ________________

She likes to wear dresses. ________________

Please give me the book. ________________

## Step3 다음 대화를 말해 보세요.

A: The wind is so strong today!
B: Yes, my hat blew right off the top of my head.
A: Oh no! Are you feeling sick?
B: No, I'm okay. I just need to wear my jacket.
A: Here, let me give you a scarf too.
B: Thank you! That will help a lot.

## Challenge 오늘 배운 단어가 활용된 영어 일기를 해석한 후, 따라서 써 보세요.

I felt sick today because of the strong wind. My mom told me to wear a warm jacket. She also gave me some soup to feel better.

<따라 쓰기>

________________

________________

## QUIZ 오늘 배운 단어로 빈칸을 채워 문장을 완성하세요.

The ________________ is blowing hard.

The cat is sitting on ________________ of the shelf.

I feel ________________ today.

She likes to ________________ dresses.

Please ________________ me the book.

DATE . . . .

DAY 63

**Step1** 단어를 익히세요.

| easy | circle | sister | cut | lip |
|---|---|---|---|---|
| 쉬운 | 원 | 여동생 | 자르다 | 입술 |

**Step2** 단어가 사용된 문장을 해석해 보세요.

This math problem is easy. ______

Draw a circle on the paper. ______

My sister is very funny. ______

Be careful not to cut yourself. ______

Her lips are red. ______

**Step3** 다음 대화를 말해 보세요.

A: This puzzle is easy!
B: Yes, it's just a circle.
A: My sister loves puzzles too.
B: Maybe she can help us cut this shape.
A: Be careful not to cut your lip.
B: Don't worry, I'll be very careful.

**Challenge** 오늘 배운 단어가 활용된 영어 일기를 해석한 후, 따라서 써 보세요.

I drew an easy circle today. My sister tried to cut it out but accidentally cut her lip. We put a bandage on it and she felt better.

<따라 쓰기>

______

______

**QUIZ** 오늘 배운 단어로 빈칸을 채워 문장을 완성하세요.

This math problem is ______.

Draw a ______ on the paper.

My ______ is very funny.

Be careful not to ______ yourself.

Her ______ are red.

DATE . . . .

DAY 64

## Step1 단어를 익히세요.

| club | cross | moon | case | fact |
|---|---|---|---|---|
| 클럽 | 십자가 | 달 | 경우 | 사실 |

## Step2 단어가 사용된 문장을 해석해 보세요.

I joined the book club. ✎ ______

The cross is a symbol of Christianity. ✎ ______

The moon is full tonight. ✎ ______

In case of emergency, call 911. ✎ ______

It's a fact that the Earth is round. ✎ ______

## Step3 다음 대화를 말해 보세요.

A: Are you going to the club tonight?
B: No, I have to finish my homework.
A: Did you see the moon last night?
B: Yes, it was so bright.
A: The club has a cross on the door.
B: Really? I didn't know that!

## Challenge 오늘 배운 단어가 활용된 영어 일기를 해석한 후, 따라서 써 보세요.

I joined a new club at school today. We learned about the moon and its phases. In case you didn't know, the moon has craters in the shape of a cross, which is a fun fact!

<따라 쓰기>

______

______

## QUIZ 오늘 배운 단어로 빈칸을 채워 문장을 완성하세요.

I joined the book ______.

The ______ is a symbol of Christianity.

The ______ is full tonight.

In ______ of emergency, call 911.

It's a ______ that the Earth is round.

DATE . . . .

DAY 65

## Step1 단어를 익히세요.

| city | window | ice | bomb | son |
|---|---|---|---|---|
| 도시 | 창문 | 얼음 | 폭탄 | 아들 |

## Step2 단어가 사용된 문장을 해석해 보세요.

The city is very crowded. ______

Open the window, please. ______

The ice is melting. ______

The bomb squad arrived quickly. ______

My son loves to play soccer. ______

## Step3 다음 대화를 말해 보세요.

A: This city is so big!
B: Yes, look out the window at all the buildings.
A: Do you see that ice on the road?
B: Yes, it looks slippery.
A: I read a story about a bomb in the city.
B: Oh no, I hope everyone was safe.

## Challenge 오늘 배운 단어가 활용된 영어 일기를 해석한 후, 따라서 써 보세요.

Today, I looked out the window and saw the city covered in ice. My son was excited to play outside. He pretended to be a superhero with a bomb. We had a lot of fun together. It was a great day!

<따라 쓰기>

______

______

## QUIZ 오늘 배운 단어로 빈칸을 채워 문장을 완성하세요.

The ______ is very crowded.

Open the ______, please.

The ______ is melting.

The ______ squad arrived quickly.

My ______ loves to play soccer.

DATE . . . .

DAY 66

## Step1 단어를 익히세요.

| angel | factory | peace | cotton | mouse |
|---|---|---|---|---|
| 천사 | 공장 | 평화 | 면 | 쥐 |

## Step2 단어가 사용된 문장을 해석해 보세요.

She is as kind as an angel. ______

The factory produces toys. ______

We all want world peace. ______

The shirt is made of cotton. ______

The mouse is small and fast. ______

## Step3 다음 대화를 말해 보세요.

A: Look, I drew an angel!

B: Wow, it looks so nice.

A: My dad works at a factory.

B: What do they make there?

A: They make cotton clothes.

B: I saw a mouse near the factory once.

## Challenge 오늘 배운 단어가 활용된 영어 일기를 해석한 후, 따라서 써 보세요.

I saw a picture of an angel today. My dad works at a factory that makes cotton clothes. We found a small mouse in the garden and let it go in peace.

<따라 쓰기>

______

______

## QUIZ 오늘 배운 단어로 빈칸을 채워 문장을 완성하세요.

She is as kind as an ______.

The ______ produces toys.

We all want world ______.

The shirt is made of ______.

The ______ is small and fast.

DATE . . . .

DAY 67

**Step1** 단어를 익히세요.

| milk | engine | much | wish | just |
|---|---|---|---|---|
| 우유 | 엔진 | 많은 | 소원 | 지금 막, 단지 |

**Step2** 단어가 사용된 문장을 해석해 보세요.

I drink milk every morning. ______________________

The engine is very powerful. ______________________

How much is this book? ______________________

Make a wish. ______________________

I just arrived. ______________________

**Step3** 다음 대화를 말해 보세요.

A: Do you want some milk?
B: Yes, I love milk very much!
A: Look at that engine. It's big!
B: Wow, it must be strong.
A: I wish I could see it work.
B: Me too. I just love big engines!

**Challenge** 오늘 배운 단어가 활용된 영어 일기를 해석한 후, 따라서 써 보세요.

I just finished my glass of milk. My brother showed me a toy car with a strong engine. I wish I had as much fun with my toys as he does!

<따라 쓰기>

______________________

______________________

**QUIZ** 오늘 배운 단어로 빈칸을 채워 문장을 완성하세요.

I drink ______________ every morning.

The ______________ is very powerful.

How ______________ is this book?

Make a ______________.

I ______________ arrived.

DATE . . . .

DAY 68

**Step1** 단어를 익히세요.

| fan | block | food | apple | stone |
|---|---|---|---|---|
| 팬, 선풍기 | 막다 | 음식 | 사과 | 돌 |

**Step2** 단어가 사용된 문장을 해석해 보세요.

I am a big fan of soccer. ______

The road is blocked. ______

What is your favorite food? ______

I ate an apple for breakfast. ______

He threw a stone into the lake. ______

**Step3** 다음 대화를 말해 보세요.

A: Do you see that big fan?
B: Yes, it's blowing air on the food.
A: Let's build a tower with these blocks.
B: Okay, I will start with this one.
A: Look, there's an apple on the ground.
B: Be careful, there's a stone next to it.

**Challenge** 오늘 배운 단어가 활용된 영어 일기를 해석한 후, 따라서 써 보세요.

I turned on the fan because it was hot. My sister used a block to stop it from moving. We ate some food, and I found a stone inside my apple!

<따라 쓰기>

______

______

**QUIZ** 오늘 배운 단어로 빈칸을 채워 문장을 완성하세요.

I am a big ______ of soccer.

The road is ______ed.

What is your favorite ______?

I ate an ______ for breakfast.

He threw a ______ into the lake.

DATE . . . .

DAY 69

**Step1** 단어를 익히세요.

| dance | congratulate | accident | love | cash |
|---|---|---|---|---|
| 춤추다 | 축하하다 | 사고 | 사랑하다 | 현금 |

**Step2** 단어가 사용된 문장을 해석해 보세요.

Let's dance to the music. ________________

I want to congratulate you on your success. ________________

There was an accident on the road. ________________

I love my family. ________________

Do you have any cash? ________________

**Step3** 다음 대화를 말해 보세요.

A: Do you like to dance?
B: Yes, I love dancing!
A: We should congratulate him on his win.
B: Yes, let's do that after the party.
A: Did you hear about the accident?
B: Yes, it was on the news.

**Challenge** 오늘 배운 단어가 활용된 영어 일기를 해석한 후, 따라서 써 보세요.

I love to dance at school. Today, my teacher congratulated me on my performance.
My friend had an accident but was fine, so we went to buy snacks with cash.

<따라 쓰기>

________________

________________

**QUIZ** 오늘 배운 단어로 빈칸을 채워 문장을 완성하세요.

Let's ________________ to the music.

I want to ________________ you on your success.

There was an ________________ on the road.

I ________________ my family.

Do you have any ________________?

DATE . . . .

DAY 70

**Step1** 단어를 익히세요.

| fail | there | meet | buy | number |
|---|---|---|---|---|
| 실패하다 | 거기 | 만나다 | 사다 | 숫자 |

**Step2** 단어가 사용된 문장을 해석해 보세요.

I failed my test. ______________________

I will wait for you there. ______________________

Let's meet at 3 P.M. ______________________

I need to buy groceries. ______________________

What is your phone number? ______________________

**Step3** 다음 대화를 말해 보세요.

A: Did you fail the test?

B: No, I passed!

A: Great! I will meet you there.

B: Can you buy some snacks?

A: Sure, how many should I get?

B: Just a small number, maybe five.

**Challenge** 오늘 배운 단어가 활용된 영어 일기를 해석한 후, 따라서 써 보세요.

I failed my math test today. My friend was there to cheer me up. We decided to meet after school to buy a number puzzle.

<따라 쓰기>

______________________

______________________

**QUIZ** 오늘 배운 단어로 빈칸을 채워 문장을 완성하세요.

I ______________ my test.

I will wait for you ______________.

Let's ______________ at 3 P.M.

I need to ______________ groceries.

What is your phone ______________?

DATE . . . .

DAY 71

**Step1** 단어를 익히세요.

| please | send | doctor | girl | ready |
|---|---|---|---|---|
| 부탁하다 | 보내다 | 의사 | 소녀 | 준비된 |

**Step2** 단어가 사용된 문장을 해석해 보세요.

Please help me with this. ______

I will send you a letter. ______

The doctor is very kind. ______

The girl is reading a book. ______

Are you ready to go? ______

**Step3** 다음 대화를 말해 보세요.

A: Can you please send this letter?
B: Sure, I will send it today.
A: The doctor is ready to see you.
B: Okay, thank you.
A: Look, the girl is playing outside.
B: She looks so happy and ready to play!

**Challenge** 오늘 배운 단어가 활용된 영어 일기를 해석한 후, 따라서 써 보세요.

I went to see the doctor today. The girl before me wasn't ready yet. My mom asked, "Please send us in when she is done."

<따라 쓰기>

______

______

**QUIZ** 오늘 배운 단어로 빈칸을 채워 문장을 완성하세요.

______ help me with this.

I will ______ you a letter.

The ______ is very kind.

The ______ is reading a book.

Are you ______ to go?

DATE . . . .

DAY 72

**Step1** 단어를 익히세요.

| grandfather | honest | subway | spoon | gentleman |
|---|---|---|---|---|
| 할아버지 | 정직한 | 지하철 | 숟가락 | 신사 |

**Step2** 단어가 사용된 문장을 해석해 보세요.

My grandfather tells great stories. ______

She is very honest. ______

I take the subway to work. ______

Use a spoon to eat soup. ______

He is a true gentleman. ______

**Step3** 다음 대화를 말해 보세요.

A: My grandfather is visiting today.
B: He sounds like an honest man.
A: Yes, he always tells the truth.
B: Did he take the subway here?
A: Yes, he did. He is such a gentleman.
B: Let's get a spoon for his tea.

**Challenge** 오늘 배운 단어가 활용된 영어 일기를 해석한 후, 따라서 써 보세요.

I visited my grandfather today. He is an honest gentleman who always tells great stories. We took the subway and he gave me a shiny spoon as a gift.

<따라 쓰기>

______

______

**QUIZ** 오늘 배운 단어로 빈칸을 채워 문장을 완성하세요.

My ______ tells great stories.

She is very ______.

I take the ______ to work.

Use a ______ to eat soup.

He is a true ______.

DATE . . . .

DAY 73

**Step1** 단어를 익히세요.

| land | twice | little | and | be |
|---|---|---|---|---|
| 땅 | 두 번 | 작은 | 그리고 | 있다 |

**Step2** 단어가 사용된 문장을 해석해 보세요.

The dog runs on the land. ____________________

I called you twice. ____________________

She has a little puppy. ____________________

He likes pizza and pasta. ____________________

I want to be a doctor. ____________________

**Step3** 다음 대화를 말해 보세요.

A: Look at this big piece of land!

B: Yes, it's twice as big as our yard.

A: There is a little house on it.

B: And there are some trees too.

A: It must be nice to live there.

B: Yes, it looks very peaceful.

**Challenge** 오늘 배운 단어가 활용된 영어 일기를 해석한 후, 따라서 써 보세요.

I saw a little piece of land today. It was there twice as big as I expected. My friend and I played there and had so much fun.

<따라 쓰기>

____________________

____________________

**QUIZ** 오늘 배운 단어로 빈칸을 채워 문장을 완성하세요.

The ____________ is fertile.

I called you ____________.

She has a ____________ puppy.

He likes pizza ____________ pasta.

I want to ____________ a doctor.

DATE . . . .

DAY 74

**Step1** 단어를 익히세요.

| tour | that | drink | because | ant |
|---|---|---|---|---|
| 여행 | 저것 | 마시다 | 왜냐하면 | 개미 |

**Step2** 단어가 사용된 문장을 해석해 보세요.

We took a tour of the city. ______________________

That is my book. ______________________

I like to drink tea. ______________________

I'm tired because I didn't sleep well. ______________________

The ant is very small. ______________________

**Step3** 다음 대화를 말해 보세요.

A: I want to go on a tour.
B: That sounds fun! Where to?
A: Look at that big building over there.
B: I need a drink because I'm thirsty.
A: Be careful, there's an ant on your cup.
B: Thanks, I didn't see it!

**Challenge** 오늘 배운 단어가 활용된 영어 일기를 해석한 후, 따라서 써 보세요.

I went on a tour with my family. We didn't drink from that cup because there was an ant in it. It was still a fun trip!

<따라 쓰기>

______________________

______________________

**QUIZ** 오늘 배운 단어로 빈칸을 채워 문장을 완성하세요.

We took a ______________ of the city.

______________ is my book.

I like to ______________ tea.

I'm tired ______________ I didn't sleep well.

The ______________ is very small.

DATE . . . .

DAY 75

**Step1** 단어를 익히세요.

| wake | talk | dad | lesson | move |
|---|---|---|---|---|
| 깨다 | 말하다 | 아빠 | 수업 | 이동하다 |

**Step2** 단어가 사용된 문장을 해석해 보세요.

I wake up early every day. ______________________

We need to talk. ______________________

My dad is very strong. ______________________

The lesson was interesting. ______________________

We will move to a new house. ______________________

**Step3** 다음 대화를 말해 보세요.

A: I wake up early every day.
B: Me too! I like talking with my dad in the morning.
A: Does he help you with your lessons?
B: Yes, he does. He's really good at math.
A: Are you going to move to a new house soon?
B: Yes, we are moving next month.

**Challenge** 오늘 배운 단어가 활용된 영어 일기를 해석한 후, 따라서 써 보세요.

I wake up early to talk with my dad. He helps me with my lessons before school. Then we move to the kitchen for breakfast.

<따라 쓰기>

______________________

______________________

**QUIZ** 오늘 배운 단어로 빈칸을 채워 문장을 완성하세요.

I ______________ up early every day.

We need to ______________.

My ______________ is very strong.

The ______________ was interesting.

We will ______________ to a new house.

DATE . . . .

DAY 76

**Step1** 단어를 익히세요.

| all | glue | wedding | enter | smart |
|---|---|---|---|---|
| 모두 | 풀 | 결혼식 | 들어가다 | 똑똑한 |

**Step2** 단어가 사용된 문장을 해석해 보세요.

All of my friends are coming. ______________________

Use glue to stick the paper. ______________________

The wedding was beautiful. ______________________

You can enter the room now. ______________________

She is very smart. ______________________

**Step3** 다음 대화를 말해 보세요.

A: Did you invite all your friends to the wedding?

B: Yes, everyone is coming.

A: We need to glue these decorations.

B: Okay, I will help with that.

A: Can we enter the hall now?

B: Yes, let's go. You are so smart for planning this!

**Challenge** 오늘 배운 단어가 활용된 영어 일기를 해석한 후, 따라서 써 보세요.

I went to a wedding with my family. We all had to enter the hall quietly. My cousin used glue to fix his shoe and said he felt very smart for doing it.

<따라 쓰기>

______________________

______________________

**QUIZ** 오늘 배운 단어로 빈칸을 채워 문장을 완성하세요.

______________ of my friends are coming.

Use ______________ to stick the paper.

The ______________ was beautiful.

You can ______________ the room now.

She is very ______________.

DATE . . . .

DAY 77

**Step1** 단어를 익히세요.

| crowd | above | eye | student | exit |
|---|---|---|---|---|
| 군중 | 위에 | 눈 | 학생 | 출구 |

**Step2** 단어가 사용된 문장을 해석해 보세요.

The crowd cheered loudly. ______

The picture is above the sofa. ______

She has green eyes. ______

The student is studying hard. ______

The exit is to the left. ______

**Step3** 다음 대화를 말해 보세요.

A: Look at the crowd over there!
B: Yes, there are so many people.
A: See the balloon above the crowd?
B: Yes, it's right above their heads.
A: I saw a student looking for the exit.
B: The exit is on the left side.

**Challenge** 오늘 배운 단어가 활용된 영어 일기를 해석한 후, 따라서 써 보세요.

I saw a big crowd at the fair today. A balloon floated above everyone's heads. As a student, I kept an eye on the exit in case I got lost.

<따라 쓰기>

______

______

**QUIZ** 오늘 배운 단어로 빈칸을 채워 문장을 완성하세요.

The ______ cheered loudly.

The picture is ______ the sofa.

She has green ______s.

The ______ is studying hard.

The ______ is to the left.

DATE . . . .

DAY 78

## Step1 단어를 익히세요.

| care | countryside | full | contest | area |
| --- | --- | --- | --- | --- |
| 돌보다 | 시골 | 가득 찬 | 대회 | 지역 |

## Step2 단어가 사용된 문장을 해석해 보세요.

I care about you. ____________________

The countryside is peaceful. ____________________

The glass is full of water. ____________________

She won the contest. ____________________

This area is very beautiful. ____________________

## Step3 다음 대화를 말해 보세요.

A: I went to the countryside with my family.

B: That sounds fun! Was it nice there?

A: Yes, it was full of flowers and trees.

B: Did you see any animals in the area?

A: Yes, lots of them. There was even a contest for the best-looking cow!

B: Wow! Did you take care of any animals?

A: Not this time, but I helped my uncle with his garden.

## Challenge 오늘 배운 단어가 활용된 영어 일기를 해석한 후, 따라서 써 보세요.

I went to the countryside to visit my grandparents. They needed help to care for their garden, which was full of flowers. We watched a local contest in the area and had so much fun!

<따라 쓰기>

____________________

____________________

## QUIZ 오늘 배운 단어로 빈칸을 채워 문장을 완성하세요.

I ____________________ about you.

The ____________________ is peaceful.

The glass is ____________________ of water.

She won the ____________________.

This ____________________ is very beautiful.

DATE . . . .

DAY 79

## Step1 단어를 익히세요.

| calender | prize | paper | near | front |
|---|---|---|---|---|
| 달력 | 상 | 종이 | 가까운 | 앞 |

## Step2 단어가 사용된 문장을 해석해 보세요.

Mark the date on your calendar. ______________________

He won a prize. ______________________

Write your name on the paper. ______________________

My house is near the park. ______________________

The car is in front of the house. ______________________

## Step3 다음 대화를 말해 보세요.

A: Look at this calendar!

B: It shows the prize dates for the contest.

A: I need some paper to write it down.

B: There's some paper near the desk.

A: Can you put it in front of me?

B: Sure, here you go!

## Challenge 오늘 배운 단어가 활용된 영어 일기를 해석한 후, 따라서 써 보세요.

I marked a prize on my calendar today. The details were on a piece of paper near my desk. It was in the front of my notebook, so I wouldn't forget.

<따라 쓰기>

______________________

______________________

## QUIZ 오늘 배운 단어로 빈칸을 채워 문장을 완성하세요.

Mark the date on your ______________.

He won a ______________.

Write your name on the ______________.

My house is ______________ the park.

The car is in ______________ of the house.

DATE . . . .

DAY 80

**Step1** 단어를 익히세요.

| war | doll | car | band | country |
|---|---|---|---|---|
| 전쟁 | 인형 | 차 | 밴드 | 나라 |

**Step2** 단어가 사용된 문장을 해석해 보세요.

The war ended last year. ______________________

She has a pretty doll. ______________________

I need to wash my car. ______________________

The band is playing music. ______________________

Korea is a beautiful country. ______________________

**Step3** 다음 대화를 말해 보세요.

A: Did you read about the war in the book?
B: Yes, it was a sad story.
A: I like this doll. It's cute!
B: It looks like it could be from another country.
A: Did you see the new car outside?
B: Yes, it belongs to the band that visited.

**Challenge** 오늘 배운 단어가 활용된 영어 일기를 해석한 후, 따라서 써 보세요.

I learned about a war in history class today. My friend showed me a doll from another country. On the way home, we saw a band playing music near a car.

<따라 쓰기>

______________________

______________________

**QUIZ** 오늘 배운 단어로 빈칸을 채워 문장을 완성하세요.

The ______________ ended last year.

She has a pretty ______________.

I need to wash my ______________.

The ______________ is playing music.

Korea is a beautiful ______________.

DATE . . . .

DAY 81

**Step1** 단어를 익히세요.

| shoe | curtain | only | leaf | along |
|---|---|---|---|---|
| 신발 | 커튼 | 오직 | 잎 | ~을 따라 |

**Step2** 단어가 사용된 문장을 해석해 보세요.

My shoe is too tight. ______________________

Open the curtain, please. ______________________

Only you can help me. ______________________

The leaf fell from the tree. ______________________

Walk along the river. ______________________

**Step3** 다음 대화를 말해 보세요.

A: I lost my shoe.
B: Let's check behind the curtain.
A: There it is! Only one shoe was missing.
B: Look, a leaf blew in through the window.
A: It must have come from the tree along the road.
B: Let's close the curtain to keep more leaves out.

**Challenge** 오늘 배운 단어가 활용된 영어 일기를 해석한 후, 따라서 써 보세요.

I found my lost shoe behind the curtain today. It was the only one missing. I saw a leaf blowing along the sidewalk.

<따라 쓰기>

______________________

______________________

**QUIZ** 오늘 배운 단어로 빈칸을 채워 문장을 완성하세요.

My ______________ is too tight.

Open the ______________, please.

______________ you can help me.

The ______________ fell from the tree.

Walk ______________ the river.

DATE . . . .

DAY 82

**Step1** 단어를 익히세요.

| power | school | both | a(n) | miss |
|---|---|---|---|---|
| 힘 | 학교 | 둘 다 | 하나 | 놓치다 |

**Step2** 단어가 사용된 문장을 해석해 보세요.

Knowledge is power. ______

School starts at 8 A.M. ______

I like both apples and oranges. ______

I have a book. ______

Don't miss the bus. ______

**Step3** 다음 대화를 말해 보세요.

A: Do you have the power to lift this?

B: Yes, I think so. Let's both try.

A: We can do it together!

B: Did you miss the bus to school today?

A: Yes, I missed it by a minute.

B: That's okay, I can give you a ride.

**Challenge** 오늘 배운 단어가 활용된 영어 일기를 해석한 후, 따라서 써 보세요.

I used all my power to run to school today. I didn't want to miss the bus. Both my friend and I had a great day learning a new lesson.

<따라 쓰기>

______

______

**QUIZ** 오늘 배운 단어로 빈칸을 채워 문장을 완성하세요.

Knowledge is ______.

______ starts at 8 A.M.

I like ______ apples and oranges.

I have ______ book.

Don't ______ the bus.

DATE . . . .

DAY 83

**Step1** 단어를 익히세요.

| or | into | farm | also | mind |
|---|---|---|---|---|
| 또는 | 안으로 | 농장 | 또한 | 마음 |

**Step2** 단어가 사용된 문장을 해석해 보세요.

Do you want tea or coffee? ____________________

She went into the house. ____________________

They have a big farm. ____________________

He is a teacher and also a writer. ____________________

Keep an open mind. ____________________

**Step3** 다음 대화를 말해 보세요.

A: Do you want to visit the farm or the park?
B: Let's go to the farm. We can see the animals.
A: We can also buy fresh vegetables there.
B: Yes, that sounds great. Keep that in mind!
A: Should we walk into the barn first?
B: Sure, let's see what's inside!

**Challenge** 오늘 배운 단어가 활용된 영어 일기를 해석한 후, 따라서 써 보세요.

I went into the farm to help or just to relax. The farm work was hard, but I also enjoyed the fresh air. It cleared my mind and made me feel better.

<따라 쓰기>

____________________

____________________

**QUIZ** 오늘 배운 단어로 빈칸을 채워 문장을 완성하세요.

Do you want tea ____________ coffee?

She went ____________ the house.

They have a big ____________.

He is a teacher and ____________ a writer.

Keep an open ____________.

DATE . . . .

DAY 84

**Step1** 단어를 익히세요.

| over | adult | air | office | divide |
|---|---|---|---|---|
| 위에 | 성인 | 공기 | 사무실 | 나누다 |

**Step2** 단어가 사용된 문장을 해석해 보세요.

The plane flew over the city. ______________________

He is now an adult. ______________________

The air is fresh in the morning. ______________________

She works in an office. ______________________

Let's divide the tasks. ______________________

**Step3** 다음 대화를 말해 보세요.

A: Look at the bird flying over the tree!
B: Yes, it's so high in the air.
A: Are we going to the office later?
B: Yes, we need to meet the new adult team member.
A: How do we divide the work for the project?
B: We will discuss that in the meeting.

**Challenge** 오늘 배운 단어가 활용된 영어 일기를 해석한 후, 따라서 써 보세요.

I watched a plane fly over our house today. My mom, who is an adult, works in an office nearby. She helps divide the tasks among her team to keep the air clean and fresh.

<따라 쓰기>

______________________

______________________

**QUIZ** 오늘 배운 단어로 빈칸을 채워 문장을 완성하세요.

The plane flew ____________ the city.

He is now an ____________.

The ____________ is fresh in the morning.

She works in an ____________.

Let's ____________ the tasks.

DATE . . . .

DAY 85

**Step1** 단어를 익히세요.

| river | tail | palace | brother | middle |
|---|---|---|---|---|
| 강 | 꼬리 | 궁전 | 형제 | 중간 |

**Step2** 단어가 사용된 문장을 해석해 보세요.

The river is flowing fast. ____________________

The cat has a long tail. ____________________

The palace is huge. ____________________

My brother is very tall. ____________________

He stood in the middle. ____________________

**Step3** 다음 대화를 말해 보세요.

A: Look at the river! It's so wide.
B: Yes, I see a fish with a long tail.
A: Imagine living in a palace by the river.
B: That would be amazing! My brother would love it.
A: We could play in the middle of the big hall.
B: Yes, and explore every room in the palace.

**Challenge** 오늘 배운 단어가 활용된 영어 일기를 해석한 후, 따라서 써 보세요.

I went to the river with my brother today. We saw a fish with a long tail swimming in the middle. We pretended the river was a palace and had lots of fun.

<따라 쓰기>

____________________

____________________

**QUIZ** 오늘 배운 단어로 빈칸을 채워 문장을 완성하세요.

The __________ is flowing fast.

The dog wagged its __________.

The __________ is huge.

My __________ is very tall.

He stood in the __________.

DATE . . . .

DAY 86

## Step1 단어를 익히세요.

| kind | end | fine | race | sell |
|---|---|---|---|---|
| 친절한 | 끝 | 좋은 | 경주 | 팔다 |

## Step2 단어가 사용된 문장을 해석해 보세요.

She is very kind. ______

This is the end of the road. ______

I'm feeling fine. ______

He won the race. ______

They sell fruit at the market. ______

## Step3 다음 대화를 말해 보세요.

A: That was a fun race!

B: Yes, it was! Everyone was so kind.

A: I'm glad it didn't end too quickly.

B: Me too. The weather was fine today.

A: Did they sell snacks at the event?

B: Yes, I bought some cookies!

## Challenge 오늘 배운 단어가 활용된 영어 일기를 해석한 후, 따라서 써 보세요.

I met a kind teacher today who helped me with my homework. At the end of the day, we watched a fun race. My friend said he will sell his old toys, which are still in fine condition.

<따라 쓰기>

______

______

## QUIZ 오늘 배운 단어로 빈칸을 채워 문장을 완성하세요.

She is very ______.

This is the ______ of the road.

I'm feeling ______.

He won the ______.

They ______ fruit at the market.

DATE . . . .

DAY 87

## Step1 단어를 익히세요.

| business | next | together | learn | cousin |
|---|---|---|---|---|
| 사업 | 다음 | 함께 | 배우다 | 사촌 |

## Step2 단어가 사용된 문장을 해석해 보세요.

He started a new business. ______________________

Who is next in line? ______________________

Let's do this together. ______________________

I want to learn a new language. ______________________

My cousin is visiting us. ______________________

## Step3 다음 대화를 말해 보세요.

A: My cousin started a new business.
B: That's great! What kind of business?
A: It's a bakery. We can visit it next week.
B: I would love to! Maybe we can learn how to bake together.
A: That sounds fun. I like doing things with you.
B: Me too. We always have a good time together.

## Challenge 오늘 배운 단어가 활용된 영어 일기를 해석한 후, 따라서 써 보세요.

My cousin and I plan to start a business together. We want to learn everything we can. Our first meeting is next week.

<따라 쓰기>

______________________

______________________

## QUIZ 오늘 배운 단어로 빈칸을 채워 문장을 완성하세요.

He started a new ______________.

Who is ______________ in line?

Let's do this ______________.

I want to ______________ a new language.

My ______________ is visiting us.

DATE . . . .

DAY 88

**Step1** 단어를 익히세요.

| problem | bug | south | train | curious |
| --- | --- | --- | --- | --- |
| 문제 | 벌레 | 남쪽 | 기차 | 호기심 많은 |

**Step2** 단어가 사용된 문장을 해석해 보세요.

I have a problem with my computer. ✎ ____________________

The bug is on the leaf. ✎ ____________________

We are traveling south. ✎ ____________________

The train is arriving. ✎ ____________________

The cat is very curious. ✎ ____________________

**Step3** 다음 대화를 말해 보세요.

A: I have a problem with my homework.
B: What's the problem? Maybe I can help.
A: There's a bug on my paper!
B: Oh no! Let's move it outside.
A: Have you ever taken the train to the south?
B: No, but I'm curious about what it's like.

**Challenge** 오늘 배운 단어가 활용된 영어 일기를 해석한 후, 따라서 써 보세요.

I had a problem with my toy train today. A bug got inside it, and I couldn't fix it.
My curious brother wanted to know if it came from the south.

<따라 쓰기>

____________________

____________________

**QUIZ** 오늘 배운 단어로 빈칸을 채워 문장을 완성하세요.

I have a ____________________ with my computer.

The ____________________ is on the leaf.

We are traveling ____________________.

The ____________________ is arriving.

The cat is very ____________________.

DATE . . . .

DAY 89

**Step1** 단어를 익히세요.

| this | tonight | museum | engineer | living room |
|---|---|---|---|---|
| 이것 | 오늘 밤 | 박물관 | 엔지니어 | 거실 |

**Step2** 단어가 사용된 문장을 해석해 보세요.

This is my favorite book. ______________________

Let's watch a movie tonight. ______________________

The museum is very interesting. ______________________

She is an engineer. ______________________

The TV is in the living room. ______________________

**Step3** 다음 대화를 말해 보세요.

A: Are you coming to the museum tonight?
B: Yes, I am! I'm excited to see everything.
A: My dad, who is an engineer, will be there too.
B: That's cool! I'd love to meet him.
A: We can talk more about this in the living room.
B: Sure, let's go there now!

**Challenge** 오늘 배운 단어가 활용된 영어 일기를 해석한 후, 따라서 써 보세요.

I am excited about visiting the museum tonight. My dad, who is an engineer, will take me there. We talked about our plans in the living room after dinner.

<따라 쓰기>

**QUIZ** 오늘 배운 단어로 빈칸을 채워 문장을 완성하세요.

__________ is my favorite book.

Let's watch a movie __________.

The __________ is very interesting.

She is an __________.

The TV is in the __________.

DATE . . . .

DAY 90

**Step1** 단어를 익히세요.

| sleep | telephone | mirror | bathroom | almost |
|---|---|---|---|---|
| 자다 | 전화기 | 거울 | 화장실 | 거의 |

**Step2** 단어가 사용된 문장을 해석해 보세요.

I need to sleep early tonight. ______

The telephone is ringing. ______

Look in the mirror. ______

The bathroom is upstairs. ______

It's almost time to go. ______

**Step3** 다음 대화를 말해 보세요.

A: I need to sleep soon. I'm so tired.
B: Me too. Let's talk more tomorrow.
A: Did you see the new telephone in the living room?
B: Yes, it looks really nice.
A: I almost dropped the mirror in the bathroom today.
B: Oh no! Be careful next time.

**Challenge** 오늘 배운 단어가 활용된 영어 일기를 해석한 후, 따라서 써 보세요.

I almost fell asleep while talking on the telephone. Before bed, I looked in the mirror in the bathroom. I had a very tiring day.

<따라 쓰기>

______

______

**QUIZ** 오늘 배운 단어로 빈칸을 채워 문장을 완성하세요.

I need to ______ early tonight.

The ______ is ringing.

Look in the ______.

The ______ is upstairs.

It's ______ time to go.

DATE . . . .

DAY 91

**Step1** 단어를 익히세요.

| part | puzzle | brand | burn | family |
|---|---|---|---|---|
| 부분 | 퍼즐 | 브랜드 | 태우다 | 가족 |

**Step2** 단어가 사용된 문장을 해석해 보세요.

This part is broken. ______

I love solving puzzles. ______

This is my favorite brand. ______

Be careful not to burn yourself. ______

My family is very important to me. ______

**Step3** 다음 대화를 말해 보세요.

A: I finished part of the puzzle.
B: Great job! What brand is it?
A: It's from a brand called "PuzzleFun."
B: I like their puzzles too!
A: Be careful with the candles; we don't want to burn it.
B: Yes, I'll keep them away. My family loves doing puzzles together.

**Challenge** 오늘 배운 단어가 활용된 영어 일기를 해석한 후, 따라서 써 보세요.

I worked on a puzzle with my family today. We finished part of it and saw the brand name on the box. My mom warned us not to burn the pieces by accident.

<따라 쓰기>

**QUIZ** 오늘 배운 단어로 빈칸을 채워 문장을 완성하세요.

This ______ is broken.

I love solving ______.

This is my favorite ______.

Be careful not to ______ yourself.

My ______ is very important to me.

DATE . . . .

DAY 92

**Step1** 단어를 익히세요.

| again | church | last | hair | picture |
|---|---|---|---|---|
| 다시 | 교회 | 마지막 | 머리카락 | 그림 |

**Step2** 단어가 사용된 문장을 해석해 보세요.

Let's do it again.

We go to church every Sunday.

This is the last piece.

She has long hair.

I took a picture of the sunset.

**Step3** 다음 대화를 말해 보세요.

A: Are you going to church again this Sunday?
B: Yes, I go every week.
A: Did you see the picture on the wall?
B: Yes, it was beautiful.
A: It shows the last supper.
B: I noticed it. The details in the hair are amazing!

**Challenge** 오늘 배운 단어가 활용된 영어 일기를 해석한 후, 따라서 써 보세요.

I went to church again with my family. I saw a beautiful picture of the last supper on the wall. My mom fixed my hair before we went inside.

<따라 쓰기>

______________________________

______________________________

**QUIZ** 오늘 배운 단어로 빈칸을 채워 문장을 완성하세요.

Let's do it ____________.

We go to ____________ every Sunday.

This is the ____________ piece.

She has long ____________.

I took a ____________ of the sunset.

DATE . . . .

DAY 93

## Step1 단어를 익히세요.

| cute | fill | cook | how | homework |
|---|---|---|---|---|
| 귀여운 | 채우다 | 요리하다 | 어떻게 | 숙제 |

## Step2 단어가 사용된 문장을 해석해 보세요.

That puppy is so cute. ________________

Fill the bottle with water. ________________

I love to cook. ________________

How are you today? ________________

I need to finish my homework. ________________

## Step3 다음 대화를 말해 보세요.

A: Your new puppy is so cute!

B: Thanks! He fills our home with joy.

A: How do you find time to cook and do homework?

B: I cook first, then do my homework.

A: That sounds like a good plan.

B: It works well for me!

## Challenge 오늘 배운 단어가 활용된 영어 일기를 해석한 후, 따라서 써 보세요.

I saw a cute cat while doing my homework. To fill the time, I decided to cook something. I wondered how to make a simple dish.

<따라 쓰기>

________________

________________

## QUIZ 오늘 배운 단어로 빈칸을 채워 문장을 완성하세요.

That puppy is so ________________.

________________ the bottle with water.

I love to ________________.

________________ are you today?

I need to finish my ________________.

DATE . . . .

DAY 94

## Step1 단어를 익히세요.

| start | might | date | nation | body |
| --- | --- | --- | --- | --- |
| 시작하다 | ~할지도 모른다 | 날짜 | 국가 | 몸 |

## Step2 단어가 사용된 문장을 해석해 보세요.

Let's start the meeting. ______

It might rain later. ______

What is today's date? ______

Korea is a beautiful nation. ______

Take care of your body. ______

## Step3 다음 대화를 말해 보세요.

A: When will the game start?

B: It might start at 5 P.M.

A: Do you know the date of the game?

B: Yes, it's on June 10th.

A: Which nation is hosting the event?

B: Our nation is hosting it this year.

## Challenge 오늘 배운 단어가 활용된 영어 일기를 해석한 후, 따라서 써 보세요.

I started a new book today about different nations. It said that the date of the festival might change. I learned how each country's culture affects the body and health.

<따라 쓰기>

______

______

## QUIZ 오늘 배운 단어로 빈칸을 채워 문장을 완성하세요.

Let's ______ the meeting.

It ______ rain later.

What is today's ______?

Korea is a beautiful ______.

Take care of your ______.

DATE . . . .

DAY 95

**Step1** 단어를 익히세요.

| discuss | good | act | trip | bird |
|---|---|---|---|---|
| 논의하다 | 좋은 | 행동하다 | 여행 | 새 |

**Step2** 단어가 사용된 문장을 해석해 보세요.

Let's discuss the plan. ______________________

This is a good book. ______________________

You should act right now. ______________________

We are planning a trip. ______________________

The bird is singing. ______________________

**Step3** 다음 대화를 말해 보세요.

A: Let's discuss the new project.
B: Sure, when do you have time? This is a good idea.
A: I agree. We need to act quickly.
B: Yes, we do. Are you planning a trip?
A: Yes, to the mountains. Look at that bird!
B: It's beautiful.

**Challenge** 오늘 배운 단어가 활용된 영어 일기를 해석한 후, 따라서 써 보세요.

I discussed our trip with my family today. We had a good plan for where to go. I saw a bird act funny in the park.

<따라 쓰기>

______________________

______________________

**QUIZ** 오늘 배운 단어로 빈칸을 채워 문장을 완성하세요.

Let's ______________ the plan.

This is a ______________ book.

You should ______________ right now.

We are planning a ______________.

The ______________ is singing.

DATE . . . .

DAY 96

**Step1** 단어를 익히세요.

| bridge | left | cover | oil | great |
|---|---|---|---|---|
| 다리 | 왼쪽 | 덮다 | 기름 | 훌륭한 |

**Step2** 단어가 사용된 문장을 해석해 보세요.

The bridge is very long. ______

Turn left at the corner. ______

Cover the pot with a lid. ______

The car needs more oil. ______

She did a great job. ______

**Step3** 다음 대화를 말해 보세요.

A: Look at that big bridge!

B: Yes, it's on the left side of the road.

A: The bridge is covered with lights.

B: That must look great at night.

A: Be careful of the oil on the road.

B: Thanks for telling me. I'll watch out.

**Challenge** 오늘 배운 단어가 활용된 영어 일기를 해석한 후, 따라서 써 보세요.

I walked across the bridge today. On the left side, it was covered with flowers. We had to be careful because there was some oil on the path, but the view was great.

<따라 쓰기>

______

______

**QUIZ** 오늘 배운 단어로 빈칸을 채워 문장을 완성하세요.

The ______ is very long.

Turn ______ at the corner.

______ the pot with a lid.

The car needs more ______.

She did a ______ job.

DATE . . . .

DAY 97

**Step1** 단어를 익히세요.

| of | back | adventure | breakfast | carry |
| --- | --- | --- | --- | --- |
| ~의 | 뒤, 등 | 모험 | 아침 식사 | 나르다 |

**Step2** 단어가 사용된 문장을 해석해 보세요.

This is the book of dreams. ______

My back hurts. ______

We went on an adventure. ______

I had toast for breakfast. ______

Can you carry this bag? ______

**Step3** 다음 대화를 말해 보세요.

A: Are you ready for a day of adventure?

B: Yes, I just need to eat breakfast first.

A: What did you have for breakfast?

B: I had cereal and juice.

A: Do you want me to carry your bag?

B: That would be great. My back is a bit sore.

**Challenge** 오늘 배운 단어가 활용된 영어 일기를 해석한 후, 따라서 써 보세요.

I had a big breakfast before our adventure. We carried our backpacks full of snacks. The trail was fun, and I loved exploring the back of the forest.

<따라 쓰기>

______

______

**QUIZ** 오늘 배운 단어로 빈칸을 채워 문장을 완성하세요.

This is the book ______ dreams.

My ______ hurts.

We went on an ______.

I had toast for ______.

Can you ______ this bag?

DATE . . . .

DAY 98

## Step1 단어를 익히세요.

| class | glove | beauty | ear | weekend |
|---|---|---|---|---|
| 수업 | 장갑 | 아름다움 | 귀 | 주말 |

## Step2 단어가 사용된 문장을 해석해 보세요.

The class is starting soon. ____________________

Wear gloves to keep your hands warm. ____________________

The beauty of nature is amazing. ____________________

My ear hurts. ____________________

What are your plans for the weekend? ____________________

## Step3 다음 대화를 말해 보세요.

A: How was your class today?

B: It was good. We learned a lot.

A: Did you see my new gloves?

B: Yes, they are beautiful!

A: What are you doing this weekend?

B: I'm going to the park to enjoy the beauty of nature.

## Challenge 오늘 배운 단어가 활용된 영어 일기를 해석한 후, 따라서 써 보세요.

I had a fun class about nature today. My teacher wore gloves to show us the beauty of different plants. I can't wait to learn more this weekend; it was music to my ears!

<따라 쓰기>

____________________

____________________

## QUIZ 오늘 배운 단어로 빈칸을 채워 문장을 완성하세요.

The ____________________ is starting soon.

Wear ____________________ to keep your hands warm.

The ____________________ of nature is amazing.

My ____________________ hurts.

What are your plans for the ____________________?

DATE . . . .

DAY 99

**Step1** 단어를 익히세요.

| eat | prince | touch | answer | carrot |
|---|---|---|---|---|
| 먹다 | 왕자 | 만지다 | 대답하다 | 당근 |

**Step2** 단어가 사용된 문장을 해석해 보세요.

I like to eat pizza. ______________________

The prince is charming. ______________________

Do not touch the painting. ______________________

Please answer the question. ______________________

Rabbits eat carrots. ______________________

**Step3** 다음 대화를 말해 보세요.

A: Did you see the prince in the movie?
B: Yes, he was very brave.
A: What did he eat for dinner?
B: He ate a big carrot.
A: Can I touch the book with his story?
B: Sure, I'll answer any questions you have.

**Challenge** 오늘 배운 단어가 활용된 영어 일기를 해석한 후, 따라서 써 보세요.

I read a story about a prince who loves to eat carrots. He let people touch his golden crown. When asked why he loves carrots, he would always answer with a smile.

<따라 쓰기>

______________________

______________________

**QUIZ** 오늘 배운 단어로 빈칸을 채워 문장을 완성하세요.

I like to ______________ pizza.

The ______________ is charming.

Do not ______________ the painting.

Please ______________ the question.

Rabbits eat ______________.

DATE . . . .

DAY 100

## Step1 단어를 익히세요.

| alright | rain | woman | balloon | sour |
|---|---|---|---|---|
| 괜찮은 | 비 | 여성 | 풍선 | 신, 시큼한 |

## Step2 단어가 사용된 문장을 해석해 보세요.

Everything is alright now. ________________

It's going to rain soon. ________________

The woman is very kind. ________________

I love balloons. ________________

This lemon is sour. ________________

## Step3 다음 대화를 말해 보세요.

A: Is everything alright?

B: Yes, just enjoying the rain.

A: Look at that woman with the balloons.

B: She looks happy.

A: I tasted a sour candy today.

B: Really? I prefer sweet ones.

## Challenge 오늘 배운 단어가 활용된 영어 일기를 해석한 후, 따라서 써 보세요.

I went outside even though it was raining. A woman gave me a balloon, which made my day. I also tried a sour candy, but it was alright.

<따라 쓰기>

________________

________________

## QUIZ 오늘 배운 단어로 빈칸을 채워 문장을 완성하세요.

Everything is ________________ now.

It's going to ________________ soon.

The ________________ is very kind.

I love ________________.

This lemon is ________________.

DATE . . . .

DAY 101

**Step1** 단어를 익히세요.

| fight | world | exercise | heart | ground |
|---|---|---|---|---|
| 싸움, 싸우다 | 세계 | 운동하다 | 심장 | 땅 |

**Step2** 단어가 사용된 문장을 해석해 보세요.

They had a big fight. ________________

The world is a big place. ________________

I exercise every morning. ________________

My heart is beating fast. ________________

The ground is wet. ________________

**Step3** 다음 대화를 말해 보세요.

A: Did you see the news about the fight?

B: Yes, it was happening in another part of the world.

A: It's important to exercise for a healthy heart.

B: I agree. I like to run on the ground outside.

A: Running outside is the best!

B: Yes, it makes my heart feel strong.

**Challenge** 오늘 배운 단어가 활용된 영어 일기를 해석한 후, 따라서 써 보세요.

I watched a movie about a fight to save the world. It reminded me to exercise and keep my heart strong. Afterward, I did push-ups on the ground.

<따라 쓰기>

________________

________________

**QUIZ** 오늘 배운 단어로 빈칸을 채워 문장을 완성하세요.

They had a big ________________.

The ________________ is a big place.

I ________________ every morning.

My ________________ is beating fast.

The ________________ is wet.

DATE . . . .

DAY 102

**Step1** 단어를 익히세요.

| type | desk | famous | fruit | lake |
|---|---|---|---|---|
| 유형 | 책상 | 유명한 | 과일 | 호수 |

**Step2** 단어가 사용된 문장을 해석해 보세요.

What type of music do you like? ______________________

The book is on the desk. ______________________

She is a famous singer. ______________________

I like to eat fruit. ______________________

The lake is very calm. ______________________

**Step3** 다음 대화를 말해 보세요.

A: What type of fruit do you like?
B: I like apples the best.
A: Have you seen that famous desk?
B: Yes, it's in the museum.
A: Do you like visiting the lake?
B: Yes, it's a great place to relax.

**Challenge** 오늘 배운 단어가 활용된 영어 일기를 해석한 후, 따라서 써 보세요.

I learned about different types of fruit in class today. We talked about a famous lake where special fruit grows. I sat at my desk and drew a picture of the lake.

<따라 쓰기>

______________________

______________________

**QUIZ** 오늘 배운 단어로 빈칸을 채워 문장을 완성하세요.

What ______________ of music do you like?

The book is on the ______________.

She is a ______________ singer.

I like to eat ______________.

The ______________ is very calm.

DATE . . . .

DAY 103

## Step1 단어를 익히세요.

| cookie | before | against | kitchen | voice |
|---|---|---|---|---|
| 쿠키 | 전에 | 반대하여 | 주방 | 목소리 |

## Step2 단어가 사용된 문장을 해석해 보세요.

I baked some cookies. ______________________

Finish your homework before dinner. ______________________

She is against the idea. ______________________

The kitchen is clean. ______________________

Her voice is beautiful. ______________________

## Step3 다음 대화를 말해 보세요.

A: Did you bake cookies before dinner?
B: Yes, they're in the kitchen.
A: I heard your voice singing while baking.
B: Yes, I love to sing when I cook.
A: Are you against eating cookies before dinner?
B: No, I think it's okay to have one!

## Challenge 오늘 배운 단어가 활용된 영어 일기를 해석한 후, 따라서 써 보세요.

I ate a cookie before dinner today. My mom was against it, but I couldn't resist. Her voice called me from the kitchen to set the table.

<따라 쓰기>

______________________

______________________

## QUIZ 오늘 배운 단어로 빈칸을 채워 문장을 완성하세요.

What ______________ of music do you like?

The book is on the ______________.

She is a ______________ singer.

I like to eat ______________.

The ______________ is very calm.

DATE . . . .

DAY 104

**Step1** 단어를 익히세요.

after | strong | than | right | hour

**Step2** 단어가 사용된 문장을 해석해 보세요.

We can leave after lunch. ______________________

He is very strong. ______________________

She is taller than me. ______________________

Turn right at the next street. ______________________

The meeting is in an hour. ______________________

**Step3** 다음 대화를 말해 보세요.

A: Let's go for a walk after dinner.
B: That sounds good. I need to get strong.
A: Walking is easier than running.
B: Yes, and we can talk while we walk.
A: Should we turn right at the corner?
B: Yes, and let's walk for an hour.

**Challenge** 오늘 배운 단어가 활용된 영어 일기를 해석한 후, 따라서 써 보세요.

I felt stronger after my workout today. My right arm is stronger than my left. I exercised for an hour.

<따라 쓰기>

______________________

______________________

**QUIZ** 오늘 배운 단어로 빈칸을 채워 문장을 완성하세요.

We can leave ______________ lunch.

He is very ______________.

She is taller ______________ me.

Turn ______________ at the next street.

The meeting is in an ______________.

DATE . . . .

DAY 105

**Step1** 단어를 익히세요.

| off | human | some | fox | arm |
|---|---|---|---|---|
| 멀리, 떨어져서 | 인간 | 몇몇 | 여우 | 팔 |

**Step2** 단어가 사용된 문장을 해석해 보세요.

Turn off the lights. ✎ ______________________

Humans are intelligent. ✎ ______________________

I need some help. ✎ ______________________

The fox is very clever. ✎ ______________________

My arm hurts. ✎ ______________________

**Step3** 다음 대화를 말해 보세요.

A: Turn off the TV, please.
B: Okay, I'll turn it off.
A: Some humans are as smart as a fox.
B: Yes, I heard that.
A: I saw a fox today.
B: Wow! I hope it doesn't bite my arm!

**Challenge** 오늘 배운 단어가 활용된 영어 일기를 해석한 후, 따라서 써 보세요.

I saw a fox run off into the woods today. Some humans were watching it from a distance. My friend waved his arm to say goodbye to the fox.

<따라 쓰기>

______________________

______________________

**QUIZ** 오늘 배운 단어로 빈칸을 채워 문장을 완성하세요.

Turn ____________ the lights.

____________ are intelligent.

I need ____________ help.

The ____________ is very clever.

My ____________ hurts.

DATE . . . .

DAY 106

## Step1 단어를 익히세요.

| art | year | cat | west | room |
|---|---|---|---|---|
| 예술 | 해, 년 | 고양이 | 서쪽 | 방 |

## Step2 단어가 사용된 문장을 해석해 보세요.

I love modern art. ______________________

This year is going by fast. ______________________

The cat is sleeping. ______________________

The sun sets in the west. ______________________

The room is messy. ______________________

## Step3 다음 대화를 말해 보세요.

A: Do you like art?

B: Yes, I love drawing.

A: I got a cat last year.

B: Really? Cats are so cute.

A: My cat likes to sleep in my room.

B: Mine likes to watch the sunset in the west.

## Challenge 오늘 배운 단어가 활용된 영어 일기를 해석한 후, 따라서 써 보세요.

I made some art in my room today. It was a picture of a cat. I showed it to my friend who lives in the west part of town; we've been friends for a year.

<따라 쓰기>

______________________

______________________

## QUIZ 오늘 배운 단어로 빈칸을 채워 문장을 완성하세요.

I love modern ______________.

This ______________ is going by fast.

The ______________ is sleeping.

The sun sets in the ______________.

The ______________ is messy.

DATE . . . .

DAY 107

## Step1 단어를 익히세요.

| pick | cart | ahead | season | bank |
|---|---|---|---|---|
| 고르다 | 카트 | 앞으로 | 계절 | 은행 |

## Step2 단어가 사용된 문장을 해석해 보세요.

Pick your favorite color. ______________________

The cart is full of groceries. ______________________

We need to plan ahead. ______________________

Spring is my favorite season. ______________________

I need to go to the bank. ______________________

## Step3 다음 대화를 말해 보세요.

A: Which fruit should we pick?
B: Let's pick apples.
A: Do we need a cart for the apples?
B: Yes, it's just ahead.
A: What's your favorite season?
B: I like summer because I can go to the river bank.

## Challenge 오늘 배운 단어가 활용된 영어 일기를 해석한 후, 따라서 써 보세요.

I went to the store to pick some fruits today. I pushed the cart ahead of me, looking for my favorite snacks. This season, we plan to visit the river bank for a picnic.

<따라 쓰기>

______________________

______________________

## QUIZ 오늘 배운 단어로 빈칸을 채워 문장을 완성하세요.

__________ your favorite color.

The __________ is full of groceries.

We need to plan __________.

Spring is my favorite __________.

I need to go to the __________.

DATE . . . .

DAY 108

**Step1** 단어를 익히세요.

| fever | fall | could | now | to |
| --- | --- | --- | --- | --- |
| 열 | 떨어지다 | 할 수 있다 | 지금 | ~로 |

**Step2** 단어가 사용된 문장을 해석해 보세요.

He has a high fever. ________________

Be careful not to fall. ________________

Could you help me? ________________

Let's go now. ________________

She went to the store. ________________

**Step3** 다음 대화를 말해 보세요.

A: Do you have a fever?
B: Yes, I think so.
A: You could fall if you don't rest.
B: I know, I should lie down now.
A: Can I get you something to drink?
B: Yes, please. That would be nice.

**Challenge** 오늘 배운 단어가 활용된 영어 일기를 해석한 후, 따라서 써 보세요.

I have a fever now, so I can't go to school. My mom said I could fall if I try to move too much. I hope to feel better soon.

<따라 쓰기>

________________

________________

**QUIZ** 오늘 배운 단어로 빈칸을 채워 문장을 완성하세요.

He has a high ________________.

Be careful not to ________________.

________________ you help me?

Let's go ________________.

She went ________________ the store.

DATE . . . .

DAY 109

**Step1** 단어를 익히세요.

| hundred | science | below | stress | can |
|---|---|---|---|---|
| 백(100) | 과학 | 아래 | 스트레스 | 할 수 있다 |

**Step2** 단어가 사용된 문장을 해석해 보세요.

There are a hundred students in the school. ______

I love studying science. ______

The cat is hiding below the table. ______

I feel a lot of stress before exams. ______

I can help you with that. ______

**Step3** 다음 대화를 말해 보세요.

A: There are a hundred stars in the sky tonight.
B: Wow, that's a lot!
A: Do you like science?
B: Yes, I love learning about the stars.
A: The temperature is below freezing tonight.
B: That can cause stress for some people.

**Challenge** 오늘 배운 단어가 활용된 영어 일기를 해석한 후, 따라서 써 보세요.

I read a science book with a hundred fun facts. One fact said that being below sea level can cause stress. It was interesting to learn how deep water can affect us.

<따라 쓰기>

______

______

**QUIZ** 오늘 배운 단어로 빈칸을 채워 문장을 완성하세요.

There are a ______ students in the school.

I love studying ______.

The cat is hiding ______ the table.

I feel a lot of ______ before exams.

I ______ help you with that.

DATE . . . .

DAY 110

**Step1** 단어를 익히세요.

| history | yesterday | however | park | gift |
|---|---|---|---|---|
| 역사 | 어제 | 하지만 | 공원 | 선물 |

**Step2** 단어가 사용된 문장을 해석해 보세요.

History is my favorite subject. ________________

I met her yesterday. ________________

However, I disagree with you. ________________

We played in the park. ________________

She gave me a gift. ________________

**Step3** 다음 대화를 말해 보세요.

A: Did you study history yesterday?
B: Yes, I did.
A: However, I still have questions.
B: We can talk about it at the park.
A: I got a gift for you!
B: Thank you! I love surprises.

**Challenge** 오늘 배운 단어가 활용된 영어 일기를 해석한 후, 따라서 써 보세요.

Yesterday, I visited a history museum. However, I also spent time in the park nearby. I bought a small gift from the museum shop to remember the day.

<따라 쓰기>

________________

________________

**QUIZ** 오늘 배운 단어로 빈칸을 채워 문장을 완성하세요.

________________ is my favorite subject.

I met her ________________.

________________, I disagree with you.

We played in the ________________.

She gave me a ________________.

DATE . . . .

DAY 111

**Step1** **단어를 익히세요.**

| borrow | study | alone | fish | giraffe |
|---|---|---|---|---|
| 빌리다 | 공부하다 | 혼자 | 물고기 | 기린 |

**Step2** **단어가 사용된 문장을 해석해 보세요.**

Can I borrow your pen? ______________________

I need to study for my exam. ______________________

She likes to be alone. ______________________

The fish is swimming. ______________________

The giraffe is very tall. ______________________

**Step3** **다음 대화를 말해 보세요.**

A: Can I borrow your book to study?

B: Sure, but why do you want to study alone?

A: I focus better when I'm alone.

B: That makes sense. Did you know I have a pet fish?

A: Really? I wish I had a pet. Maybe a giraffe!

B: A giraffe? That's funny!

**Challenge** **오늘 배운 단어가 활용된 영어 일기를 해석한 후, 따라서 써 보세요.**

I borrowed a book to study alone. While reading, I saw pictures of a fish and a giraffe. It made my study time more interesting.

<따라 쓰기>

______________________

______________________

**QUIZ** **오늘 배운 단어로 빈칸을 채워 문장을 완성하세요.**

Can I ______________ your pen?

I need to ______________ for my exam.

She likes to be ______________.

The ______________ is swimming.

The ______________ is very tall.

DATE . . . .

DAY 112

**Step1** **단어를 익히세요.**

| concert | play | sand | evening | fast |
|---|---|---|---|---|
| 콘서트 | 놀다 | 모래 | 저녁 | 빠른 |

**Step2** **단어가 사용된 문장을 해석해 보세요.**

The concert was amazing. ____________________

Let's play outside. ____________________

The sand is warm. ____________________

Good evening! ____________________

The car is very fast. ____________________

**Step3** **다음 대화를 말해 보세요.**

A: Are you going to the concert tonight?
B: Yes, I am! Are you going too?
A: No, I'm going to play in the sand with my brother.
B: That sounds fun! What time are you going?
A: We're going in the evening, around 6 P.M.
B: Have a great time! Time goes by so fast when you're having fun.

**Challenge** **오늘 배운 단어가 활용된 영어 일기를 해석한 후, 따라서 써 보세요.**

In the evening, I went to a concert. Afterward, I watched children play in the sand. It was a fast-paced day but very enjoyable.

<따라 쓰기>

____________________

____________________

**QUIZ** **오늘 배운 단어로 빈칸을 채워 문장을 완성하세요.**

The ____________ was amazing.

Let's ____________ outside.

The ____________ is warm.

Good ____________!

The car is very ____________.

DATE . . . .

DAY 113

**Step1** 단어를 익히세요.

| cloud | basketball | duck | die | bone |
|---|---|---|---|---|
| 구름 | 농구 | 오리 | 죽다 | 뼈 |

**Step2** 단어가 사용된 문장을 해석해 보세요.

The cloud looks like a sheep. ____________________

We played basketball at school. ____________________

The duck is swimming. ____________________

The plant will die without water. ____________________

The bone is strong. ____________________

**Step3** 다음 대화를 말해 보세요.

A: Look at that cloud!
B: It looks like a duck.
A: Do you want to play basketball later?
B: Sure, that sounds fun.
A: Did you hear about the old duck that died?
B: Yes, it was sad. Ducks have weak bones.

**Challenge** 오늘 배운 단어가 활용된 영어 일기를 해석한 후, 따라서 써 보세요.

I saw clouds in the sky while playing basketball. A duck was nearby, looking for food. Sadly, I found a bone, and it made me think of animals that die.

<따라 쓰기>

**QUIZ** 오늘 배운 단어로 빈칸을 채워 문장을 완성하세요.

The ____________________ looks like a sheep.

We played ____________________ at school.

The ____________________ is swimming.

The plant will ____________________ without water.

The ____________________ is strong.

DATE . . . .

DAY 114

**Step1** 단어를 익히세요.

| word | grass | pig | king | jeans |
|---|---|---|---|---|
| 단어 | 잔디 | 돼지 | 왕 | 청바지 |

**Step2** 단어가 사용된 문장을 해석해 보세요.

This word is difficult to spell. ______

The grass is green. ______

The pig is eating. ______

The king is wise. ______

I wear jeans every day. ______

**Step3** 다음 대화를 말해 보세요.

A: Can you spell this word?

B: Yes, I can spell it.

A: Look at the pig on the grass.

B: It's rolling around!

A: Did you see the king in the movie?

B: Yes, he was wearing jeans!

**Challenge** 오늘 배운 단어가 활용된 영어 일기를 해석한 후, 따라서 써 보세요.

I learned a new word today: "king." We read a story about a king who loved to play on the grass. He even wore jeans while playing with his pet pig.

<따라 쓰기>

______

______

**QUIZ** 오늘 배운 단어로 빈칸을 채워 문장을 완성하세요.

This ______ is difficult to spell.

The ______ is green.

The ______ is eating.

The ______ is wise.

I wear ______ every day.

DATE . . . .

DAY 115

**Step1** 단어를 익히세요.

| pencil | time | memory | holiday | work |
|---|---|---|---|---|
| 연필 | 시간 | 기억 | 휴일 | 일하다 |

**Step2** 단어가 사용된 문장을 해석해 보세요.

I need a new pencil. ______________________________

What time is it? ______________________________

This is a great memory. ______________________________

The holiday starts tomorrow. ______________________________

I work from home. ______________________________

**Step3** 다음 대화를 말해 보세요.

A: Do you have a pencil I can use?
B: Yes, here you go.
A: What time is it now?
B: It's 3 P.M.
A: Do you have a favorite holiday memory?
B: Yes, I remember when we didn't have to work and had fun!

**Challenge** 오늘 배운 단어가 활용된 영어 일기를 해석한 후, 따라서 써 보세요.

I used a pencil to write about my holiday memories. It took some time, but it was worth it. Now, I have a nice story to remember when I work.

<따라 쓰기>

______________________________

______________________________

**QUIZ** 오늘 배운 단어로 빈칸을 채워 문장을 완성하세요.

I need a new ____________.

What ____________ is it?

This is a great ____________.

The ____________ starts tomorrow.

I ____________ from home.

DATE . . . .

DAY 116

## Step1 단어를 익히세요.

| people | lazy | must | aunt | fly |
|---|---|---|---|---|
| 사람들 | 게으른 | 해야 한다 | 이모, 고모 | 날다 |

## Step2 단어가 사용된 문장을 해석해 보세요.

People are very kind here. ______________________

Don't be lazy. ______________________

You must finish your homework. ______________________

My aunt is visiting us. ______________________

Birds can fly. ______________________

## Step3 다음 대화를 말해 보세요.

A: Some people can be lazy.
B: Yes, but we must work hard.
A: My aunt always says that.
B: She sounds very wise.
A: Did you see the bird fly?
B: Yes, it flew so high!

## Challenge 오늘 배운 단어가 활용된 영어 일기를 해석한 후, 따라서 써 보세요.

My aunt says that people should not be lazy. She told me we must work hard to reach our goals. She also said, "If you work hard, you can fly high like a bird!"

<따라 쓰기>

______________________

______________________

## QUIZ 오늘 배운 단어로 빈칸을 채워 문장을 완성하세요.

______________ are very kind here.

Don't be ______________.

You ______________ finish your homework.

My ______________ is visiting us.

Birds can ______________.

DATE . . . .

DAY 117

**Step1** 단어를 익히세요.

| tomorrow | night | blue | birth | every |
|---|---|---|---|---|
| 내일 | 밤 | 파란, 파란색 | 출생 | 모든 |

**Step2** 단어가 사용된 문장을 해석해 보세요.

See you tomorrow. ______________________

Good night! ______________________

The sky is blue. ______________________

Her birth was a blessing. ______________________

I walk every day. ______________________

**Step3** 다음 대화를 말해 보세요.

A: What are you doing tomorrow?

B: I'm going out at night to see the stars.

A: The sky will be so blue!

B: Yes, it will be beautiful.

A: Do you know your birth date?

B: Yes, it's in every memory I have!

**Challenge** 오늘 배운 단어가 활용된 영어 일기를 해석한 후, 따라서 써 보세요.

Tomorrow night, I will see the blue moon. It only happens once in a while, like a special birth. Every time it happens, it feels magical.

<따라 쓰기>

______________________

______________________

**QUIZ** 오늘 배운 단어로 빈칸을 채워 문장을 완성하세요.

See you ______________.

Good ______________!

The sky is ______________.

Her ______________ was a blessing.

I walk ______________ day.

DATE . . . .

DAY 118

## Step1 단어를 익히세요.

| lie | ring | push | goodbye | cage |
| --- | --- | --- | --- | --- |
| 거짓말하다 | 반지 | 밀다 | 안녕 | 우리 |

## Step2 단어가 사용된 문장을 해석해 보세요.

Don't lie to me. ______

She wore a diamond ring. ______

Can you push the door? ______

Goodbye, see you soon. ______

The bird is in the cage. ______

## Step3 다음 대화를 말해 보세요.

A: Did you lie about the ring?

B: No, I told the truth.

A: Can you push the door open?

B: Sure, no problem.

A: It's time to say goodbye to the bird.

B: Yes, let's open the cage and let it go.

## Challenge 오늘 배운 단어가 활용된 영어 일기를 해석한 후, 따라서 써 보세요.

I saw my friend lie about losing his ring. He tried to push the blame on someone else. Before saying goodbye, we let the bird out of its cage.

<따라 쓰기>

______

______

## QUIZ 오늘 배운 단어로 빈칸을 채워 문장을 완성하세요.

Don't ______ to me.

She wore a diamond ______.

Can you ______ the door?

______, see you soon.

The bird is in the ______.

DATE . . . .

DAY 119

**Step1** 단어를 익히세요.

| quick | tape | in | cow | drop |
|---|---|---|---|---|
| 빠른 | 테이프 | ~안에 | 소 | 떨어트리다 |

**Step2** 단어가 사용된 문장을 해석해 보세요.

He is a quick learner. ✎ ______

Use tape to fix it. ✎ ______

The cat is in the box. ✎ ______

The cow is in the field. ✎ ______

Don't drop the glass. ✎ ______

**Step3** 다음 대화를 말해 보세요.

A: Can you make a quick fix with this tape?

B: Sure, I'll put it in place.

A: Be careful not to drop it.

B: I got it! Did you see the cow in the field?

A: Yes, it was walking slowly.

B: It's a nice contrast to our quick work!

**Challenge** 오늘 배운 단어가 활용된 영어 일기를 해석한 후, 따라서 써 보세요.

I fixed my book with quick tape today. I saw a cow in the field while walking.

I was careful not to drop my snack on the way.

<따라 쓰기>

______

______

**QUIZ** 오늘 배운 단어로 빈칸을 채워 문장을 완성하세요.

He is a ______ learner.

Use ______ to fix it.

The cat is ______ the box.

The ______ is in the field.

Don't ______ the glass.

DATE . . . .

DAY 120

**Step1** 단어를 익히세요.

| hot | change | want | coin | ugly |
|---|---|---|---|---|
| 뜨거운 | 변하다 | 원하다 | 동전 | 못생긴 |

**Step2** 단어가 사용된 문장을 해석해 보세요.

The soup is very hot. ______________________

People change over time. ______________________

I want to go home. ______________________

He found a coin on the ground. ______________________

That painting is ugly. ______________________

**Step3** 다음 대화를 말해 보세요.

A: The weather is so hot today!
B: Yes, I wish it would change soon.
A: Do you want to get some ice cream?
B: That sounds perfect!
A: Look at this old coin I found.
B: It's a bit ugly, but it's interesting!

**Challenge** 오늘 배운 단어가 활용된 영어 일기를 해석한 후, 따라서 써 보세요.

It was so hot today, I wanted a cold drink. I found an old coin that changed color over time. It looked a bit ugly but still interesting.

<따라 쓰기>

______________________

______________________

**QUIZ** 오늘 배운 단어로 빈칸을 채워 문장을 완성하세요.

The soup is very ______________.

People ______________ over time.

I ______________ to go home.

He found a ______________ on the ground.

That painting is ______________.

DATE . . . .

DAY 121

**Step1** 단어를 익히세요.

| not | grey | shop | sit | strawberry |
|---|---|---|---|---|
| 아닌 | 회색 | 가게 | 앉다 | 딸기 |

**Step2** 단어가 사용된 문장을 해석해 보세요.

I am not ready yet. ______

The sky is grey today. ______

The shop is open. ______

Please sit down. ______

I like strawberry ice cream. ______

**Step3** 다음 대화를 말해 보세요.

A: That's not a grey shirt, is it?

B: No, it's actually blue.

A: Do you want to go to the shop?

B: Sure, let's sit and plan first.

A: I want to buy some strawberries.

B: Sounds delicious! Let's go.

**Challenge** 오늘 배운 단어가 활용된 영어 일기를 해석한 후, 따라서 써 보세요.

I did not buy the grey shirt at the shop. Instead, I sat down and enjoyed a strawberry smoothie. It was a fun day!

<따라 쓰기>

______

______

**QUIZ** 오늘 배운 단어로 빈칸을 채워 문장을 완성하세요.

I am ______ ready yet.

The sky is ______ today.

The ______ is open.

Please ______ down.

I like ______ ice cream.

DATE . . . .

DAY 122

**Step1** 단어를 익히세요.

| airplane | map | beside | headache | board |
|---|---|---|---|---|
| 비행기 | 지도 | ~옆에 | 두통 | 판자 |

**Step2** 단어가 사용된 문장을 해석해 보세요.

The airplane is taking off. ______________________________

Do you have a map? ______________________________

The cat is sitting beside me. ______________________________

I have a headache. ______________________________

The board is broken. ______________________________

**Step3** 다음 대화를 말해 보세요.

A: Have you ever been on an airplane?
B: Yes, I have. It's so exciting!
A: Do you use a map when you travel?
B: Yes, I keep one beside me all the time.
A: Do you get headaches on planes?
B: Sometimes, but I rest and feel better.

**Challenge** 오늘 배운 단어가 활용된 영어 일기를 해석한 후, 따라서 써 보세요.

I saw an airplane in the sky today. I looked at a map beside my desk to see where it was going. I got a headache, so I rested on a wooden board.

<따라 쓰기>

______________________________

______________________________

**QUIZ** 오늘 배운 단어로 빈칸을 채워 문장을 완성하세요.

The ______________ is taking off.

Do you have a ______________?

The cat is sitting ______________ me.

I have a ______________.

The ______________ is broken.

DATE . . . .

DAY 123

## Step1 단어를 익히세요.

| sugar | green | weather | pocket | face |
|---|---|---|---|---|
| 설탕 | 녹색 | 날씨 | 주머니 | 얼굴 |

## Step2 단어가 사용된 문장을 해석해 보세요.

Add some sugar to the tea. ______

Her dress is green. ______

The weather is nice today. ______

My keys are in my pocket. ______

He has a friendly face. ______

## Step3 다음 대화를 말해 보세요.

A: Do you want some sugar in your tea?

B: Yes, just a little, please.

A: Look at that green tree outside.

B: It's so beautiful, especially in this weather.

A: Do you have any tissues in your pocket?

B: Yes, here you go.

## Challenge 오늘 배운 단어가 활용된 영어 일기를 해석한 후, 따라서 써 보세요.

I put some sugar in my tea today. I wore a green jacket because the weather was cool. I found a coin in my pocket and it brought a smile to my face.

<따라 쓰기>

______

______

## QUIZ 오늘 배운 단어로 빈칸을 채워 문장을 완성하세요.

Add some ______ to the tea.

Her dress is ______.

The ______ is nice today.

My keys are in my ______.

He has a friendly ______.

DATE . . . .

DAY 124

## Step1 단어를 익히세요.

| begin | she | animal | delicious | early |
|---|---|---|---|---|
| 시작하다 | 그녀 | 동물 | 맛있는 | 일찍 |

## Step2 단어가 사용된 문장을 해석해 보세요.

Let's begin the meeting. ______________________

She is my best friend. ______________________

The zoo has many animals. ______________________

This cake is delicious. ______________________

I wake up early every day. ______________________

## Step3 다음 대화를 말해 보세요.

A: When does the movie begin?

B: It begins at 7 P.M.

A: She loves animals so much.

B: Yes, she always talks about them.

A: We had a delicious meal today.

B: That's nice! Did you eat early?

## Challenge 오늘 배운 단어가 활용된 영어 일기를 해석한 후, 따라서 써 보세요.

I began my day early today. My grandmother made a delicious breakfast for us. After eating, we visited the zoo to see the animals.

<따라 쓰기>

______________________

______________________

## QUIZ 오늘 배운 단어로 빈칸을 채워 문장을 완성하세요.

Let's ______________ the meeting.

______________ is my best friend.

The zoo has many ______________.

This cake is ______________.

I wake up ______________ every day.

DATE . . . .

DAY 125

**Step1** 단어를 익히세요.

| cool | drive | clip | teen | company |
|---|---|---|---|---|
| 시원한 | 운전하다 | 클립 | 십대 | 회사 |

**Step2** 단어가 사용된 문장을 해석해 보세요.

The weather is cool today. ✎ ______

He can drive very well. ✎ ______

Use a clip to hold the papers together. ✎ ______

He is a teen. ✎ ______

She works at a big company. ✎ ______

**Step3** 다음 대화를 말해 보세요.

A: The weather is so cool today.
B: Yes, it's nice and refreshing.
A: Do you know how to drive?
B: Not yet, but I want to learn when I'm a teen.
A: I need a clip for these papers.
B: I have one from my dad's company.

**Challenge** 오늘 배운 단어가 활용된 영어 일기를 해석한 후, 따라서 써 보세요.

It was a cool day today. My dad let me drive the car. As a teen, it was exciting!
At home, I used a clip to hold my papers from the company.

<따라 쓰기>

______

______

**QUIZ** 오늘 배운 단어로 빈칸을 채워 문장을 완성하세요.

The weather is ______ today.

He can ______ very well.

Use a ______ to hold the papers together.

He is a ______.

She works at a big ______.

DATE . . . .

DAY 126

**Step1** 단어를 익히세요.

| crazy | shy | day | exam | fix |
|---|---|---|---|---|
| 미친 | 수줍은 | 날 | 시험 | 고치다 |

**Step2** 단어가 사용된 문장을 해석해 보세요.

Are you crazy? ______

She is very shy. ______

Today is a sunny day. ______

I have an exam tomorrow. ______

Can you fix my bike? ______

**Step3** 다음 대화를 말해 보세요.

A: Today was a crazy day!
B: Really? What happened?
A: I was so shy during my exam.
B: Don't worry, you did your best.
A: I need to fix my computer.
B: Maybe we can work on it together.

**Challenge** 오늘 배운 단어가 활용된 영어 일기를 해석한 후, 따라서 써 보세요.

I had a crazy day today. I felt shy during the exam. After school, I helped my friend fix his bike.

<따라 쓰기>

______

______

**QUIZ** 오늘 배운 단어로 빈칸을 채워 문장을 완성하세요.

Are you ______?

She is very ______.

Today is a sunny ______.

I have an ______ tomorrow.

Can you ______ my bike?

DATE . . . .

DAY 127

## Step1 단어를 익히세요.

| should | fog | he | kill | introduce |
|---|---|---|---|---|
| 해야 한다 | 안개 | 그 | 죽이다 | 소개하다 |

## Step2 단어가 사용된 문장을 해석해 보세요.

You should study more. ______

The fog is very thick. ______

He is my brother. ______

They want to kill the bugs. ______

Let me introduce you to my friend. ______

## Step3 다음 대화를 말해 보세요.

A: Should we go outside in the fog?
B: No, it's too hard to see.
A: He said he will introduce his friend to us.
B: That sounds nice.
A: Did you hear about the story where the hero tries to kill the dragon?
B: Yes, it was very exciting.

## Challenge 오늘 배운 단어가 활용된 영어 일기를 해석한 후, 따라서 써 보세요.

He should be careful in the fog. He talked about a hero killing a monster. I want to introduce him to my favorite book.

<따라 쓰기>

______

______

## QUIZ 오늘 배운 단어로 빈칸을 채워 문장을 완성하세요.

You ______ study more.

The ______ is very thick.

______ is my brother.

They want to ______ the bugs.

Let me ______ you to my friend.

DATE . . . .

DAY 128

## Step1 단어를 익히세요.

| draw | accent | home | battery | many |
|---|---|---|---|---|
| 그리다 | 악센트 | 집 | 배터리 | 많은 |

## Step2 단어가 사용된 문장을 해석해 보세요.

She loves to draw pictures. ______

He has a strong accent. ______

I want to go home. ______

My phone's battery is low. ______

There are many books on the shelf. ______

## Step3 다음 대화를 말해 보세요.

A: Do you like to draw pictures?

B: Yes, I draw every day.

A: I love your accent when you speak.

B: Thank you! I learned it at home.

A: Do you have many batteries?

B: Yes, we have many in the drawer.

## Challenge 오늘 배운 단어가 활용된 영어 일기를 해석한 후, 따라서 써 보세요.

At home, I decided to draw a picture. My friend with a strong accent called, asking if I had any extra batteries. I found many and gave them to him.

<따라 쓰기>

______

______

## QUIZ 오늘 배운 단어로 빈칸을 채워 문장을 완성하세요.

She loves to ______ pictures.

He has a strong ______.

I want to go ______.

My phone's ______ is low.

There are ______ books on the shelf.

DATE . . . .

DAY 129

## Step1 단어를 익히세요.

| point | safe | warm | basket | new |
|---|---|---|---|---|
| 가리키다 | 안전한 | 따듯한 | 바구니 | 새로운 |

## Step2 단어가 사용된 문장을 해석해 보세요.

Point to the picture. ______________________

Is this place safe? ______________________

The soup is warm. ______________________

Put the fruits in the basket. ______________________

I bought a new phone. ______________________

## Step3 다음 대화를 말해 보세요.

A: Can you point to the new book?

B: Sure, it's right there on the table.

A: Is your home safe?

B: Yes, it feels very safe and warm.

A: Look at the basket. It's full of fruit.

B: I love having fresh fruit. It's a nice new basket.

## Challenge 오늘 배운 단어가 활용된 영어 일기를 해석한 후, 따라서 써 보세요.

I pointed to the new basket on the shelf. It looked safe and strong. I felt warm inside when I held it.

<따라 쓰기>

______________________

______________________

## QUIZ 오늘 배운 단어로 빈칸을 채워 문장을 완성하세요.

__________ to the picture.

Is this place __________?

The soup is __________.

Put the fruits in the __________.

I bought a __________ phone.

DATE . . . .

DAY 130

**Step1** 단어를 익히세요.

| short | dark | low | egg | walk |
|---|---|---|---|---|
| 짧은 | 어두운 | 낮은 | 계란 | 걷다 |

**Step2** 단어가 사용된 문장을 해석해 보세요.

She has short hair. ____________________

The room is very dark. ____________________

The table is too low. ____________________

I had an egg for breakfast. ____________________

Let's go for a walk. ____________________

**Step3** 다음 대화를 말해 보세요.

A: I took a short walk today.

B: Was it nice outside?

A: Yes, but it got dark quickly.

B: Did you see anything interesting?

A: I saw a nest with low branches and eggs.

B: That sounds lovely! I love nature.

**Challenge** 오늘 배운 단어가 활용된 영어 일기를 해석한 후, 따라서 써 보세요.

I took a short walk today. The sky was dark, and the sun was low. I found an egg on the ground.

<따라 쓰기>

____________________

____________________

**QUIZ** 오늘 배운 단어로 빈칸을 채워 문장을 완성하세요.

She has ____________ hair.

The room is very ____________.

The table is too ____________.

I had an ____________ for breakfast.

Let's go for a ____________.

DATE . . . .

DAY 131

## Step1 단어를 익히세요.

| sad | test | store | guess | elephant |
|---|---|---|---|---|
| 슬픈 | 시험 | 가게 | 추측하다 | 코끼리 |

## Step2 단어가 사용된 문장을 해석해 보세요.

She looked very sad. ______________________

I have a test tomorrow. ______________________

The store is closed. ______________________

Can you guess the answer? ______________________

The elephant is very big. ______________________

## Step3 다음 대화를 말해 보세요.

A: I feel sad today.

B: Why? Did something happen?

A: I didn't do well on the test.

B: I'm sorry to hear that. Want to go to the store?

A: Sure, that might cheer me up.

B: Guess what? I saw a toy elephant there!

## Challenge 오늘 배운 단어가 활용된 영어 일기를 해석한 후, 따라서 써 보세요.

I felt sad after the test today. I went to the store to feel better. I guess I saw a toy elephant there.

<따라 쓰기>

______________________

______________________

## QUIZ 오늘 배운 단어로 빈칸을 채워 문장을 완성하세요.

She looked very ______________.

I have a ______________ tomorrow.

The ______________ is closed.

Can you ______________ the answer?

The ______________ is very big.

DATE . . . .

DAY 132

**Step1** 단어를 익히세요.

| roof | do | heavy | come | button |
|---|---|---|---|---|
| 지붕 | 하다 | 무거운 | 오다 | 단추 |

**Step2** 단어가 사용된 문장을 해석해 보세요.

The roof needs repairing. ______________________

What do you want to do? ______________________

This bag is very heavy. ______________________

Can you come to my party? ______________________

The button is missing. ______________________

**Step3** 다음 대화를 말해 보세요.

A: What should we do today?
B: Let's fix the roof. It's leaking.
A: That sounds like a heavy job.
B: Yes, but we can do it together.
A: Did you see the new button on my coat?
B: Yes, it looks nice. Where did you get it?

**Challenge** 오늘 배운 단어가 활용된 영어 일기를 해석한 후, 따라서 써 보세요.

I saw a worker on the roof today. He had to do a heavy job. My mom asked him to come inside to fix a button on her coat.

<따라 쓰기>

______________________

______________________

**QUIZ** 오늘 배운 단어로 빈칸을 채워 문장을 완성하세요.

The ______________ needs repairing.

What do you want to ______________?

This bag is very ______________.

Can you ______________ to my party?

The ______________ is missing.

DATE . . . .

DAY 133

**Step1** 단어를 익히세요.

| dialogue | important | cinema | build | file |
|---|---|---|---|---|
| 대화 | 중요한 | 영화관 | 짓다 | 파일 |

**Step2** 단어가 사용된 문장을 해석해 보세요.

The dialogue in the movie was great. ______________________

It's important to exercise. ______________________

We are going to the cinema. ______________________

They will build a new school. ______________________

The file is on my desk. ______________________

**Step3** 다음 대화를 말해 보세요.

A: The dialogue was so funny.

B: Yes, I loved it. Exercise is very important.

A: I agree. Let's go to the cinema tonight.

B: Sure, what time? They're building a new park.

A: That's great. I need to find my file.

B: It's on your desk.

**Challenge** 오늘 배운 단어가 활용된 영어 일기를 해석한 후, 따라서 써 보세요.

I had an important dialogue with my friend today. We talked about the new cinema they built. I saved our conversation in a file.

<따라 쓰기>

______________________

______________________

**QUIZ** 오늘 배운 단어로 빈칸을 채워 문장을 완성하세요.

The ______________ in the movie was great.

It's ______________ to exercise.

We are going to the ______________.

They will ______________ a new school.

The ______________ is on my desk.

DATE . . . .

DAY 134

**Step1** **단어를 익히세요.**

| nothing | know | make | late | dish |
|---|---|---|---|---|
| 아무것도 | 알다 | 만들다 | 늦은 | 접시 |

**Step2** **단어가 사용된 문장을 해석해 보세요.**

There's nothing in the fridge. ______________________

Do you know her? ______________________

Let's make a cake. ______________________

I'm late for the meeting. ______________________

Wash the dishes, please. ______________________

**Step3** **다음 대화를 말해 보세요.**

A: What are you doing today?
B: Nothing much. You?
A: I know how to make a great dish.
B: Really? Can you teach me?
A: Sure, but don't be late.
B: I won't be! I want to learn.

**Challenge** **오늘 배운 단어가 활용된 영어 일기를 해석한 후, 따라서 써 보세요.**

I know I should not make noise at night. Last night, I made a dish in the kitchen. Now it's late, so I will do nothing and rest.

<따라 쓰기>

______________________

______________________

**QUIZ** **오늘 배운 단어로 빈칸을 채워 문장을 완성하세요.**

There's ______________ in the fridge.

Do you ______________ her?

Let's ______________ a cake.

I'm ______________ for the meeting.

Wash the ______________, please.

DATE . . . .

DAY 135

**Step1** 단어를 익히세요.

| forest | corner | airport | decide | flag |
| --- | --- | --- | --- | --- |
| 숲 | 모퉁이 | 공항 | 결정하다 | 깃발 |

**Step2** 단어가 사용된 문장을 해석해 보세요.

The forest is very dense. ______________________

The store is on the corner. ______________________

We need to get to the airport early. ______________________

I can't decide what to wear. ______________________

The flag is waving in the wind. ______________________

**Step3** 다음 대화를 말해 보세요.

A: Have you ever been to the forest near the corner?

B: Yes, it's very peaceful there.

A: We need to go to the airport soon.

B: Did you decide what time we should leave?

A: Yes, we should leave when the flag is lowered.

B: Okay, I'll be ready by then.

**Challenge** 오늘 배운 단어가 활용된 영어 일기를 해석한 후, 따라서 써 보세요.

I went for a walk in the forest. At the corner, I saw a flag. My family decided to visit the airport next.

<따라 쓰기>

______________________

______________________

**QUIZ** 오늘 배운 단어로 빈칸을 채워 문장을 완성하세요.

The ______________ is very dense.

The store is on the ______________.

We need to get to the ______________ early.

I can't ______________ what to wear.

The ______________ is waving in the wind.

DATE . . . .

DAY 136

**Step1** 단어를 익히세요.

| it | deep | parent | clever | skin |
|---|---|---|---|---|
| 그것 | 깊은 | 부모 | 영리한 | 피부 |

**Step2** 단어가 사용된 문장을 해석해 보세요.

It is very cold today. ______________________

The lake is very deep. ______________________

My parents are kind. ______________________

She is very clever. ______________________

Her skin is soft. ______________________

**Step3** 다음 대화를 말해 보세요.

A: I saw a cartoon movie yesterday.
B: What was it about?
A: It was about a clever dolphin living in the deep sea.
B: That sounds exciting! Did your parents watch it with you?
A: Yes, they did. The dolphin had shiny, smooth skin.
B: Wow, that's amazing!

**Challenge** 오늘 배운 단어가 활용된 영어 일기를 해석한 후, 따라서 써 보세요.

I found a deep hole in the yard. My parent said to be careful. They are always so clever about keeping our skin safe.

<따라 쓰기>

______________________

______________________

**QUIZ** 오늘 배운 단어로 빈칸을 채워 문장을 완성하세요.

__________ is very cold today.

The lake is very __________.

My __________ are kind.

She is very __________.

Her __________ is soft.

DATE . . . .

DAY 137

**Step1** 단어를 익히세요.

| if | restroom | finger | tree | fresh |
|---|---|---|---|---|
| 만약 | 화장실 | 손가락 | 나무 | 신선한 |

**Step2** 단어가 사용된 문장을 해석해 보세요.

If it rains, we will stay inside. ✎ ____________________

Where is the restroom? ✎ ____________________

I hurt my finger. ✎ ____________________

The tree is very tall. ✎ ____________________

The fruit is fresh. ✎ ____________________

**Step3** 다음 대화를 말해 보세요.

A: If you need to go, the restroom is over there.
B: Thanks! I'll go in a minute.
A: Look at this tree. It's so big!
B: Yes, and the air here feels fresh.
A: Ouch, I hurt my finger.
B: Be careful next time!

**Challenge** 오늘 배운 단어가 활용된 영어 일기를 해석한 후, 따라서 써 보세요.

If you need the restroom, it's near the tree. I hurt my finger climbing it. The air feels so fresh today.

<따라 쓰기>

____________________

____________________

**QUIZ** 오늘 배운 단어로 빈칸을 채워 문장을 완성하세요.

__________ it rains, we will stay inside.

Where is the __________?

I hurt my __________.

The __________ is very tall.

The fruit is __________.

DATE . . . .

DAY 138

**Step1** 단어를 익히세요.

| tall | husband | get | pants | teach |
|---|---|---|---|---|
| 키 큰 | 남편 | 얻다 | 바지 | 가르치다 |

**Step2** 단어가 사용된 문장을 해석해 보세요.

He is very tall. ____________________

Her husband is a chef. ____________________

I need to get a new phone. ____________________

These pants are too tight. ____________________

She loves to teach. ____________________

**Step3** 다음 대화를 말해 보세요.

A: Your husband is very tall!
B: Yes, he is. He plays basketball.
A: Where did he get those pants?
B: He got them from the store downtown.
A: Does he teach basketball?
B: Yes, he loves to teach kids.

**Challenge** 오늘 배운 단어가 활용된 영어 일기를 해석한 후, 따라서 써 보세요.

My dad is very tall. He bought new pants today. He will teach me how to play basketball.

<따라 쓰기>

____________________

____________________

**QUIZ** 오늘 배운 단어로 빈칸을 채워 문장을 완성하세요.

He is very ____________.

Her ____________ is a chef.

I need to ____________ a new phone.

These ____________ are too tight.

She loves to ____________.

DATE . . . .

DAY 139

**Step1** 단어를 익히세요.

| on | hold | wet | line | bicycle |
|---|---|---|---|---|
| 위에 | 잡다 | 젖은 | 줄 | 자전거 |

**Step2** 단어가 사용된 문장을 해석해 보세요.

The book is on the table. ______________________

Hold my hand. ______________________

The floor is wet. ______________________

Stand in line. ______________________

I ride my bicycle to school. ______________________

**Step3** 다음 대화를 말해 보세요.

A: Can you put the book on the table?
B: Sure, I'll do that now.
A: Hold on, is the table wet?
B: Yes, it is. Let me dry it first.
A: Do you see the line of bicycles outside?
B: Yes, they're all parked in a row.

**Challenge** 오늘 배운 단어가 활용된 영어 일기를 해석한 후, 따라서 써 보세요.

I saw a bicycle on the sidewalk. I tried to hold it, but the seat was wet. There was a long line of bikes next to it.

<따라 쓰기>

______________________

______________________

**QUIZ** 오늘 배운 단어로 빈칸을 채워 문장을 완성하세요.

The book is ______________ the table.

______________ my hand.

The floor is ______________.

Stand in ______________.

I ride my ______________ to school.

DATE . . . .

DAY 140

## Step1 단어를 익히세요.

| poor | wall | pass | crown | danger |
|---|---|---|---|---|
| 가난한 | 벽 | 통과하다 | 왕관 | 위험 |

## Step2 단어가 사용된 문장을 해석해 보세요.

The family is very poor. ______________________

The wall needs painting. ______________________

Did you pass the test? ______________________

The king wore a crown. ______________________

Be aware of the danger. ______________________

## Step3 다음 대화를 말해 보세요.

A: The family in the story is very poor.

B: Yes, it made me sad to read about them.

A: Did you see the crown on the wall?

B: Yes, it looks so shiny and bright.

A: They had to pass through many dangers to get it.

B: Yes, the adventure was full of danger!

## Challenge 오늘 배운 단어가 활용된 영어 일기를 해석한 후, 따라서 써 보세요.

I read a story about a poor boy. He found a crown behind a wall. He had to pass through danger to get it.

<따라 쓰기>

______________________

______________________

## QUIZ 오늘 배운 단어로 빈칸을 채워 문장을 완성하세요.

The family is very ______________________.

The ______________________ needs painting.

Did you ______________________ the test?

The king wore a ______________________.

Be aware of the ______________________.

DATE . . . .

DAY 141

**Step1** **단어를 익히세요.**

| sun | foot | save | ask | red |
|---|---|---|---|---|
| 태양 | 발 | 구하다 | 묻다 | 빨간색 |

**Step2** **단어가 사용된 문장을 해석해 보세요.**

The sun is shining. ______________________

My foot hurts. ______________________

We need to save money. ______________________

Ask me anything. ______________________

Her dress is red. ______________________

**Step3** **다음 대화를 말해 보세요.**

A: The sun is very bright today.
B: Yes, it's a beautiful day. My foot is sore.
A: You should rest it. We need to save more money.
B: I agree. Can I ask you a question?
A: Sure, go ahead.
B: Where did you buy your read shoes?

**Challenge** **오늘 배운 단어가 활용된 영어 일기를 해석한 후, 따라서 써 보세요.**

I played outside in the sun today. I hurt my foot and needed help. My friend asked, "Is your foot red?" before helping me.

<따라 쓰기>

______________________

______________________

**QUIZ** **오늘 배운 단어로 빈칸을 채워 문장을 완성하세요.**

The ______________ is shining.

My ______________ hurts.

We need to ______________ money.

______________ me anything.

Her dress is ______________.

DATE . . . .

DAY 142

**Step1** 단어를 익히세요.

| door | never | way | hospital | close |
|---|---|---|---|---|
| 문 | 결코 | 길 | 병원 | 닫다 |

**Step2** 단어가 사용된 문장을 해석해 보세요.

The door is open. ______

I will never forget you. ______

This is the way home. ______

She works at a hospital. ______

Please close the window. ______

**Step3** 다음 대화를 말해 보세요.

A: Can you close the door, please?
B: Sure, I'll do it now.
A: I hope we never have to go to the hospital again.
B: Yes, I agree. It was a scary experience.
A: Do you know the way to the park?
B: Yes, I can guide you there.

**Challenge** 오늘 배운 단어가 활용된 영어 일기를 해석한 후, 따라서 써 보세요.

I went to the hospital today. The doctor said never to close the door completely. It must stay open for safety.

<따라 쓰기>

______

______

**QUIZ** 오늘 배운 단어로 빈칸을 채워 문장을 완성하세요.

The ______ is open.

I will ______ forget you.

This is the ______ home.

She works at a ______.

Please ______ the window.

DATE . . . .

DAY 143

**Step1** 단어를 익히세요.

| stay | favorite | hunt | humor | scissors |
|---|---|---|---|---|
| 머무르다 | 가장 좋아하는 | 사냥하다 | 유머 | 가위 |

**Step2** 단어가 사용된 문장을 해석해 보세요.

You can stay here. ____________________

Pizza is my favorite food. ____________________

They went to hunt in the forest. ____________________

He has a good sense of humor. ____________________

I need the scissors. ____________________

**Step3** 다음 대화를 말해 보세요.

A: I had to stay home today.
B: Really? What did you do at home?
A: I watched my favorite show. It was about a treasure hunt.
B: That sounds fun! Did it have a lot of humor?
A: Yes, it was very funny. One character even tried to cut a rope with scissors.
B: That sounds interesting.

**Challenge** 오늘 배운 단어가 활용된 영어 일기를 해석한 후, 따라서 써 보세요.

I stayed at my friend's house today. We watched my favorite show about a lion who likes to hunt. The humor was funny, and we used scissors to make paper animals.

<따라 쓰기>

____________________

____________________

**QUIZ** 오늘 배운 단어로 빈칸을 채워 문장을 완성하세요.

You can ____________________ here.

Pizza is my ____________________ food.

They went to ____________________ in the forest.

He has a good sense of ____________________.

I need the ____________________.

DATE . . . .

DAY 144

## Step1 단어를 익히세요.

| behind | side | at | smile | song |
|---|---|---|---|---|
| 뒤에 | 쪽 | 에 | 미소 짓다 | 노래 |

## Step2 단어가 사용된 문장을 해석해 보세요.

The cat is hiding behind the curtain. ______

Please sit on this side. ______

He is at the store. ______

She has a beautiful smile. ______

I like this song. ______

## Step3 다음 대화를 말해 보세요.

A: Look behind the curtain.
B: There's nothing there. It's just a wall.
A: Did you check the other side?
B: Yes, I looked at both sides.
A: Can you smile for the picture?
B: Sure! What song should we play while we take the picture?

## Challenge 오늘 배운 단어가 활용된 영어 일기를 해석한 후, 따라서 써 보세요.

I found my book behind the chair. It was at the side of the room. I smiled when I heard my favorite song playing.

<따라 쓰기>

______

______

## QUIZ 오늘 배운 단어로 빈칸을 채워 문장을 완성하세요.

The cat is hiding ______ the curtain.

Please sit on this ______.

He is ______ the store.

She has a beautiful ______.

I like this ______.

DATE . . . .

DAY 145

**Step1** 단어를 익히세요.

| stand | across | glad | birthday | double |
| --- | --- | --- | --- | --- |
| 서다 | 건너편 | 기쁜 | 생일 | 두 배 |

**Step2** 단어가 사용된 문장을 해석해 보세요.

Please stand up. ____________________

The park is across the street. ____________________

I'm glad you came. ____________________

Today is my birthday. ____________________

The price is double. ____________________

**Step3** 다음 대화를 말해 보세요.

A: Can you stand here for a moment?
B: Sure, what do you need?
A: Look across the street. Do you see that sign?
B: Yes, I see it. What does it say?
A: I'm so glad you're here for my birthday.
B: Me too! Let's have double the fun today!

**Challenge** 오늘 배운 단어가 활용된 영어 일기를 해석한 후, 따라서 써 보세요.

Today was my birthday, and I was very glad. I got a double scoop of ice cream.
My friend and I stood across from each other, eating ice cream.

<따라 쓰기>

____________________

____________________

**QUIZ** 오늘 배운 단어로 빈칸을 채워 문장을 완성하세요.

Please ____________ up.

The park is ____________ the street.

I'm ____________ you came.

Today is my ____________.

The price is ____________.

DATE . . . .

DAY 146

**Step1** 단어를 익히세요.

| very | cycle | classroom | sea | hero |
|---|---|---|---|---|
| 매우 | 자전거, 순환 | 교실 | 바다 | 영웅 |

**Step2** 단어가 사용된 문장을 해석해 보세요.

I'm very tired. ______

We went for a cycle ride. ______

The classroom is clean. ______

I love the sea. ______

He is a hero. ______

**Step3** 다음 대화를 말해 보세요.

A: The sea is very calm today.
B: Yes, it's perfect for sailing.
A: Did you finish the cycling race?
B: Yes, it was very challenging.
A: Who is your favorite hero?
B: I like the one who saved the classroom from the fire.

**Challenge** 오늘 배운 단어가 활용된 영어 일기를 해석한 후, 따라서 써 보세요.

I was very happy in the classroom today. We learned about the sea and its creatures. My hero is a diver who explores the ocean.

<따라 쓰기>

______

______

**QUIZ** 오늘 배운 단어로 빈칸을 채워 문장을 완성하세요.

I'm ______ tired.

We went for a ______ ride.

The ______ is clean.

I love the ______.

He is a ______.

DATE . . . .

DAY 147

**Step1** 단어를 익히세요.

| but | true | speak | supper | house |
|---|---|---|---|---|
| 그러나 | 진실 | 말하다 | 저녁식사 | 집 |

**Step2** 단어가 사용된 문장을 해석해 보세요.

I like apples, but I don't like bananas. ______________________

Her story is true. ______________________

Can you speak louder? ______________________

We had supper at 7 P.M. ______________________

The house is big. ______________________

**Step3** 다음 대화를 말해 보세요.

A: Is it true that you speak three languages?
B: Yes, it is, but I'm still learning.
A: Are you coming for supper tonight?
B: I'd love to, but I have to help at home.
A: Can I visit your house this weekend?
B: Sure, that sounds great!

**Challenge** 오늘 배운 단어가 활용된 영어 일기를 해석한 후, 따라서 써 보세요.

I wanted to play outside, but I had to do homework. It is true that I love to speak with my friends. After supper, I stayed at my house.

<따라 쓰기>

______________________

______________________

**QUIZ** 오늘 배운 단어로 빈칸을 채워 문장을 완성하세요.

I like apples, ____________ I don't like bananas.

Her story is ____________.

Can you ____________ louder?

We had ____________ at 7 P.M.

The ____________ is big.

DATE . . . .

DAY 148

## Step1 단어를 익히세요.

| bed | fry | enjoy | paint | win |
|---|---|---|---|---|
| 침대 | 튀기다 | 즐기다 | 그리다 | 이기다 |

## Step2 단어가 사용된 문장을 해석해 보세요.

The cat is sleeping on the bed. ____________________

I will fry the chicken. ____________________

I enjoy reading books. ____________________

She likes to paint. ____________________

Our team will win. ____________________

## Step3 다음 대화를 말해 보세요.

A: The bed is too soft.

B: I like it that way. Are you going to fry the fish?

A: Yes, it tastes better that way. Do you enjoy movies?

B: Yes, especially comedies. She loves to paint.

A: She's very talented. I hope we win the game.

B: Me too.

## Challenge 오늘 배운 단어가 활용된 영어 일기를 해석한 후, 따라서 써 보세요.

I jumped on my bed this morning. My mom fried some eggs, and I enjoyed breakfast. Later, I painted a picture and won a small prize at school.

<따라 쓰기>

____________________

____________________

## QUIZ 오늘 배운 단어로 빈칸을 채워 문장을 완성하세요.

The __________ is very comfortable.

I will __________ the chicken.

I __________ reading books.

She likes to __________.

Our team will __________.

DATE . . . .

DAY 149

## Step1 단어를 익히세요.

| skirt | clear | you | meat | bedroom |
|---|---|---|---|---|
| 치마 | 명확한 | 너 | 고기 | 침실 |

## Step2 단어가 사용된 문장을 해석해 보세요.

She wore a red skirt. ______________________

The instructions are clear. ______________________

How are you today? ______________________

I don't eat much meat. ______________________

The bedroom is upstairs. ______________________

## Step3 다음 대화를 말해 보세요.

A: Do you like my new skirt?
B: Yes, it's very pretty on you.
A: Thank you! Are you cooking meat for dinner?
B: Yes, we're having steak tonight.
A: Can you help me clear the table?
B: Sure, then I'll go to my bedroom to rest.

## Challenge 오늘 배운 단어가 활용된 영어 일기를 해석한 후, 따라서 써 보세요.

I wore my favorite skirt today. It's clear that you like it too. We talked about our favorite meat dishes in my bedroom.

<따라 쓰기>

______________________

______________________

## QUIZ 오늘 배운 단어로 빈칸을 채워 문장을 완성하세요.

She wore a red ______________.

The instructions are ______________.

How are ______________ today?

I don't eat much ______________.

The ______________ is upstairs.

DATE . . . .

DAY 150

**Step1** 단어를 익히세요.

| live | fun | helicopter | hungry | elementary |
|---|---|---|---|---|
| 살다 | 재밌는 | 헬리콥터 | 배고픈 | 초급의 |

**Step2** 단어가 사용된 문장을 해석해 보세요.

I live in Seoul. ____________________

This game is fun. ____________________

The helicopter is flying overhead. ____________________

I'm very hungry. ____________________

She is in elementary school. ____________________

**Step3** 다음 대화를 말해 보세요.

A: Do you live near the park?

B: Yes, it's a fun place to visit.

A: Have you ever seen a helicopter up close?

B: No, but I think it would be exciting.

A: Are you hungry? Let's eat something.

B: Yes, I'm so hungry. What's for dinner?

**Challenge** 오늘 배운 단어가 활용된 영어 일기를 해석한 후, 따라서 써 보세요.

I live in a fun neighborhood. Today, I saw a helicopter flying overhead. After that, I felt hungry and ate lunch at my elementary school.

<따라 쓰기>

____________________

____________________

**QUIZ** 오늘 배운 단어로 빈칸을 채워 문장을 완성하세요.

I ____________ in Seoul.

This game is ____________.

The ____________ is flying overhead.

I'm very ____________.

She is in ____________ school.

DATE . . . .

DAY 151

**Step1** 단어를 익히세요.

| tell | hand | salt | money | condition |
| --- | --- | --- | --- | --- |
| 말하다 | 손 | 소금 | 돈 | 조건, 상태 |

**Step2** 단어가 사용된 문장을 해석해 보세요.

Can you tell me a story? ______

My hand is cold. ______

Add some salt to the soup. ______

I need some money. ______

The car is in good condition. ______

**Step3** 다음 대화를 말해 보세요.

A: Can you tell me what happened?

B: Sure, I'll explain everything.

A: Do you need a hand with that?

B: Yes, please. Can you pass the salt?

A: Here you go. Do you have enough money for lunch?

B: Yes, I do. Thanks for asking.

**Challenge** 오늘 배운 단어가 활용된 영어 일기를 해석한 후, 따라서 써 보세요.

My mom told me to wash my hands before dinner. She asked for salt to add to the soup. I saved my money under the condition that I could buy a toy later.

<따라 쓰기>

______

**QUIZ** 오늘 배운 단어로 빈칸을 채워 문장을 완성하세요.

Can you ______ me a story?

My ______ is cold.

Add some ______ to the soup.

I need some ______.

The car is in good ______.

DATE . . . .

DAY 152

**Step1** 단어를 익히세요.

| bright | place | dolphin | snow | street |
|---|---|---|---|---|
| 밝은 | 장소 | 돌고래 | 눈 | 거리 |

**Step2** 단어가 사용된 문장을 해석해 보세요.

The sun is very bright. ______________________

This is a nice place. ______________________

The dolphin is swimming. ______________________

I love watching snow fall. ______________________

The street is busy. ______________________

**Step3** 다음 대화를 말해 보세요.

A: The sun is so bright today.
B: Yes, it's a perfect day to go to the beach.
A: I love that place where we can see dolphins.
B: Me too! They are so playful.
A: Did you see the snow last night?
B: Yes, it covered the entire street.

**Challenge** 오늘 배운 단어가 활용된 영어 일기를 해석한 후, 따라서 써 보세요.

I visited a bright place today near the beach. I saw a dolphin jumping out of the water. On the way home, snow started to fall on the street.

<따라 쓰기>

______________________

______________________

**QUIZ** 오늘 배운 단어로 빈칸을 채워 문장을 완성하세요.

The sun is very ____________.

This is a nice ____________.

The ____________ is swimming.

I love watching ____________ fall.

The ____________ is busy.

DATE . . . .

DAY 153

**Step1** 단어를 익히세요.

| arrive | thirst | present | break | baby |
|---|---|---|---|---|
| 도착하다 | 목마름 | 선물 | 깨다 | 아기 |

**Step2** 단어가 사용된 문장을 해석해 보세요.

They will arrive soon. ______________________

I have a thirst for knowledge. ______________________

Here is a present for you. ______________________

Don't break the glass. ______________________

The baby is sleeping. ______________________

**Step3** 다음 대화를 말해 보세요.

A: What time will you arrive?
B: I'll arrive at 3 P.M.
A: I feel a strong thirst for coffee right now.
B: No problem! I will get some on the way.
A: Did you get the present for the baby?
B: Yes, I hope it doesn't break.

**Challenge** 오늘 배운 단어가 활용된 영어 일기를 해석한 후, 따라서 써 보세요.

I arrived at the party and felt a thirst. I gave a present to the baby. Be careful not to break it.

<따라 쓰기>

**QUIZ** 오늘 배운 단어로 빈칸을 채워 문장을 완성하세요.

They will ______________ soon.

I have a ______________ for knowledge.

Here is a ______________ for you.

Don't ______________ the glass.

The ______________ is sleeping.

DATE . . . .

DAY 154

## Step1 단어를 익히세요.

| dry | pretty | age | hello | read |
|---|---|---|---|---|
| 마른, 건조한 | 예쁜 | 나이 | 안녕하세요 | 읽다 |

## Step2 단어가 사용된 문장을 해석해 보세요.

The clothes are dry. ________

She is very pretty. ________

What is your age? ________

Hello, how are you? ________

I like to read books. ________

## Step3 다음 대화를 말해 보세요.

A: Hello! How are you today?

B: Hi! I'm good, thank you.

A: Have you read this book?

B: Yes, it's pretty interesting.

A: Your skin looks dry. Do you need lotion?

B: No, thanks. At my age, it's normal.

## Challenge 오늘 배운 단어가 활용된 영어 일기를 해석한 후, 따라서 써 보세요.

Hello! Today, I read a pretty storybook. Even at my age, I still enjoy it. The pages were dry and crisp.

<따라 쓰기>

________

________

## QUIZ 오늘 배운 단어로 빈칸을 채워 문장을 완성하세요.

The clothes are ________.

She is very ________.

What is your ________?

________, how are you?

I like to ________ books.

DATE . . . .

DAY 155

**Step1** 단어를 익히세요.

| find | table | as | grow | mouth |
|---|---|---|---|---|
| 찾다 | 테이블 | ~처럼, ~로서 | 자라다 | 입 |

**Step2** 단어가 사용된 문장을 해석해 보세요.

Can you help me find my keys? ______________________

The table is set. ______________________

She works as a teacher. ______________________

Plants grow with sunlight. ______________________

Open your mouth wide. ______________________

**Step3** 다음 대화를 말해 보세요.

A: Did you find your book?
B: Yes, it was on the table.
A: Great! You read as much as you can.
B: Yes, I want to grow smarter.
A: Look at that plant! It grew so tall.
B: Wow! It almost reaches my mouth.

**Challenge** 오늘 배운 단어가 활용된 영어 일기를 해석한 후, 따라서 써 보세요.

I found my book on the table. As I grow older, I read more and more. The story made my mouth smile.

<따라 쓰기>

______________________

______________________

**QUIZ** 오늘 배운 단어로 빈칸을 채워 문장을 완성하세요.

Can you help me ______________ my keys?

The ______________ is set.

She works ______________ a teacher.

Plants ______________ with sunlight.

Open your ______________ wide.

DATE . . . .

DAY 156

**Step1** 단어를 익히세요.

| hang | wait | use | airline | wrong |
|---|---|---|---|---|
| 걸다 | 기다리다 | 사용하다 | 항공사 | 잘못된 |

**Step2** 단어가 사용된 문장을 해석해 보세요.

Hang your coat here. ✎ ______

Please wait for me. ✎ ______

How do you use this? ✎ ______

Which airline are you flying with? ✎ ______

Something is wrong. ✎ ______

**Step3** 다음 대화를 말해 보세요.

A: Can you hang up your coat?
B: Sure, I'll do it now.
A: We need to wait for the next bus.
B: Okay, I can wait a bit longer.
A: Which airline did you use for your trip?
B: I used SkyAir, but they got my luggage wrong.

**Challenge** 오늘 배운 단어가 활용된 영어 일기를 해석한 후, 따라서 써 보세요.

I hang my coat by the door. We had to wait for our flight because the airline had the wrong time. I used my phone to check for updates.

<따라 쓰기>

______

______

**QUIZ** 오늘 배운 단어로 빈칸을 채워 문장을 완성하세요.

______ your coat here.

Please ______ for me.

How do you ______ this?

Which ______ are you flying with?

Something is ______.

DATE . . . .

DAY 157

**Step1** 단어를 익히세요.

| write | have | cry | kid | high |
|---|---|---|---|---|
| 쓰다 | 가지다 | 울다 | 아이 | 높은 |

**Step2** 단어가 사용된 문장을 해석해 보세요.

I like to write stories. ________________

Do you have a pen? ________________

The baby is crying. ________________

The kid is playing outside. ________________

The mountain is very high. ________________

**Step3** 다음 대화를 말해 보세요.

A: Did you write your homework?

B: Yes, I finished it yesterday.

A: Do you have any plans for today?

B: I have to watch my little brother.

A: Why is that kid crying?

B: I think he lost his toy. He was so high up on the slide.

**Challenge** 오늘 배운 단어가 활용된 영어 일기를 해석한 후, 따라서 써 보세요.

I wrote a story about a kid today. He lost his toy and began to cry. His dad picked him up high to make him feel better.

<따라 쓰기>

________________

________________

**QUIZ** 오늘 배운 단어로 빈칸을 채워 문장을 완성하세요.

I like to ________________ stories.

Do you ________________ a pen?

The baby is ________________.

The ________________ is playing outside.

The mountain is very ________________.

DATE . . . .

DAY 158

**Step1** 단어를 익히세요.

| may | out | busy | here | choose |
| --- | --- | --- | --- | --- |
| ~할지도 모른다 | 밖에 | 바쁜 | 여기 | 선택하다 |

**Step2** 단어가 사용된 문장을 해석해 보세요.

It may rain tomorrow. ____________________

Let's go out. ____________________

I am very busy today. ____________________

Come here, please. ____________________

Choose your favorite color. ____________________

**Step3** 다음 대화를 말해 보세요.

A: You may want to go out for a walk.
B: I might, but I'm very busy today.
A: If you finish early, come here.
B: Okay, I'll try my best.
A: What do you want for lunch? You can choose.
B: I may choose a sandwich.

**Challenge** 오늘 배운 단어가 활용된 영어 일기를 해석한 후, 따라서 써 보세요.

I may go out to play later. I am busy with homework right now. When I'm done, I will choose a game to play here.

<따라 쓰기>

____________________

____________________

**QUIZ** 오늘 배운 단어로 빈칸을 채워 문장을 완성하세요.

It __________ rain tomorrow.

Let's go __________.

I am very __________ today.

Come __________, please.

__________ your favorite color.

DATE . . . .

DAY 159

**Step1** 단어를 익히세요.

| they | always | question | show | thank |
|---|---|---|---|---|
| 그들, 그것들 | 항상 | 질문 | 보여주다 | 감사하다 |

**Step2** 단어가 사용된 문장을 해석해 보세요.

They are my friends. ______________________

She is always happy. ______________________

Do you have a question? ______________________

Let me show you something. ______________________

Thank you for your help. ______________________

**Step3** 다음 대화를 말해 보세요.

A: They always have good ideas.
B: Yes, I learn a lot from them.
A: Did they ask you a question today?
B: Yes, they asked me to show my project.
A: That sounds interesting! How did it go?
B: It went well. They thanked me for my work.

**Challenge** 오늘 배운 단어가 활용된 영어 일기를 해석한 후, 따라서 써 보세요.

They always ask good questions in class. The teacher likes to show them the answers. I want to thank them for being helpful.

<따라 쓰기>

______________________

______________________

**QUIZ** 오늘 배운 단어로 빈칸을 채워 문장을 완성하세요.

__________ are my friends.

She is __________ happy.

Do you have a __________?

Let me __________ you something.

__________ you for your help.

DATE . . . .

DAY 160

**Step1** 단어를 익히세요.

| focus | bath | letter | movie | uncle |
| --- | --- | --- | --- | --- |
| 집중하다 | 목욕 | 편지 | 영화 | 삼촌 |

**Step2** 단어가 사용된 문장을 해석해 보세요.

Please focus on your work. ______________________

I like to take a bath. ______________________

I received a letter. ______________________

The movie was exciting. ______________________

My uncle is very funny. ______________________

**Step3** 다음 대화를 말해 보세요.

A: Can you focus on your homework now?
B: Yes, I'll start in a minute.
A: Did you take a bath today?
B: Yes, I did. It was very relaxing.
A: Have you written a letter to your uncle?
B: Not yet, but I'll do it after watching a movie.

**Challenge** 오늘 배운 단어가 활용된 영어 일기를 해석한 후, 따라서 써 보세요.

I need to focus on my homework. Afterward, I will take a bath. My uncle sent me a letter about a new movie we can watch together.

<따라 쓰기>

______________________

______________________

**QUIZ** 오늘 배운 단어로 빈칸을 채워 문장을 완성하세요.

Please ____________ on your work.

I like to take a ____________.

I received a ____________.

The ____________ was exciting.

My ____________ is very funny.

# 정답 및 해설

## DAY 1

### Step 2

The heat is very strong today. 오늘 열기가 너무 강하다.
Let's go to the park. 공원에 가자.
This dress is different from mine. 이 드레스는 내 것과 다르다.
The glass broke into pieces. 유리가 산산조각 났다.
Can you catch the ball? 공을 잡을 수 있니?

### Step 3

A: The heat is very strong today. 오늘 열기가 너무 강하다.
B: Yes, it is. Where should we go? 맞아, 어디로 갈까?
A: Let's go to a different place today. 오늘은 다른 곳에 가자.
B: Okay. How about the park with the glass house? 좋아. 유리 집이 있는 공원은 어때?
A: That sounds good. Can we catch the bus from here? 좋아. 여기서 버스를 탈 수 있을까?
B: Yes, if we hurry, we can catch it. 응, 서두르면 탈 수 있어.

### Challenge

It was very hot, so I went to a different room. I saw a glass of water and caught it. Drinking the water made me feel better. 날씨가 너무 더워서 다른 방으로 갔다. 물 한 잔을 보고 그것을 잡았다. 물을 마시니 기분이 나아졌다.

## DAY 2

### Step 2

The cat is climbing down the tree. 고양이가 나무를 내려오고 있다.
We are traveling north for the vacation. 우리는 휴가를 위해 북쪽으로 여행을 가고 있다.
She felt a great joy. 그녀는 큰 기쁨을 느꼈다.
I bought some fresh bread. 나는 신선한 빵을 샀다.
The giant tower is very tall. 거대한 탑이 매우 높다.

### Step 3

A: Look down there! What is that? 저기 봐! 저게 뭐야?
B: It looks like a giant statue. 거대한 조각상처럼 보여.
A: Wow, it's so big. Let's go north to see it. 와, 정말 크다. 북쪽으로 가서 보자.
B: Sure. We can bring some bread for a picnic. 좋아. 소풍용 빵을 가져가자.
A: Yes, that would be a joy! 그래, 정말 기쁠 거야!
B: I'm excited. Let's go now! 신난다. 지금 가자!

### Challenge

Today, I went north. I felt joy when I bought a giant bread. I walked down the street to go home. 오늘 나는 북쪽으로 갔다. 거대한 빵을 사니 기쁨을 느꼈다. 집으로 가려고 길을 걸었다.

## DAY 3

### Step 2

A guide showed us the way to the hospital. 가이드가 병원으로 가는 길을 안내해 주었다.
She is always happy in the morning. 그녀는 항상 아침에 행복하다.
Drink a lot of water every day. 매일 많은 물을 마셔라.
The puppy is very cute. 강아지가 매우 귀엽다.
There is a treasure at the bottom of the sea. 바다 밑바닥에 보물이 있다.

### Step 3

A: Look at that puppy by the water! 저기 물가에 있는 강아지 좀 봐!
B: It's so cute! It's playing at the bottom of the hill. 정말 귀엽다! 언덕 아래에서 놀고 있어.
A: Do you want to go see it? I can guide you there. 보러 갈래? 내가 안내해줄게.
B: Yes, I would be happy to see the puppy up close. 응, 가까이서 강아지를 보면 행복할 거야.
A: Let's go! It will be a happy day. 가자! 오늘은 행복한 날이 될 거야.
B: I agree. Let's go now! 맞아. 지금 가자!

### Challenge

I guided my puppy to the park, and we played near the water. The puppy was very happy as it splashed around. Seeing my puppy's joy made me feel happy, too. 나는 강아지를 공원으로 데려가서 물가에서 놀았다. 강아지가 물장난을 치며 매우 행복해했다. 강아지가 즐거워하는 것을 보니 나도 행복했다.

## DAY 4

### Step 2

The cat is a bit fat. 고양이가 조금 뚱뚱하다.
Don't worry about the test. 시험 걱정하지 마.
Can I taste your cake? 네 케이크를 맛봐도 될까?
Listen to the music. 음악을 들어봐.
He acted like a fool. 그는 바보처럼 행동했다.

### Step 3

A: Do you think this dog is fat? 이 개가 뚱뚱하다고 생각해?
B: No, don't worry about it. 아니, 걱정하지 마.
A: Have you tasted this cookie? 이 쿠키를 맛봤어?
B: Yes, I did. It tastes delicious! 응, 맛봤어. 맛있더라!
A: Let's listen to some music while we eat. 먹으면서 음악 좀 듣자.
B: Great idea! We don't want to look like fools just by sitting here.
좋은 생각이야! 그냥 앉아있으면 바보처럼 보일 거야.

### Challenge

I tasted the new dish and didn't worry about getting fat. My friend called me a fool, but I listened and enjoyed the meal. The taste made me very happy. 나는 새로운 요리를 맛보고 살찔 걱정을 하지 않았다. 친구가 나를 바보라고 불렀지만, 나는 듣고 맛있게 먹었다. 그 맛은 나를 매우 행복하게 만들었다.

## DAY 5

### Step 2

That is a big house. 저것은 큰 집이다.
I heard a strange sound. 나는 이상한 소리를 들었다.
We play football every weekend. 우리는 매 주말마다 축구를 한다.
She has already left. 그녀는 이미 떠났다.
Hurry up, we are late! 서둘러, 우리 늦었어!

### Step 3

A: Did you hear that loud sound? 저 큰 소리 들었어?
B: Yes, I did. What was it? 응, 들었어. 뭐였어?
A: It was from the football game. 축구 경기에서 나온 소리였어.
B: Oh, I see. The big game has already started? 아, 그렇구나. 중요한 경기가 벌써 시작했어?
A: Yes, it started a few minutes ago. 응, 몇 분 전에 시작했어.
B: Let's hurry! We don't want to miss it. 빨리 가자! 놓치고 싶지 않아.

### Challenge

I heard a big sound from the stadium and hurried over. The football game had already started. The cheers from the crowd were very exciting. 나는 경기장에서 큰 소리를 듣고 서둘러 갔다. 축구 경기는 이미 시작됐었다. 군중의 환호는 매우 흥미진진했다.

## DAY 6

### Step 2

I hope you feel better soon. 빨리 나아지길 바란다.
The cat is sleeping. 고양이가 자고 있다.
What did you say? 뭐라고 말했니?
He hurt his head. 그는 머리를 다쳤다.
The lady is very kind. 그 숙녀는 매우 친절하다.

### Step 3

A: I hope the lady is okay. 그 숙녀가 괜찮길 바란다.
B: What happened to her? 그녀에게 무슨 일이 있었니?
A: She hit her head. 그녀가 머리를 부딪혔어.
B: Oh no! What did the doctor say? 오, 안돼! 의사가 뭐라고 했어?
A: The doctor said she will be fine. 의사는 그녀가 괜찮을 거라고 했어.
B: That's good to hear. I hope she recovers soon. 다행이다. 빨리 회복하길 바란다.

### Challenge

I hope I did well on the test today. The teacher said I was very focused. A nice lady patted my head and said I did a great job. 오늘 시험을 잘 봤으면 좋겠다. 선생님이 내가 매우 집중했다고 하셨다. 친절한 숙녀 한 분이 내 머리를 쓰다듬으며 잘했다고 말했다.

## DAY 7

### Step 2

She likes to design clothes. 그녀는 옷을 디자인하는 것을 좋아한다.
We run every morning. 우리는 매일 아침 달린다.
He collects stamps. 그는 우표를 수집한다.
He is very handsome. 그는 매우 잘생겼다.
I am happy today. 나는 오늘 행복하다.

### Step 3

A: Did you design this poster? 이 포스터 네가 디자인했니?
B: Yes, I did. Do you like it? 응, 내가 했어. 마음에 들어?
A: It's very nice! By the way, do you like to run? 정말 멋져! 그런데, 달리는 걸 좋아해?
B: Yes, I run every morning. What about you? 응, 나는 매일 아침 달려. 너는?
A: I collect stamps. It's my hobby. 나는 우표를 수집해. 그게 내 취미야.
B: That's interesting. You're also very handsome, by the way. 흥미롭네. 그런데, 너도 정말 잘생겼다.
A: Thank you! I appreciate that. 고마워! 고맙게 생각해.

### Challenge

I designed a new poster and then went for a run. On the way, I collected some beautiful flowers. A handsome man smiled at me, and I felt happy. 나는 새로운 포스터를 디자인하고 달리기를 했다. 가는 길에 아름다운 꽃을 몇 개 모았다. 잘생긴 남자가 나에게 웃어줬고, 나는 행복했다.

## DAY 8

### Step 2

The gate is open. 문이 열려 있다.
I am sorry for being late. 늦어서 미안하다.
This is a basic recipe. 이것은 기본적인 레시피이다.
What is the cost of this book? 이 책의 가격은 얼마인가요?
Can you print this document? 이 문서를 인쇄할 수 있나요?

### Step 3

A: Can you open the gate for me? 문을 열어줄 수 있나요?
B: Sure, no problem. Here you go. 물론이죠, 문제없어요. 여기요.
A: Thank you! I'm sorry for asking. 감사합니다! 부탁해서 죄송해요.
B: It's okay. It's a basic thing to do. 괜찮아요. 기본적인 일이에요.
A: By the way, do you know the cost to print this document?
그런데, 이 문서를 인쇄하는 비용을 아세요?

### Challenge

I printed a basic flyer about the event and posted it on the gate. Someone pointed out a mistake, and I felt sorry. I promised to reprint it despite the extra cost. 나는 행사에 대한 기본적인 전단지를 인쇄하여 문에 붙였다. 누군가가 실수를 지적했고, 나는 미안함을 느꼈다. 추가 비용이 들더라도 다시 인쇄하겠다고 약속했다.

## DAY 9

### Step 2

Don't forget your homework. 숙제를 잊지 마세요.
The cat is under the table. 고양이가 테이블 아래에 있다.
He wore a red cap. 그는 빨간 모자를 썼다.
Can you check my answer? 내 답을 확인해 줄 수 있나요?
The horse is very fast. 말은 매우 빠르다.

### Step 3

A: Did you forget your cap? 모자를 잊었니?
B: Oh no, I think I did. It must be under the table. 오, 안돼, 그런 것 같아. 테이블 아래에 있을 거야.
A: Let me check for you. 내가 확인해줄게.
B: Thanks. By the way, did you see the horse in the field? 고마워. 그런데, 들판에서 말 봤어?
A: Yes, I did. It's a beautiful horse. 응, 봤어. 아름다운 말이야.
B: I agree. Let's go see it after you find my cap. 동의해. 네가 모자를 찾은 후에 보러 가자.
A: Sure, I'll find it quickly. 좋아, 빨리 찾을게.

### Challenge

I forgot my cap under the tree and went to check on my horse. The horse was fine, but I still needed to find my cap. Eventually, I found it and put it on. 나는 나무 아래에 모자를 두고 말 상태를 확인하러 갔다. 말은 괜찮았지만, 여전히 모자를 찾아야 했다. 결국 모자를 찾아 쓰게 되었다.

## DAY 10

### Step 2

The future looks bright. 미래는 밝아 보인다.
The death of the hero was sad. 영웅의 죽음은 슬펐다.
He is very rich. 그는 매우 부유하다.
The customer is always right. 고객은 항상 옳다.
I met him two years ago. 나는 그를 2년 전에 만났다.

### Step 3

A: What do you think about the future? 미래에 대해 어떻게 생각해?
B: The future looks bright. 미래는 밝아 보인다.
A: Did you hear about the hero's death? 그 영웅의 죽음에 대해 들었어?
B: Yes, it was very sad. 응, 매우 슬펐어.
A: He was very rich, you know. 그는 매우 부유했었어, 알지?
B: Really? I didn't know that. 정말? 몰랐어.

### Challenge

I want to be rich in the future and have many customers. I learned about someone who died a long time ago in history class. It was fun to see how they changed the future. 나는 미래에 부유해지고 많은 고객을 갖고 싶다. 역사 수업에서 오래 전에 죽은 사람에 대해 배웠다. 그들이 어떻게 미래를 바꿨는지 보는 것은 재미있었다.

## DAY 11

### Step 2

Bees make honey. 벌은 꿀을 만든다.
A triangle has three sides. 삼각형은 세 변을 가지고 있다.
The meeting is at 2 P.M. 회의는 오후 2시에 있다.
I understand what you mean. 나는 네가 무슨 말 하는지 이해해.
It's very cold outside. 밖이 매우 춥다.

### Step 3

A: Do you like honey in your tea? 차에 꿀 넣는 거 좋아해?
B: Yes, especially when it's cold. 응, 특히 추울 때.
A: Did you learn about the triangle? 너는 삼각형에 대해 배웠니?
B: Yes, I did it in math class at 3 P.M. 응, 나는 오후 3시에 있던 수학시간에 배웠어.
A: Did you understand its meaning? 그 의미를 이해했니?
B: Not really, it was a bit confusing. 사실 잘 모르겠어, 좀 헷갈렸어.

### Challenge

In the cold afternoon, I enjoyed some honey. I looked at a triangle puzzle and tried to understand it. By 3 P.M., I finally figured it out and felt accomplished. 추운 오후에 나는 꿀을 즐겼다. 삼각형 퍼즐을 보며 이해하려고 애썼다. 오후 3시까지 결국 그것을 이해하고 성취감을 느꼈다.

## DAY 12

### Step 2

I often go to the park. 나는 자주 공원에 간다.
Don't forget your umbrella. 우산을 잊지 마세요.
That guy is my friend. 저 남자는 내 친구다.
Can you copy this paper for me? 이 종이를 복사해 줄 수 있나요?
She wore a pink dress. 그녀는 분홍색 드레스를 입었다.

### Step 3

A: Do you often need an umbrella? 너는 자주 우산이 필요해?
B: Yes, especially in this weather. 응, 특히 이런 날씨에는.
A: Did you see the guy with the pink umbrella? 분홍색 우산 든 남자 봤어?
B: Yes, he stood out a lot. 응, 정말 눈에 띄었어.
A: He was trying to copy my style, I think. 그는 내 스타일을 따라하려고 했던 것 같아.
B: Really? That's funny! 정말? 웃기다!

### Challenge

I often see a guy with a pink umbrella. He uses it to stand out in the crowd. One day, I decided to copy his idea and bought a bright pink umbrella too. 나는 자주 분홍색 우산을 든 남자를 본다. 그는 군중 속에서 돋보이기 위해 그것을 사용한다. 어느 날, 나는 그의 아이디어를 따라하기로 결심하고 밝은 분홍색 우산을 샀다.

## DAY 13

### Step 2

We went to the zoo yesterday. 우리는 어제 동물원에 갔다.
Let's meet at noon. 정오에 만나자.
The boy is playing soccer. 소년은 축구를 하고 있다.
My daughter loves to read. 내 딸은 독서를 좋아한다.
The chair is made of wood. 의자는 나무로 만들어졌다.

### Step 3

A: Are we going to the zoo today? 오늘 동물원에 갈 거야?
B: Yes, let's go at noon. 응, 정오에 가자.
A: Did you meet the boy at the park? 공원에서 그 소년을 만났니?
B: Yes, I did. Tom's daughter was playing nearby. 응, 만났어. 톰의 딸이 근처에서 놀고 있었어.
A: They were playing near the wood. 그들은 나무 근처에서 놀고 있었어.
B: It looked like they were having so much fun. 정말 재미있어 보였어.

### Challenge

I went to the zoo at noon with my family. A boy was showing his daughter a big animal made of wood. We had so much fun looking at all the animals. 나는 가족과 함께 정오에 동물원에 갔다. 한 소년이 딸에게 나무로 만든 큰 동물을 보여주고 있었다. 우리는 모든 동물을 보며 정말 즐거운 시간을 보냈다.

## DAY 14

### Step 2

I feel happy today. 나는 오늘 행복하다.
Can you open the door? 문을 열 수 있나요?
It's not for sale. 그것은 판매용이 아니다.
The garden is full of flowers. 정원은 꽃으로 가득하다.
Look at the beautiful rainbow. 아름다운 무지개를 봐.

### Step 3

A: How do you feel today? 오늘 기분이 어때?
B: I feel great! The garden is open now. 정말 좋아! 정원이 이제 열려 있어.
A: I heard there is a sale on plants. 식물 세일이 있다고 들었어.
B: Yes, I bought some flowers. 응, 꽃을 좀 샀어.
A: Did you see the rainbow over the garden? 정원 위에 무지개 봤어?
B: Yes, it was beautiful! 응, 정말 아름다웠어!

### Challenge

I felt happy when I saw a rainbow in the garden. I decided to open a small sale stand there. Many people came to buy items, enjoying the colorful view. 정원에서 무지개를 보았을 때 행복감을 느꼈다. 거기에서 작은 세일 가판대를 열기로 했다. 많은 사람들이 화려한 풍경을 즐기며 물건을 사러 왔다.

## DAY 15

### Step 2

The police are here to help. 경찰이 도와주기 위해 여기에 있다.
Look up at the sky. 하늘을 봐.
What are you doing? 무엇을 하고 있니?
She wore a gold necklace. 그녀는 금목걸이를 했다.
The movie was fantastic. 그 영화는 환상적이었다.

### Step 3

A: Did you see the police car? 경찰차 봤어?
B: Yes, it went up the hill. 응, 언덕 위로 갔어.
A: What did they find? 그들은 무엇을 찾았어?
B: I heard they found gold there. 거기서 금을 찾았다고 들었어.
A: Really? That's fantastic! 정말? 대단하다!
B: Yes, it's all over the news. 응, 뉴스에 다 나왔어.

### Challenge

I saw a police car drive up the street today. The officer asked us, "What are you doing?" and showed us his gold badge. It was fantastic! 오늘 경찰차가 길을 올라가는 것을 보았다. 경찰관이 우리에게 "무엇을 하고 있나요?"라고 물었고, 그의 금 배지를 보여주었다. 정말 대단했다!

## DAY 16

### Step 2

Turn left at the corner. 모퉁이에서 좌회전하세요.
I need to finish my homework. 나는 숙제를 끝내야 해.
She goes to college. 그녀는 대학에 다닌다.
This problem is very hard. 이 문제는 매우 어렵다.
Let's meet in the afternoon. 오후에 만나자.

### Step 3

A: Did you finish your work? 일을 끝냈니?
B: Yes, I finished it this afternoon. 응, 오늘 오후에 끝냈어.
A: How was college today? 오늘 대학 어땠어?
B: It was hard, but I managed. 힘들었지만, 해냈어.
A: Can you turn fast? 너는 빠르게 돌 수 있어?
B: Sure, I can. 물론, 할 수 있어.

### Challenge

I turned in my homework and finished my tasks. My brother in college says it's hard work. In the afternoon, I played outside. 나는 숙제를 제출하고 과제를 끝냈다. 대학에 다니는 내 형은 그것이 힘든 일이라고 말한다. 오후에는 밖에서 놀았다.

## DAY 17

### Step 2

Blood is red. 피는 빨갛다.
What are you doing today? 오늘 무엇을 하고 있니?
I love spending time in nature. 나는 자연 속에서 시간을 보내는 것을 좋아한다.
He is my best friend. 그는 내 가장 친한 친구다.
I like to eat candy. 나는 사탕 먹는 것을 좋아한다.

### Step 3

A: Did you see the blood on my knee? 내 무릎의 피 봤어?
B: Yes, what happened? 응, 무슨 일이야?
A: I fell while hiking today. 오늘 하이킹하다가 넘어졌어.
B: Oh no! Nature can be tough sometimes. 오, 안돼! 자연은 가끔 거칠 수 있어.
A: My friend gave me some candy to make me feel better.
내 친구가 나를 기분 좋게 하려고 사탕을 줬어.
B: That's nice of your friend. 친구가 참 착하네.

### Challenge

Today, I learned about blood in science class. My friend and I talked about how amazing nature is. After school, we shared some candy. 오늘 과학 수업에서 피에 대해 배웠다. 내 친구와 나는 자연이 얼마나 놀라운지에 대해 이야기했다. 학교가 끝난 후, 우리는 사탕을 나누어 먹었다.

## DAY 18

### Step 2

Please sit on the chair. 의자에 앉으세요.
Where are you going? 어디 가니?
Can you help me? 도와줄 수 있니?
The queen lives in a palace. 여왕은 궁전에 산다.
I wake up at 7 A.M. 나는 오전 7시에 일어난다.

### Step 3

A: Where is the new chair that you bought? 네가 산 새 의자는 어디에 있어?
B: It's in the dining room. 식당에 있어.
A: Can you help me move it? 그것을 옮기는 데 도와줄래?
B: Sure. Did you see the queen on TV this morning? 물론이지. 오늘 아침 TV에서 여왕 봤어?
A: Yes, I saw her at 10 A.M. 응, 오전 10시에 봤어.
B: She looked very elegant. 그녀는 매우 우아해 보였어.

### Challenge

I saw a fancy chair today and wondered where it came from. My teacher said it looked like a chair for a queen. In the A.M., I asked for help with my homework. 오늘 멋진 의자를 보았고, 그것이 어디서 왔는지 궁금해졌다. 선생님은 그것이 여왕을 위한 의자처럼 보인다고 말했다. 오전에 나는 숙제에 대해 도움을 요청했다.

## DAY 19

### Step 2

I can see you. 나는 너를 볼 수 있다.

I received the bill. 나는 청구서를 받았다.

This is for you. 이것은 너를 위한 것이다.

Leave a note for me. 나를 위해 메모를 남겨줘.

It's the first month of the year. 올해의 첫 번째 달이다.

### Step 3

A: Did you see the bill for this month? 이번 달 청구서 봤어?

B: Yes, it's on the table. 응, 테이블 위에 있어.

A: Can you write a note for me? 나를 위해 메모를 써줄 수 있니?

B: Sure, what should it say? 물론이지, 뭐라고 써야 해?

A: Just remind me to pay the bill. 청구서를 지불해야 한다고 상기시켜줘.

B: Okay, I will write it now. 좋아, 지금 쓸게.

### Challenge

I saw a bill on the table today. It was a note for my mom to pay next month. I reminded her so she wouldn't forget. 오늘 테이블 위에서 청구서를 봤다. 그것은 다음 달에 지불하라는 엄마를 위한 메모였다. 나는 그녀가 잊지 않도록 상기시켰다.

## DAY 20

### Step 2

We ate at a nice restaurant. 우리는 좋은 식당에서 식사했다.

Do you have enough money? 충분한 돈이 있나요?

He wore a scarf around his neck. 그는 목에 스카프를 둘렀다.

She reads the newspaper every morning. 그녀는 매일 아침 신문을 읽는다.

He couldn't hide his anger. 그는 화를 숨길 수 없었다.

### Step 3

A: Did you like the restaurant we visited? 우리가 간 식당 어땠어?

B: Yes, but the food wasn't enough. 응, 하지만 음식이 충분하지 않았어.

A: I saw the manager's neck turn red with anger. 나는 매니저의 목이 화로 인해 붉어지는 것을 봤어.

B: Yes, he was very angry. Did you read the newspaper today?
응, 그는 매우 화났어. 오늘 신문 읽었어?

A: Yes, it talked about the restaurant. 응, 그 식당에 대해 얘기했어.

B: I hope they get better soon. 빨리 나아지길 바란다.

### Challenge

I went to a restaurant today. The food was delicious and there was enough for everyone. I saw a man reading a newspaper and rubbing his neck, as if he was trying to control his anger.
오늘 식당에 갔다. 음식은 맛있었고 모두에게 충분했다. 나는 신문을 읽으며 목을 문지르는 남자를 보았는데, 그는 화를 억누르려는 것처럼 보였다

## DAY 21

### Step 2

My mother is very kind. 나의 어머니는 매우 친절하시다.
He stood by the door. 그는 문 옆에 서 있었다.
The dog is barking. 개가 짖고 있다.
She is afraid of spiders. 그녀는 거미를 무서워한다.
What is your name? 네 이름이 뭐니?

### Step 3

A: What is your dog's name? 네 개의 이름이 뭐야?
B: His name is Max. 그의 이름은 맥스야.
A: Is he by your mother? 그는 네 어머니 옆에 있어?
B: Yes, he is. She loves him. 응, 그래. 그녀는 그를 사랑해.
A: Are you afraid of big dogs? 너 큰 개들 무서워하니?
B: No, I'm not. I like big dogs a lot. 아니, 안 무서워. 나는 큰 개들을 정말 좋아해.

### Challenge

I was with my mother by the park today. We saw a dog named Max. I was afraid at first, but he was very friendly. 오늘 공원 옆에서 어머니와 함께 있었다. 우리는 맥스라는 개를 봤다. 처음엔 무서웠지만, 그는 매우 친절했다.

## DAY 22

### Step 2

We are in the same group. 우리는 같은 그룹에 있다.
I saw a bat in the cave. 나는 동굴에서 박쥐를 보았다.
He stood at the base of the mountain. 그는 산 기슭에 서 있었다.
The bell rang loudly. 종이 크게 울렸다.
I have an appointment with the dentist. 나는 치과 의사와 약속이 있다.

### Step 3

A: Did you see the group of bats? 박쥐 무리를 봤어?
B: Yes, they were flying near the bell. 응, 그들은 종 근처에서 날고 있었어.
A: They made a loud sound when they flew by. 그들이 날 때 큰 소리를 냈어.
B: Yes, they did. Do you have a dentist appointment today? 응, 맞아. 오늘 치과 예약 있어?
A: Yes, I do. I need to check the base of my tooth. 응, 있어. 치아의 기초를 점검해야 해.
B: I hope it goes well! 잘 되길 바랄게!

### Challenge

I went to the zoo with my group today. We saw a bat hanging upside down. At school, we learned the base facts about animals. The bell rang, and I remembered I had a dentist appointment. 오늘 그룹과 함께 동물원에 갔다. 우리는 거꾸로 매달린 박쥐를 보았다. 학교에서는 동물에 대한 기초 사실을 배웠다. 종이 울리고, 나는 치과 예약이 있다는 것을 기억했다.

## DAY 23

### Step 2

The man is very tall. 그 남자는 매우 키가 크다.
The car is going at a high speed. 차가 고속으로 달리고 있다.
She borrowed a book from the library. 그녀는 도서관에서 책을 빌렸다.
He is wearing a yellow shirt. 그는 노란 셔츠를 입고 있다.
I like to bake cookies. 나는 쿠키를 굽는 것을 좋아한다.

### Step 3

A: Did you see the man running at high speed? 고속으로 달리는 남자를 봤어?
B: Yes, he ran past the library. 응, 그는 도서관을 지나 달렸어.
A: He was wearing a yellow shirt. 그는 노란 셔츠를 입고 있었어.
B: I saw that too. Are you going to the library? 나도 봤어. 너 도서관 갈 거야?
A: Yes, but I need to bake some cookies first. 응, 하지만 먼저 쿠키를 구워야 해.
B: That sounds delicious! 맛있겠다!

### Challenge

I saw a man running at high speed today. He was heading to the library. He wore a yellow shirt. After school, my mom and I baked cookies. 오늘 고속으로 달리는 남자를 봤다. 그는 도서관으로 향하고 있었다. 그는 노란 셔츠를 입고 있었다. 방과 후, 엄마와 나는 쿠키를 구웠다.

## DAY 24

### Step 2

Keep your room clean. 방을 깨끗하게 유지하세요.
The news was a shock to everyone. 그 소식은 모두에게 충격이었다.
The tickets are free. 티켓은 무료다.
We sailed on a boat. 우리는 배를 타고 항해했다.
I need to pay the bill. 나는 청구서를 지불해야 한다.

### Step 3

A: How do you keep your boat in good condition? 배를 어떻게 좋은 상태로 유지하니?
B: I clean it every week. 매주 청소해.
A: Did you hear about the free boat rides? 무료 보트 타기에 대해 들었니?
B: Yes, it was a shock to me. 응, 나에게 충격이었어.
A: Usually, you have to pay a lot for that. 보통은 그걸 위해 많은 돈을 내야 해.
B: I know! It's such a great offer. 나도 알아! 정말 좋은 제안이야.

### Challenge

I saw a free boat ride sign today. It was a shock because we usually have to pay. I hope they keep it free for a long time. 오늘 무료 보트 타기 표지판을 봤다. 우리는 보통 돈을 내야 하기 때문에 충격이었다. 오랫동안 무료로 유지되길 바란다.

## DAY 25

### Step 2

Who is your favorite teacher? 네가 가장 좋아하는 선생님은 누구니?
The field is full of flowers. 들판은 꽃으로 가득하다.
My boss is very kind. 내 상사는 매우 친절하다.
Brushing your teeth is a good habit. 양치질은 좋은 습관이다.
When is your birthday? 네 생일은 언제니?

### Step 3

A: Who is that in the field? 들판에 저 사람 누구야?
B: That's my boss. 저 사람은 내 상사야.
A: What is he doing there? 그는 거기서 뭐 하고 있어?
B: He has a habit of walking there. 그는 거기서 산책하는 습관이 있어.
A: When does he usually go? 그는 보통 언제 가?
B: He goes every morning. 그는 매일 아침 가.

### Challenge

I went to the field today with my class. Our teacher asked us, "Who knows the names of these plants?" It's his habit to quiz us when we go on trips. 오늘 반 친구들과 들판에 갔다. 선생님이 우리에게 "이 식물들의 이름을 아는 사람?"이라고 물으셨다. 여행을 갈 때마다 퀴즈를 내는 것이 그의 습관이다.

## DAY 26

### Step 2

I love listening to music. 나는 음악 듣는 것을 좋아한다.
The rabbit is hopping around. 토끼가 여기저기 뛰어다닌다.
That movie is a comedy. 저 영화는 코미디다.
This math problem is difficult. 이 수학 문제는 어렵다.
My hobby is painting. 내 취미는 그림 그리기다.

### Step 3

A: What is your favorite hobby? 네가 가장 좋아하는 취미는 뭐야?
B: I love listening to music. 나는 음악 듣는 것을 좋아해.
A: Do you have any pets? 애완동물 있어?
B: Yes, I have a rabbit. 응, 토끼가 있어.
A: Do you enjoy watching comedy shows? 코미디 쇼 보는 거 좋아해?
B: Yes, but some jokes are difficult to understand. 응, 하지만 어떤 농담은 이해하기 어려워.

### Challenge

I shared my hobby with the class today. I like music, watching comedy shows, and taking care of my pet rabbit. It was difficult to choose just one to talk about! 오늘 반 친구들과 내 취미를 공유했다. 나는 음악 듣기, 코미디 쇼 보기, 애완 토끼 돌보기를 좋아한다. 무엇 하나만 이야기하기 어려웠다!

# DAY 27

## Step 2

She bought a new pair of boots. 그녀는 새 부츠를 샀다.
I have one apple left. 나는 사과가 하나 남았다.
The child is playing. 아이가 놀고 있다.
He can kick the ball far. 그는 공을 멀리 찰 수 있다.
Look around for clues. 단서를 찾아 주위를 둘러봐.

## Step 3

A: Whose boot is this? 이 부츠 누구 거야?
B: It belongs to one of the children. 그 아이들 중 하나의 것이야.
A: Did the child lose it? 그 아이가 잃어버렸어?
B: Yes, they were playing around here. 응, 여기서 놀고 있었어.
A: Did you see them kick the ball? 그들이 공을 차는 거 봤어?
B: Yes, that's when they lost the boot. 응, 그때 부츠를 잃어버렸어.

## Challenge

I lost one of my boots at recess today. A child found it and kicked it around the playground. We all laughed as we ran to get it back. 오늘 쉬는 시간에 부츠 하나를 잃어버렸다. 어떤 아이가 그것을 찾아 운동장에서 차고 놀았다. 우리는 그것을 다시 찾으려고 뛰어가면서 모두 웃었다.

# DAY 28

## Step 2

Some people believe in ghosts. 어떤 사람들은 유령을 믿는다.
The tiger is a strong animal. 호랑이는 강한 동물이다.
He wore a funny hat. 그는 웃긴 모자를 썼다.
Tell me about your day. 너의 하루에 대해 말해줘.
What is the weight of this box? 이 상자의 무게가 얼마인가요?

## Step 3

A: Did you hear about the ghost in the old house? 오래된 집에 유령 이야기를 들었니?
B: Yes, and the story about the tiger too. 응, 그리고 호랑이에 대한 이야기까지도.
A: That's scary. Did you see my hat? 무섭다. 내 모자 봤어?
B: Yes, it's over there by the door. 응, 저기 문 옆에 있어.
A: Do you know anything about its weight? 그 무게에 대해 아는 거 있어?
B: It's very light, like a feather. 깃털처럼 매우 가벼워.

## Challenge

I read a book about a ghost and a tiger today. The ghost wore a funny hat, and the tiger talked about its weight. It was a very interesting story! 오늘 유령과 호랑이에 관한 책을 읽었다. 유령은 웃긴 모자를 썼고, 호랑이는 자신의 무게에 대해 이야기했다. 매우 흥미로운 이야기였다!

## DAY 29

### Step 2

The car's brakes are very strong. 그 차의 브레이크는 매우 강력하다.
The dog is tied with a chain. 그 개는 사슬에 묶여 있다.
No, I don't want it. 아니, 나는 원하지 않는다.
I lost my key. 나는 열쇠를 잃어버렸다.
They climbed the hill. 그들은 언덕을 올랐다.

### Step 3

A: Did you check the brakes on your bike? 네 자전거의 브레이크를 확인했니?
B: No, not yet. 아니, 아직.
A: You should, especially on this hill. 해야 해, 특히 이 언덕에서는.
B: Yes, and the chain looks loose too. 응, 그리고 사슬도 헐거워 보여.
A: Do you have the key to the lock? 자물쇠 열쇠 가지고 있어?
B: Yes, it's in my pocket. 응, 내 주머니에 있어.

### Challenge

The brakes didn't work, so I had to stop with my feet. I used a chain to lock my bike because I didn't have the key. 오늘 나는 자전거를 타고 언덕을 내려갔다. 브레이크가 작동하지 않아서 발로 멈춰야 했다. 열쇠가 없어서 체인으로 자전거를 잠갔다.

## DAY 30

### Step 2

He studies at an academy. 그는 학원에서 공부한다.
Stay calm in an emergency. 비상시에는 침착하세요.
That's a great idea. 그것은 좋은 아이디어다.
Let's try this new game. 이 새로운 게임을 해보자.
The sun rises in the east. 해는 동쪽에서 뜬다.

### Step 3

A: Hey, there's a new academy in the east. 야, 동쪽에 새 학원이 생겼어.
B: Really? That sounds fun. I want to go. 정말? 재밌겠는데. 가고 싶어.
A: Yeah, it's a good idea. You can learn new things there.
응, 좋은 생각이야. 거기서 새로운 걸 배울 수 있어.
B: That sounds nice. Should I try it? 좋다. 내가 해볼까?
A: Yes, try it. It's very calm and nice. 응, 해봐. 아주 조용하고 좋아.
B: Great! I'll tell my mom. 멋지다! 엄마한테 말해야겠다.

### Challenge

I went to my new academy in the east part of town today. I had an idea to try and stay calm during my first class. It helped me learn a lot! 오늘 시내 동쪽에 있는 새 학원에 갔다. 첫 수업 동안 침착하려고 시도하는 아이디어가 있었다. 그것은 나에게 많은 것을 배우게 했다!

## DAY 31

### Step 2

I ate a bowl of soup. 나는 국 한 그릇을 먹었다.
The lion is the king of the jungle. 사자는 정글의 왕이다.
Mathematics is my favorite subject. 수학은 내가 가장 좋아하는 과목이다.
I need some help. 나는 도움이 필요하다.
Are you certain about that? 그것에 대해 확신하니?

### Step 3

A: Do you need a bowl for the soup? 국을 담을 그릇이 필요하니?
B: Yes, I do. Thanks. 응, 필요해. 고마워.
A: Have you seen the lion at the zoo? 동물원에서 사자를 본 적 있어?
B: Yes, it was amazing. 응, 정말 놀라웠어.
A: Are you good at mathematics? 수학 잘해?
B: I'm not certain, but I try my best. 확신은 없지만, 최선을 다해.

### Challenge

I need help with my mathematics homework. My teacher said I should be certain of my answers. After school, I saw a lion in a picture on my cereal bowl. 나는 수학 숙제에 도움이 필요하다. 선생님이 내 답에 대해 확신을 가져야 한다고 하셨다. 방과 후, 시리얼 그릇의 그림에서 사자를 보았다.

## DAY 32

### Step 2

I got this gift from my friend. 나는 이 선물을 친구에게 받았다.
We live on Earth. 우리는 지구에 산다.
The frog is green. 개구리는 녹색이다.
Do not play with fire. 불장난 하지 마라.
I hate getting up early. 나는 일찍 일어나는 것을 싫어한다.

### Step 3

A: Where is this frog from? 이 개구리는 어디서 왔니?
B: It's from the earth's wetlands. 지구의 습지에서 왔어.
A: Do you think frogs hate fire? 개구리가 불을 싫어한다고 생각해?
B: Yes, they do. Fire is dangerous for them. 응, 그래. 불은 그들에게 위험해.
A: Did you see the fire in the forest? 숲에서 불 본 적 있어?
B: Yes, it was scary. 응, 무서웠어.

### Challenge

I learned about frogs in science class today. They need water from the earth to live. I also learned they hate fire and stay far away from it. 오늘 과학 수업에서 개구리에 대해 배웠다. 그들은 지구의 물이 필요하다. 또한 그들은 불을 싫어하고 멀리 떨어져 있다는 것을 배웠다.

## DAY 33

### Step 2

I write in my diary every night. 나는 매일 밤 일기를 쓴다.
She ate a sweet pear. 그녀는 달콤한 배를 먹었다.
The couple is very happy. 그 커플은 매우 행복하다.
His wife is a doctor. 그의 아내는 의사이다.
Yes, I can help you. 네, 도와드릴 수 있습니다.

### Step 3

A: Do you keep a diary? 너 일기 쓰니?
B: Yes, I write in it every night. 응, 매일 밤 써.
A: Did you see the couple with the pears? 배를 들고 있는 커플 봤어?
B: Yes, they were sharing them. 응, 그들은 배를 나눠 먹고 있었어.
A: Is the woman his wife? 그 여자가 그의 아내야?
B: Yes, she is. They seem very happy. 응, 맞아. 그들은 매우 행복해 보여.

### Challenge

I wrote in my diary about my day at school. I saw a couple sharing a pear during lunch. The boy asked, "Is this for your wife?" and the girl laughed and said, "Yes, it's for you!" 학교에서 보낸 하루를 일기에 썼다. 점심시간에 배를 나눠 먹는 커플을 봤다. 소년이 "이거 네 아내 줄 거야?"라고 물었고, 소녀는 웃으며 "네, 너에게 줄 거야!"라고 말했다.

## DAY 34

### Step 2

Do you have any questions? 질문이 있습니까?
I love the smell of flowers. 나는 꽃 냄새를 좋아한다.
Can I have another piece? 한 조각 더 먹어도 될까요?
Baseball is my favorite sport. 야구는 내가 가장 좋아하는 스포츠다.
He fell asleep during the movie. 그는 영화 도중에 잠들었다.

### Step 3

A: Do you smell something strange? 이상한 냄새가 나지 않아?
B: Yes, I do. It's coming from the kitchen. 응, 부엌에서 나는 것 같아.
A: Do you have any idea what it is? 그게 뭔지 알아?
B: Maybe it's the food. Let's check. 아마 음식일 거야. 확인해보자.
A: Do you want to watch another baseball game? 또 다른 야구 경기 볼래?
B: Sure, during the next break. 물론, 다음 휴식 시간에.

### Challenge

I played baseball during recess today. I didn't like any of the snacks they had. Another kid shared his chips with me, and they had a weird smell. 오늘 쉬는 시간에 야구를 했다. 제공된 간식 중 아무것도 마음에 들지 않았다. 다른 아이가 나에게 칩을 나눠줬는데, 이상한 냄새가 났다.

## DAY 35

### Step 2

I like to eat potatoes. 나는 감자 먹는 것을 좋아한다.
My shoes are dirty. 내 신발은 더럽다.
She blew a big bubble. 그녀는 큰 거품을 불었다.
We climbed the mountain. 우리는 산을 올랐다.
The dog is brown. 그 개는 갈색이다.

### Step 3

A: Did you see the brown potato chips on the table? 테이블 위에 있는 갈색 감자칩 봤어?
B: Yes, they look delicious, but my hands are dirty. 응, 맛있어 보이는데 손이 더러워.
A: Do you need some soap to wash them? 손 씻으려고 비누 필요해?
B: Yes, please. Do you have the soap that makes big bubbles? 응, 부탁해. 큰 거품이 나는 비누 있어?
A: Have you been to the mountain nearby? 근처 산에 가본 적 있어?
B: Yes, it's beautiful there. 응, 거기 정말 아름다워.

### Challenge

I helped plant potatoes in the school garden today. My hands got dirty with the brown soil. Later, I blew bubbles and watched them float towards the mountain. 오늘 학교 정원에서 감자를 심는 것을 도왔다. 내 손은 갈색 흙으로 더러워졌다. 나중에 나는 거품을 불었고 그것들이 산을 향해 떠가는 것을 보았다.

## DAY 36

### Step 2

The library is very quiet. 도서관은 매우 조용하다.
Can you advise me on this? 이것에 대해 조언해 줄 수 있나요?
The nurse was very kind. 간호사는 매우 친절했다.
We visited an old castle. 우리는 오래된 성을 방문했다.
The sky is clear today. 오늘 하늘이 맑다.

### Step 3

A: The castle looks beautiful against the sky. 성이 하늘 배경으로 아름다워 보인다.
B: Yes, it's so quiet here. 응, 여기는 정말 조용해.
A: I need some advice. Can you help? 나는 조언이 필요해. 도와줄 수 있어?
B: Sure, what do you need? 물론, 뭐가 필요해?
A: Should I become a nurse? 내가 간호사가 되어야 할까?
B: Yes, I think you would be great at it. 응, 너는 잘할 것 같아.

### Challenge

I went to a quiet place to read today. A nurse came by and advised me to rest more. I imagined living in a castle under the bright blue sky. 오늘 조용한 곳에 가서 책을 읽었다. 간호사가 와서 더 쉬라고 조언했다. 나는 밝은 파란 하늘 아래 성에서 사는 것을 상상했다.

## DAY 37

### Step 2

I love to swim in the pool. 나는 수영장에서 수영하는 것을 좋아한다.
Be careful with the knife. 칼을 조심해라.
I think it's a good idea. 나는 그것이 좋은 생각이라고 생각한다.
What is that thing? 저것은 무엇인가요?
I broke my nose in the fight. 나는 싸움에서 코가 부러졌다.

### Step 3

A: Do you like to swim? 수영하는 것을 좋아하니?
B: Yes, I love it. 응, 좋아해.
A: What do you think of this knife? 이 칼에 대해 어떻게 생각해?
B: It's sharp. Be careful! 그것은 날카로워. 조심해!
A: What's your favorite thing to do? 네가 가장 좋아하는 것은 무엇이니?
B: I think it's reading. 나는 독서인 것 같아.

### Challenge

I went to the pool to swim today. I saw a shiny thing in the water and thought it was a knife. When I looked closer, it was just a toy near my nose. 오늘 수영하러 수영장에 갔다. 물속에서 반짝이는 것을 보고 칼이라고 생각했다. 가까이에서 보니 그것은 내 코 근처에 있는 장난감이었다.

## DAY 38

### Step 2

The room is very clean. 방이 매우 깨끗하다.
She is a nice person. 그녀는 좋은 사람이다.
A bee stung me on my neck. 벌이 내 목을 쏘았다.
They will marry next year. 그들은 내년에 결혼할 것이다.
He got a high score on the test. 그는 시험에서 높은 점수를 받았다.

### Step 3

A: Look, I cleaned my room! 봐, 내 방을 청소했어!
B: It looks so nice and clean. 정말 깨끗하고 좋다.
A: Do you think we can marry our dolls now? 우리 인형들을 결혼시킬 수 있을 것 같아?
B: Yes, let's have a wedding. My doll can be the bride. 응, 결혼식을 하자. 내 인형이 신부가 될 수 있어.
A: And my doll can be the groom. Oh no, there's a bee!
그리고 내 인형이 신랑이 될 수 있어. 오, 저기 벌이 있어!
B: Don't worry, the bee will go away. Let's play and score points in our game.
걱정 마, 벌은 곧 갈 거야. 우리 게임에서 점수를 얻자.

### Challenge

I helped clean the classroom today. My teacher said I did a nice job and gave me a good score. At recess, we saw a bee and talked about how bees help flowers "marry" to make seeds.
오늘 교실 청소를 도왔다. 선생님이 내가 잘했다고 하시며 좋은 점수를 주셨다. 쉬는 시간에 우리는 벌을 보았고, 벌이 꽃이 씨를 만들도록 돕는 방법에 대해 이야기했다.

## DAY 39

### Step 2

The turtle is slow. 거북이는 느리다.
She loves to sing. 그녀는 노래하는 것을 좋아한다.
Please stop talking. 말 그만해 주세요.
This is my chance to shine. 이것은 내가 빛날 기회이다.
There is a lot of space here. 여기 공간이 많다.

### Step 3

A: Do you think bees are slow? 벌이 느리다고 생각해?
B: No, they move very fast. 아니, 그들은 매우 빨리 움직여.
A: Have you ever heard them sing? 그들이 노래하는 것을 들어본 적 있어?
B: No, they never stop working. 아니, 그들은 일하는 것을 멈추지 않아.
A: Do you think we have a chance to see them up close?
우리가 가까이서 그들을 볼 기회가 있다고 생각해?
B: Yes, if we find a safe space to watch. 응, 우리가 안전하게 볼 공간을 찾으면.

### Challenge

I sang a slow song in music class today. The teacher asked me to stop and then gave me another chance. I felt happy because I had space to improve. 오늘 음악 수업에서 느린 노래를 불렀다. 선생님이 나에게 그만하라고 하셨다가 다시 기회를 주셨다. 발전할 공간이 있어서 기뻤다.

## DAY 40

### Step 2

We need to fill out a form. 우리는 양식을 작성해야 한다.
The toy is broken. 장난감이 부러졌다.
My favorite color is blue. 내가 가장 좋아하는 색깔은 파란색이다.
We play soccer every Saturday. 우리는 매주 토요일에 축구를 한다.
She washes her clothes every Sunday. 그녀는 매주 일요일마다 옷을 세탁한다.

### Step 3

A: What form does this toy take? 이 장난감은 어떤 형태를 띠고 있니?
B: It's in the shape of a car. 그것은 자동차 모양이야.
A: I like its color. It's bright red. 나는 그 색깔이 좋아. 밝은 빨간색이야.
B: Yes, it's very nice. Do you play soccer? 응, 정말 좋아. 너 축구 하니?
A: Yes, I do. It's my favorite sport. 응, 해. 내가 가장 좋아하는 스포츠야.
B: Make sure to wash your hands after playing! 놀고 나서 손 씻는 거 잊지 마!

### Challenge

I played with a toy that was in the form of a car today. It changed color when I washed it. Afterward, I played soccer with my friends. 오늘 자동차 형태의 장난감을 가지고 놀았다. 그것을 씻을 때 색깔이 변했다. 그 후, 친구들과 축구를 했다.

## DAY 41

### Step 2

The clock is ticking. 시계가 똑딱거리고 있다.
She has long hair. 그녀는 긴 머리카락을 가지고 있다.
The shirt was cheap. 그 셔츠는 쌌다.
This is an old book. 이것은 오래된 책이다.
Do you remember my name? 내 이름을 기억하니?

### Step 3

A: Do you see that old clock on the wall? 벽에 있는 저 오래된 시계 보이니?
B: Yes, it's been there for a long time. 응, 오랫동안 저기 있었어.
A: I remember when we bought it. 우리가 그걸 샀을 때를 기억해.
B: Was it cheap? 그때 쌌었어?
A: Yes, it was very cheap back then. 응, 그때는 아주 쌌어.
B: I can't believe it still works! 아직도 작동하다니 믿기지 않아!

### Challenge

I saw an old clock in the attic today. It had a long pendulum and still worked. I remember my grandma saying it was very cheap when she bought it. 오늘 다락방에서 오래된 시계를 봤다. 긴 진자가 있었고 아직도 작동했다. 할머니가 그걸 샀을 때 매우 쌌다고 말씀하신 것이 기억난다.

## DAY 42

### Step 2

The park is between the school and the store. 공원은 학교와 가게 사이에 있다.
The cat is inside the house. 고양이는 집 안에 있다.
We will visit our grandparents this weekend. 우리는 이번 주말에 조부모님을 방문할 것이다.
I love learning about different cultures. 나는 다양한 문화를 배우는 것을 좋아한다.
Do you have a plan? 계획이 있니?

### Step 3

A: Do you plan to visit any new places soon? 곧 새로운 곳을 방문할 계획이 있니?
B: Yes, I'm planning to visit Japan. 응, 일본을 방문할 계획이야.
A: That's exciting! What's your plan? 신나겠다! 계획이 뭐야?
B: I want to explore the culture and visit museums. 나는 문화를 탐험하고 박물관을 방문하고 싶어.
A: Will you travel between cities? 도시들 사이를 여행할 거니?
B: Yes, and I also want to see the inside of old temples. 응, 그리고 오래된 사원의 내부도 보고 싶어.

### Challenge

I have a plan to visit the museum this weekend. It's interesting to see the culture inside. I'll walk between the exhibits to learn more. 나는 이번 주말에 박물관을 방문할 계획이 있다. 내부의 문화를 보는 것이 흥미롭다. 더 많이 배우기 위해 전시물들 사이를 걸어다닐 것이다.

## DAY 43

### Step 2

Use an eraser to fix your mistake. 실수를 고치기 위해 지우개를 사용해라.
We are going to the beach tomorrow. 우리는 내일 해변에 갈 것이다.
The background of the picture is beautiful. 사진의 배경이 아름답다.
Please read aloud. 소리 내어 읽어 주세요.
I like ice cream. 나는 아이스크림을 좋아한다.

### Step 3

A: Do you have an eraser I can use? 내가 쓸 수 있는 지우개가 있니?
B: Yes, it's right here. 응, 바로 여기 있어.
A: Do you like the beach? 해변을 좋아하니?
B: Yes, I love it, especially with the sunset in the background.
응, 특히 배경에 석양이 있을 때 정말 좋아해.
A: Can you read this aloud? 이것을 소리 내어 읽어줄 수 있니?
B: Sure, I like reading out loud. 물론, 나는 소리 내어 읽는 것을 좋아해.

### Challenge

I found an eraser shaped like a star today. I took it to the beach and drew pictures in the sand. The waves in the background sounded nice as I said aloud, "I like the beach!" 오늘 별 모양의 지우개를 발견했다. 그걸 해변에 가져가서 모래에 그림을 그렸다. 배경의 파도 소리가 좋았고 나는 "나는 해변을 좋아해!"라고 소리 내어 말했다.

## DAY 44

### Step 2

The ship is sailing on the sea. 배가 바다에서 항해하고 있다.
I will see you next week. 다음 주에 보자.
The dog tried to bite me. 개가 나를 물려고 했다.
The flower is blooming. 꽃이 피고 있다.
Look at the stars. 별들을 봐.

### Step 3

A: Did you see the big ship in the harbor? 항구에 있는 큰 배 봤어?
B: Yes, it arrived last week. 응, 지난주에 도착했어.
A: Look at those beautiful flowers on the deck. 갑판 위에 있는 아름다운 꽃들을 봐.
B: They are lovely. Did you get a bite to eat? 정말 사랑스럽다. 뭐 먹을 거 샀어?
A: Yes, I did. The food on the ship was great. 응, 샀어. 배에서 먹은 음식이 훌륭했어.
B: I would love to go on a trip like that. 나도 그런 여행 가고 싶다.

### Challenge

I saw a big ship at the harbor this week. While I was there, a bug tried to bite me. I looked at a pretty flower to distract myself. 이번 주에 항구에서 큰 배를 봤다. 그곳에 있는 동안 벌레가 나를 물려고 했다. 나는 주의를 돌리기 위해 예쁜 꽃을 보았다.

## DAY 45

### Step 2

Please bring your book. 책을 가져오세요.
I need my math textbook. 수학 교과서가 필요해.
My sock has a hole in it. 내 양말에 구멍이 났어.
This cloth is very soft. 이 천은 매우 부드럽다.
My tooth hurts. 이가 아프다.

### Step 3

A: Can you bring my textbook to me? 내 교과서를 가져다 줄 수 있니?
B: Sure, where is it? 물론, 어디에 있어?
A: It's next to the blue cloth on the table. 테이블 위 파란 천 옆에 있어.
B: Okay, I see it. Do you need anything else? 알았어, 보여. 다른 건 필요 없어?
A: Yes, my sock and toothbrush, please. 응, 양말과 칫솔도 부탁해.
B: Got it. I'll bring everything to you. 알았어. 다 가져다 줄게.

### Challenge

I forgot to bring my textbook to school today. My friend helped me clean my desk with a cloth. I also found a lost sock and a tooth inside my drawer! 오늘 교과서를 학교에 가져오는 것을 잊었다. 친구가 천으로 내 책상을 청소하는 것을 도와줬다. 서랍 안에서 잃어버린 양말과 이를 찾았다!

## DAY 46

### Step 2

Good luck on your test. 시험 잘 봐.
She did well on her exam. 그녀는 시험을 잘 봤다.
There was an error in the report. 보고서에 오류가 있었다.
We had a picnic in the park. 우리는 공원에서 소풍을 갔다.
It's too hot today. 오늘은 너무 덥다.

### Step 3

A: Are we going on a picnic today? 오늘 소풍 갈 거야?
B: Yes, if the weather is good. 응, 날씨가 좋다면.
A: I hope we have good luck. 행운이 있길 바란다.
B: Me too. I hope everything goes well. 나도 그래. 모든 일이 잘 되길 바란다.
A: Did you check for any errors in the plan? 계획에 오류가 없는지 확인했니?
B: Yes, everything is ready. Let's go! 응, 다 준비됐어. 가자!

### Challenge

I had good luck at the picnic today. Everything went well and there were no errors. We had fun, but I ate too much! 오늘 소풍에서 행운이 있었다. 모든 일이 잘 됐고 오류가 없었다. 우리는 즐거웠지만, 너무 많이 먹었다!

## DAY 47

### Step 2

I need a new brush for painting. 나는 그림 그리기 위한 새 붓이 필요하다.

The branch broke in the wind. 나뭇가지가 바람에 부러졌다.

Turn off the light. 불을 꺼라.

I will go with you. 내가 너와 함께 갈게.

I will call you later. 나중에 전화할게.

### Step 3

A: Can you hand me the brush? 붓 좀 건네줄 수 있니?

B: Sure, here it is. 물론, 여기 있어.

A: Look at that branch with the bird. 저 나뭇가지에 있는 새를 봐.

B: It's beautiful in the morning light. 아침 햇빛 속에서 아름답다.

A: Do you want to call Sarah to join us? 사라를 불러서 함께하자.

B: Yes, I'll call her right now. 응, 지금 바로 전화할게.

### Challenge

I saw a bird on a branch today. The sunlight made the leaves look bright and pretty. I used a brush to paint the scene and called my friend to share it with him. 오늘 나뭇가지에 있는 새를 보았다. 햇빛이 잎을 밝고 예쁘게 보이게 했다. 나는 붓을 사용해서 그 장면을 그렸고, 친구에게 전화를 걸어 그 순간을 나눴다.

## DAY 48

### Step 2

This pillow is very soft. 이 베개는 매우 부드럽다.

We will climb the mountain tomorrow. 우리는 내일 산을 오를 것이다.

I will invite you to my party. 나는 너를 내 파티에 초대할 것이다.

He made a friendly gesture. 그는 친절한 제스처를 취했다.

The captain led the team. 캡틴이 팀을 이끌었다.

### Step 3

A: The blanket is so soft. 이 담요는 정말 부드럽다.

B: Yes, it feels nice. Did you see the captain? 응, 느낌이 좋다. 캡틴 봤어?

A: Yes, he waved to us to climb aboard. 응, 그가 우리에게 배에 오르라고 손을 흔들었어.

B: Should we invite him to join us? 그를 초대할까?

A: Yes, let's invite him. 응, 초대하자.

B: I'll go ask him now. 지금 가서 물어볼게.

### Challenge

I climbed a tree and felt the soft leaves today. My friend invited me to play a game, and I accepted with a big gesture. I became the captain of our team. 오늘 나무에 올라 부드러운 잎을 느꼈다. 친구가 나를 게임하자고 초대했고, 나는 큰 제스처로 수락했다. 나는 우리 팀의 캡틴이 되었다.

## DAY 49

### Step 2

My leg hurts. 다리가 아프다.
The bird flew away. 새가 날아갔다.
I believe in you. 나는 너를 믿는다.
The watermelon is sweet. 수박이 달다.
I had a strange dream. 나는 이상한 꿈을 꾸었다.

### Step 3

A: My leg hurts from walking so much. 너무 많이 걸어서 다리가 아파.
B: Let's rest for a while. Look at that watermelon. 좀 쉬자. 저 수박을 봐.
A: It looks delicious. I can't believe how big it is. 맛있어 보인다. 얼마나 큰지 믿을 수가 없어.
B: Yes, it's huge. Do you ever dream about flying? 응, 정말 커. 날아가는 꿈을 꿔 본 적 있어?
A: Sometimes. I dream of flying away to a new place. 가끔. 나는 새로운 곳으로 날아가는 꿈을 꿔.
B: That sounds amazing. I believe you can do anything in your dreams.
정말 멋지다. 꿈에서는 무엇이든 할 수 있다고 믿어.

### Challenge

I had a dream last night about a giant watermelon. I tried to carry it, but my legs felt too weak. I believe it rolled away down the hill! 어젯밤 거대한 수박에 대한 꿈을 꾸었다. 그것을 들려고 했지만, 다리가 너무 약해 보였다. 그것이 언덕 아래로 굴러갔다고 믿는다!

## DAY 50

### Step 2

I love to travel. 나는 여행하는 것을 좋아한다.
The bear is sleeping. 곰이 자고 있다.
This book is very interesting. 이 책은 매우 흥미롭다.
I eat a lot of vegetables. 나는 많은 채소를 먹는다.
Let's watch a movie. 영화를 보자.

### Step 3

A: Do you like to travel? 여행하는 것을 좋아하니?
B: Yes, I love it. Have you read this book about bears? 응, 좋아해. 이 곰에 관한 책을 읽어봤니?
A: No, but it sounds interesting. Do you like vegetables? 아니, 하지만 흥미로울 것 같아. 채소 좋아하니?
B: Yes, I eat them every day. Do you want to watch a movie? 응, 매일 먹어. 영화 볼래?
A: Sure, let's watch one about nature. 물론, 자연에 관한 영화를 보자.
B: Great idea! 좋은 생각이야!

### Challenge

I love to travel and see new places. On my last trip, I saw a bear in the forest. I brought a book with me to read while eating vegetables and watching the sunset. 나는 여행하는 것을 좋아하고 새로운 장소를 보는 것을 좋아한다. 마지막 여행에서 숲에서 곰을 보았다. 채소를 먹으면서 해넘이를 보며 읽기 위해 책을 가져갔다.

## DAY 51

### Step 2

The bottle is full of water. 병은 물로 가득 차 있다.

The clerk helped me find a book. 직원이 내가 책을 찾는 것을 도와줬다.

Why are you late? 왜 늦었니?

This town is very quiet. 이 마을은 매우 조용하다.

She is young and energetic. 그녀는 젊고 활기차다.

### Step 3

A: Hi! Can you help me find a bottle? 안녕하세요! 병을 좀 찾는데 도와 주실 수 있나요?

B: Sure! What kind of bottle? 그럼요. 어떤 종류의 병이요?

A: A water bottle, please. 물병이요.

B: Here are some water bottles. Do you like this one? 여기 물병이 있는데 이거 어때요?

A: Yes, I do! Why do you have so many? 네, 좋아요. 왜 이렇게 많이 있어요?

B: Many young kids in town need them for school. 이 동네 아이들이 학교에서 다들 필요하거든요.

### Challenge

I went to the store in town and talked to a young clerk. I asked, "Why are there so many bottles here?" He smiled and said, "People in this town love to recycle." 나는 마을 가게에 가서 젊은 직원과 이야기를 나눴다. 내가 "여기에 왜 이렇게 많은 병이 있나요?"라고 물었다. 그는 미소 지으며 "이 마을 사람들은 재활용을 좋아해요."라고 말했다.

## DAY 52

### Step 2

The battle was intense. 전투는 격렬했다.

He has a strong will. 그는 강한 의지를 가지고 있다.

The soldier is very brave. 그 군인은 매우 용감하다.

Please put your books here. 여기에 책을 놓아 주세요.

He got a bad grade on his test. 그는 시험에서 나쁜 성적을 받았다.

### Step 3

A: Look, there is a battle in the storybook! 봐, 이야기책에 전투가 있어!

B: Yes, the brave knight will fight. 응, 용감한 기사가 싸울 거야.

A: Why will he fight? 왜 그는 싸울까?

B: He wants to stop the bad dragon. 그는 나쁜 용을 막고 싶어해.

A: He is so brave! 그는 정말 용감해!

B: Yes, he is! He will put an end to the battle. 응, 그래! 그는 전투를 끝낼 거야.

### Challenge

I read a story about a brave knight today. He showed his will to win the battle against the bad dragon. He put his shield down only when the dragon was defeated. 오늘 용감한 기사에 대한 이야기를 읽었다. 그는 나쁜 용과의 전투에서 승리하기 위한 의지를 보였다. 그는 용이 패배했을 때만 방패를 내려놓았다.

## DAY 53

### Step 2

Take an umbrella with you. 우산을 가지고 가라.
Don't hit your brother. 동생을 때리지 마라.
She wore a white dress. 그녀는 흰 드레스를 입었다.
I like to eat beans. 나는 콩 먹는 것을 좋아한다.
The plant is dead. 식물이 죽었다.

### Step 3

A: What are you going to take? 무엇을 가져갈 거야?
B: I will take a white bean. 나는 흰 콩을 가져갈 거야.
A: Why do you need a white bean? 왜 흰 콩이 필요해?
B: I want to plant it in my garden. 내 정원에 심고 싶어.
A: Be careful not to hit the plants! 식물을 때리지 않도록 조심해!
B: I will. Look, there is a dead leaf. 그럴게. 봐, 죽은 잎이 있어.
A: Yes, let's pick it up. 응, 그걸 주워보자.

### Challenge

I saw a white bean on the ground today. I tried to take it, but it hit my foot. Then, I noticed a dead leaf beside it. 오늘 땅에 흰 콩을 보았다. 그것을 가져가려고 했지만, 내 발에 맞았다. 그러고 나서 그 옆에 죽은 잎이 있는 것을 보았다.

## DAY 54

### Step 2

The rock is heavy. 그 바위는 무겁다.
He got a new job. 그는 새 직장을 구했다.
I received a mail today. 오늘 우편을 받았다.
We had pasta for dinner. 우리는 저녁으로 파스타를 먹었다.
Will you join us? 우리와 함께할래?

### Step 3

A: What is that big rock? 저 큰 바위는 뭐야?
B: It's part of my job to move it. 그것을 옮기는 것이 내 일의 일부야.
A: Wow! That sounds hard. 와! 정말 힘들겠다.
B: Yes, but I enjoy it. 응, 하지만 즐거워.
A: Did you get the mail? 우편 받았니?
B: Yes, I did. It came after dinner. 응, 저녁 먹고 왔어.

### Challenge

I climbed a big rock after school. My job was to check the mail before dinner. After that, I joined my family for a nice meal. 방과 후 큰 바위에 올랐다. 저녁 전에 우편을 확인하는 것이 내 일이었다. 그 후 가족과 함께 좋은 식사를 했다.

## DAY 55

### Step 2

The brain is a complex organ. 뇌는 복잡한 기관이다.
Add some sugar to the tea. 차에 설탕을 좀 더해라.
We are friends. 우리는 친구다.
You need to control your emotions. 너는 감정을 통제할 필요가 있다.
They believe in heaven. 그들은 천국을 믿는다.

### Step 3

A: What does the brain do? 우리의 뇌는 무엇을 하나?
B: It helps us think and control our body. 그것은 우리가 생각하고 몸을 통제하는 데 도움을 준다.
A: Can we add more knowledge to our brain? 우리는 뇌에 더 많은 지식을 더할 수 있나?
B: Yes, we can learn new things every day. 응, 우리는 매일 새로운 것을 배울 수 있다.
A: Is it true that some people believe in heaven? 어떤 사람들이 천국을 믿는다는 것이 사실인가?
B: Yes, many people believe in heaven. 응, 많은 사람들이 천국을 믿는다.

### Challenge

I learned that our brain helps us think and control our body. When we add new information, we get smarter. My teacher said that learning new things is like adding a little bit of heaven to our minds. 우리의 뇌가 생각하고 몸을 통제하는 데 도움을 준다는 것을 배웠다. 새로운 정보를 더할 때 우리는 더 똑똑해진다. 선생님은 새로운 것을 배우는 것이 마음에 작은 천국을 더하는 것과 같다고 말씀하셨다.

## DAY 56

### Step 2

My father is very tall. 내 아버지는 매우 키가 크다.
We have the same shoes. 우리는 같은 신발을 가지고 있다.
What is your shoe size? 네 신발 사이즈는 무엇이니?
Welcome to my house. 우리 집에 온 것을 환영해.
I like beef steak. 나는 소고기 스테이크를 좋아한다.

### Step 3

A: Is your father coming to dinner? 네 아버지 저녁 먹으러 오시니?
B: Yes, he is. We will welcome him. 응, 오셔. 우리는 그를 환영할 거야.
A: Do you like beef for dinner? 저녁으로 소고기를 좋아하니?
B: Yes, we both like the same food. 응, 우리는 둘 다 같은 음식을 좋아해.
A: Do you want the same size steak? 같은 크기의 스테이크를 원하니?
B: Yes, the same size would be perfect! 응, 같은 크기가 딱 좋아!

### Challenge

I had dinner with my father today. We both had the same size steak because we love beef. He said, "Welcome home," and we enjoyed our meal together. 오늘 아버지와 저녁을 먹었다. 우리는 둘 다 소고기를 좋아해서 같은 크기의 스테이크를 먹었다. 그는 "집에 온 것을 환영해"라고 말했고, 우리는 함께 식사를 즐겼다.

## DAY 57

### Step 2

I forgot my keys, so I went back. 나는 열쇠를 잊어버려서 돌아갔다.
The ball is round. 공은 둥글다.
They live in a large house. 그들은 큰 집에 산다.
I like eating grapes. 나는 포도 먹는 것을 좋아한다.
I will love you forever. 나는 너를 영원히 사랑할 것이다.

### Step 3

A: Look at this ball! 이 공을 봐!
B: Wow, it's very large! 와, 정말 크다!
A: Yes, it's bigger than a grape. 응, 포도보다 커.
B: Do you want to play with it? 그걸로 놀고 싶니?
A: Yes, let's play forever! 응, 영원히 놀자!
B: Okay, so let's go outside! 좋아, 그럼 밖으로 나가자!

### Challenge

I found a large ball in the yard today. It was as big as a bunch of grapes, so we played with it for hours. We had so much fun, and I wished we could play forever. 오늘 마당에서 큰 공을 발견했다. 그것은 한 다발의 포도만큼 컸고, 그래서 우리는 몇 시간 동안 그것으로 놀았다. 우리는 너무 재미있어서 영원히 놀기를 바랐다.

## DAY 58

### Step 2

My goal is to become a doctor. 내 목표는 의사가 되는 것이다.
Good morning! 좋은 아침!
She was mad at him. 그녀는 그에게 화가 났다.
They believe in one god. 그들은 한 신을 믿는다.
He told an interesting story. 그는 흥미로운 이야기를 했다.

### Step 3

A: What is your goal for today? 오늘의 목표가 뭐야?
B: My goal is to finish my story. 내 목표는 내 이야기를 끝내는 것이야.
A: Did you start writing it this morning? 오늘 아침에 쓰기 시작했니?
B: Yes, I did. But I got mad because my pen broke. 응, 하지만 펜이 부러져서 화가 났어.
A: Oh no! Maybe it's a sign from god to take a break. 이런! 어쩌면 신이 쉬라고 보내는 신호일지도 몰라.
B: Maybe! I'll finish it later. 그럴지도! 나중에 끝낼게.

### Challenge

My goal this morning was to read a story. I got mad when I couldn't find the book. Then, my mom said, "Don't worry, even the gods lose things sometimes." 오늘 아침 내 목표는 이야기를 읽는 것이었다. 책을 찾을 수 없을 때 화가 났다. 그러자 엄마가 "걱정 마, 신들도 때때로 물건을 잃어버려"라고 말했다.

## DAY 59

### Step 2

The tower is very tall. 그 탑은 매우 높다.
She wore a black dress. 그녀는 검정 드레스를 입었다.
The ocean is vast. 대양은 넓다.
This is an example of good work. 이것은 좋은 일의 예다.
The kitten is small. 그 새끼 고양이는 작다.

### Step 3

A: Look at that tall tower! 저 높은 탑을 봐!
B: Yes, it looks so big next to the ocean. 응, 바다 옆에 있어서 정말 커 보인다.
A: The tower is black. 탑은 검정색이다.
B: It's a good example of a tall building. 그것은 높은 건물의 좋은 예다.
A: I see a small boat near it. 그 근처에 작은 배가 보여.
B: Yes, the boat looks tiny next to the tower. 응, 배가 탑 옆에서 정말 작아 보인다.

### Challenge

I saw a tall tower by the ocean today. It was black and stood out against the blue water. It was a great example of how a small thing can look big in the right place. 오늘 바다 옆에 높은 탑을 보았다. 그것은 검정색이었고 푸른 물과 대조되었다. 그것은 작은 것이 적절한 장소에서 어떻게 크게 보일 수 있는지에 대한 훌륭한 예였다.

## DAY 60

### Step 2

I agree with your idea. 나는 네 생각에 동의한다.
The road is long and winding. 그 길은 길고 구불구불하다.
The floor is clean. 바닥이 깨끗하다.
The monkey is eating a banana. 원숭이가 바나나를 먹고 있다.
How far is the station? 역까지 얼마나 먼가요?

### Step 3

A: Do you agree with this plan? 이 계획에 동의하니?
B: Yes, I agree. Let's take that road. 응, 동의해. 저 길을 가자.
A: Look, there's a monkey on the road! 봐, 길에 원숭이가 있어!
B: Oh wow, it's sitting on the floor. 와, 바닥에 앉아 있네.
A: How did it get so far from the forest? 어떻게 숲에서 이렇게 멀리 왔지?
B: I don't know, but it looks happy. 모르겠어, 하지만 행복해 보여.

### Challenge

I saw a monkey at school today. It was sitting on the floor near the road. I agree with my friend that it must have come from far away. 오늘 학교에서 원숭이를 봤다. 그것은 길 근처 바닥에 앉아 있었다. 나는 그것이 멀리서 왔음이 틀림없다는 친구의 말에 동의한다.

## DAY 61

### Step 2

Please return the book to the library. 책을 도서관에 돌려주세요.
What is your home address? 집 주소가 무엇인가요?
She wants to become a teacher. 그녀는 선생님이 되고 싶어해요.
The zebra has black and white stripes. 얼룩말은 검정색과 흰색 줄무늬를 가지고 있어요.
What's for lunch? 점심으로 뭐 먹나요?

### Step 3

A: When will you return home? 언제 집에 돌아오니?
B: I will return after lunch. 점심 후에 돌아올 거야.
A: Do you need my address? 내 주소가 필요하니?
B: Yes, please. I will write it down. 응, 적어둘게.
A: Look, there's a zebra in the book! 봐, 책에 얼룩말이 있어!
B: It has become my favorite animal! 그게 내 가장 좋아하는 동물이 되었어!

### Challenge

I returned home after lunch today. I wrote my address and sent a letter to a zoo to learn how zebras become striped. It was fun to learn new things. 오늘 점심 후 집에 돌아왔다. 나는 주소를 적고 얼룩말이 어떻게 줄무늬를 가지게 되는지 배우기 위해 동물원에 편지를 보냈다. 새로운 것을 배우는 것은 재미있었다.

## DAY 62

### Step 2

The wind is blowing hard. 바람이 세게 불고 있다.
The cat is sitting on top of the shelf. 고양이가 선반 위에 앉아 있다.
I feel sick today. 오늘 몸이 아프다.
She likes to wear dresses. 그녀는 드레스를 입는 것을 좋아한다.
Please give me the book. 책을 주세요.

### Step 3

A: The wind is so strong today! 오늘 바람이 정말 세다!
B: Yes, my hat blew right off the top of my head. 응, 내 모자가 머리에서 날아가 버렸어.
A: Oh no! Are you feeling sick? 이런! 몸이 안 좋니?
B: No, I'm okay. I just need to wear my jacket. 아니, 괜찮아. 그냥 자켓을 입으면 돼.
A: Here, let me give you a scarf too. 여기, 스카프도 줄게.
B: Thank you! That will help a lot. 고마워! 큰 도움이 될 거야.

### Challenge

I felt sick today because of the strong wind. My mom told me to wear a warm jacket. She also gave me some soup to feel better. 오늘 강한 바람 때문에 아팠다. 엄마가 따뜻한 자켓을 입으라고 했다. 그녀는 또한 나에게 기운을 차리도록 수프를 주셨다.

## DAY 63

### Step 2

This math problem is easy. 이 수학 문제는 쉽다.
Draw a circle on the paper. 종이에 원을 그려라.
My sister is very funny. 내 여동생은 매우 재미있다.
Be careful not to cut yourself. 자르지 않도록 조심해라.
Her lips are red. 그녀의 입술은 빨갛다.

### Step 3

A: This puzzle is easy! 이 퍼즐은 쉽다!
B: Yes, it's just a circle. 응, 그냥 원이야.
A: My sister loves puzzles too. 내 여동생도 퍼즐을 좋아해.
B: Maybe she can help us cut this shape. 아마 그녀가 이 모양을 자르는 걸 도와줄 수 있을 거야.
A: Be careful not to cut your lip. 입술을 자르지 않도록 조심해.
B: Don't worry, I'll be very careful. 걱정 마, 아주 조심할게.

### Challenge

I drew an easy circle today. My sister tried to cut it out but accidentally cut her lip. We put a bandage on it and she felt better. 오늘 쉬운 원을 그렸다. 내 여동생이 그것을 자르려고 했지만 실수로 입술을 잘랐다. 우리는 그것에 반창고를 붙였고 그녀는 기분이 나아졌다.

## DAY 64

### Step 2

I joined the book club. 나는 독서 클럽에 가입했다.
The cross is a symbol of Christianity. 십자가는 기독교의 상징이다.
The moon is full tonight. 오늘 밤 달이 가득 차 있다.
In case of emergency, call 911. 비상시에는 911에 전화하세요.
It's a fact that the Earth is round. 지구가 둥글다는 것은 사실이다.

### Step 3

A: Are you going to the club tonight? 오늘 밤 클럽에 갈 거니?
B: No, I have to finish my homework. 아니, 숙제를 끝내야 해.
A: Did you see the moon last night? 어젯밤 달 봤어?
B: Yes, it was so bright. 응, 정말 밝았어.
A: The club has a cross on the door. 클럽 문에 십자가가 있어.
B: Really? I didn't know that! 정말? 몰랐어!

### Challenge

I joined a new club at school today. We learned about the moon and its phases. In case you didn't know, the moon has craters in the shape of a cross, which is a fun fact! 오늘 학교에서 새로운 클럽에 가입했다. 우리는 달과 그 위상을 배웠다. 혹시 모르겠지만, 달에는 십자가 모양의 분화구가 있다는 재미있는 사실을 알게 되었다!

## DAY 65

### Step 2

The city is very crowded. 도시는 매우 붐빈다.
Open the window, please. 창문을 열어 주세요.
The ice is melting. 얼음이 녹고 있다.
The bomb squad arrived quickly. 폭탄 처리반이 빠르게 도착했다.
My son loves to play soccer. 내 아들은 축구하는 것을 좋아한다.

### Step 3

A: This city is so big! 이 도시는 정말 크다!
B: Yes, look out the window at all the buildings. 응, 창문 밖에 있는 모든 건물을 봐.
A: Do you see that ice on the road? 도로에 얼음 보이니?
B: Yes, it looks slippery. 응, 미끄러워 보인다.
A: I read a story about a bomb in the city. 도시에서 폭탄에 대한 이야기를 읽었어.
B: Oh no, I hope everyone was safe. 오, 모두가 안전하길 바래.

### Challenge

Today, I looked out the window and saw the city covered in ice. My son was excited to play outside. He pretended to be a superhero with a bomb. We had a lot of fun together. It was a great day! 오늘 창밖을 보니 도시가 얼음으로 덮여 있었다. 내 아들은 밖에서 놀 수 있어서 신이 났다. 그는 슈퍼히어로가 되어 폭탄 놀이를 했다. 우리는 함께 많은 재미를 느꼈다. 정말 좋은 하루였다!

## DAY 66

### Step 2

She is as kind as an angel. 그녀는 천사처럼 친절하다.
The factory produces toys. 그 공장은 장난감을 생산한다.
We all want world peace. 우리는 모두 세계 평화를 원한다.
The shirt is made of cotton. 그 셔츠는 면으로 만들어졌다.
The mouse is small and fast. 그 쥐는 작고 빠르다.

### Step 3

A: Look, I drew an angel! 봐, 천사를 그렸어!
B: Wow, it looks so nice. 와, 정말 예쁘다.
A: My dad works at a factory. 우리 아빠는 공장에서 일해.
B: What do they make there? 거기서 뭘 만드니?
A: They make cotton clothes. 면 옷을 만들어.
B: I saw a mouse near the factory once. 공장 근처에서 쥐를 본 적이 있어.

### Challenge

I saw a picture of an angel today. My dad works at a factory that makes cotton clothes. We found a small mouse in the garden and let it go in peace. 오늘 천사의 그림을 보았다. 아빠는 면 옷을 만드는 공장에서 일하신다. 우리는 정원에서 작은 쥐를 발견하고 평화롭게 놓아주었다.

## DAY 67

### Step 2

I drink milk every morning. 나는 매일 아침 우유를 마신다.
The engine is very powerful. 그 엔진은 매우 강력하다.
How much is this book? 이 책은 얼마인가요?
Make a wish. 소원을 빌어라.
I just arrived. 나는 지금 막 도착했다.

### Step 3

A: Do you want some milk? 우유 좀 마실래?
B: Yes, I love milk very much! 응, 나는 우유를 정말 좋아해!
A: Look at that engine. It's big! 저 엔진을 봐. 정말 크다!
B: Wow, it must be strong. 와, 정말 강력하겠어.
A: I wish I could see it work. 그것이 작동하는 것을 보고 싶다.
B: Me too. I just love big engines! 나도 그래. 나는 큰 엔진을 정말 좋아해!

### Challenge

I just finished my glass of milk. My brother showed me a toy car with a strong engine. I wish I had as much fun with my toys as he does! 나는 방금 우유 한 잔을 다 마셨다. 형이 강력한 엔진이 달린 장난감 자동차를 보여주었다. 나도 형처럼 내 장난감 가지고 놀 때 재미있었으면 좋겠다!

## DAY 68

### Step 2

I am a big fan of soccer. 나는 축구의 큰 팬이다.
The road is blocked. 길이 막혔다.
What is your favorite food? 네가 가장 좋아하는 음식은 무엇이니?
I ate an apple for breakfast. 나는 아침으로 사과를 먹었다.
He threw a stone into the lake. 그는 돌을 호수에 던졌다.

### Step 3

A: Do you see that big fan? 저 큰 선풍기 보이니?
B: Yes, it's blowing air on the food. 응, 음식에 바람을 불고 있어.
A: Let's build a tower with these blocks. 이 블록들로 탑을 쌓자.
B: Okay, I will start with this one. 좋아, 이걸로 시작할게.
A: Look, there's an apple on the ground. 봐, 땅에 사과가 있어.
B: Be careful, there's a stone next to it. 조심해, 그 옆에 돌이 있어.

### Challenge

I turned on the fan because it was hot. My sister used a block to stop it from moving. We ate some food, and I found a stone inside my apple! 더워서 선풍기를 켰다. 여동생이 블록을 사용해 선풍기가 움직이지 않도록 막았다. 우리는 음식을 먹었고, 나는 사과 안에서 돌을 발견했다!

## DAY 69

### Step 2

Let's dance to the music. 음악에 맞춰 춤추자.
I want to congratulate you on your success. 너의 성공을 축하하고 싶어.
There was an accident on the road. 도로에 사고가 있었다.
I love my family. 나는 내 가족을 사랑한다.
Do you have any cash? 현금이 있니?

### Step 3

A: Do you like to dance? 춤추는 거 좋아하니?
B: Yes, I love dancing! 응, 춤추는 거 정말 좋아해!
A: We should congratulate him on his win. 그의 승리를 축하해줘야 해.
B: Yes, let's do that after the party. 그래, 파티 후에 그렇게 하자.
A: Did you hear about the accident? 그 사고 소식 들었니?
B: Yes, it was on the news. 응, 뉴스에 나왔어.

### Challenge

I love to dance at school. Today, my teacher congratulated me on my performance. My friend had an accident but was fine, so we went to buy snacks with cash. 나는 학교에서 춤추는 것을 좋아한다. 오늘 선생님이 내 공연을 축하해주셨다. 내 친구가 사고를 당했지만 괜찮아서 우리는 현금으로 간식을 사러 갔다.

## DAY 70

### Step 2

I failed my test. 나는 시험에 떨어졌다.
I will wait for you there. 나는 거기서 너를 기다릴게.
Let's meet at 3 P.M. 오후 3시에 만나자.
I need to buy groceries. 나는 식료품을 사야 해.
What is your phone number? 전화번호가 뭐야?

### Step 3

A: Did you fail the test? 시험에 떨어졌니?
B: No, I passed! 아니, 합격했어!
A: Great! I will meet you there. 잘했어! 거기서 만나자.
B: Can you buy some snacks? 간식 좀 사줄 수 있니?
A: Sure, how many should I get? 물론, 몇 개 사면 될까?
B: Just a small number, maybe five. 적은 수로, 아마 다섯 개 정도.

### Challenge

I failed my math test today. My friend was there to cheer me up. We decided to meet after school to buy a number puzzle. 오늘 수학 시험에 떨어졌다. 친구가 나를 응원해주러 와줬다. 우리는 방과 후에 만나 숫자 퍼즐을 사기로 했다.

## DAY 71

### Step 2

Please help me with this. 이것 좀 도와주세요.
I will send you a letter. 너에게 편지를 보낼게.
The doctor is very kind. 그 의사는 매우 친절하다.
The girl is reading a book. 그 소녀는 책을 읽고 있다.
Are you ready to go? 갈 준비 되었니?

### Step 3

A: Can you please send this letter? 이 편지 좀 보내줄래?
B: Sure, I will send it today. 물론, 오늘 보낼게.
A: The doctor is ready to see you. 진료실로 들어 오세요.
B: Okay, thank you. 네, 감사합니다.
A: Look, the girl is playing outside. 봐, 그 소녀가 밖에서 놀고 있어.
B: She looks so happy and ready to play! 그녀는 정말 행복해 보이고 놀 준비가 되어 있어 보여!

### Challenge

I went to see the doctor today. The girl before me wasn't ready yet. My mom asked, "Please send us in when she is done." 오늘 의사 선생님을 보러 갔다. 내 앞에 있던 소녀는 아직 준비가 안 되어 있었다. 엄마가 "그녀가 끝나면 우리를 보내주세요."라고 부탁하셨다.

## DAY 72

### Step 2

My grandfather tells great stories. 우리 할아버지는 멋진 이야기를 들려주신다.
She is very honest. 그녀는 매우 정직하다.
I take the subway to work. 나는 지하철을 타고 출근한다.
Use a spoon to eat soup. 숟가락을 사용해서 수프를 먹어라.
He is a true gentleman. 그는 진정한 신사다.

### Step 3

A: My grandfather is visiting today. 할아버지가 오늘 방문하셔.
B: He sounds like an honest man. 그는 정직한 분 같아.
A: Yes, he always tells the truth. 응, 그는 항상 진실만 말씀하셔.
B: Did he take the subway here? 여기 지하철 타고 오셨니?
A: Yes, he did. He is such a gentleman. 응, 오셨어. 그는 정말 신사야.
B: Let's get a spoon for his tea. 그의 차를 위한 숟가락을 가져오자.

### Challenge

I visited my grandfather today. He is an honest gentleman who always tells great stories. We took the subway and he gave me a shiny spoon as a gift. 오늘 할아버지를 방문했다. 그는 항상 멋진 이야기를 해주시는 정직한 신사다. 우리는 지하철을 타고 갔고, 할아버지는 반짝이는 숟가락을 선물로 주셨다.

## DAY 73

### Step 2

The dog runs on the land. 개가 땅 위를 달립니다.
I called you twice. 나는 너에게 두 번 전화했다.
She has a little puppy. 그녀는 작은 강아지를 가지고 있다.
He likes pizza and pasta. 그는 피자와 파스타를 좋아한다.
I want to be a doctor. 나는 의사가 되고 싶다.

### Step 3

A: Look at this big piece of land! 이 큰 땅덩어리를 봐!
B: Yes, it's twice as big as our yard. 응, 우리 마당보다 두 배 크다.
A: There is a little house on it. 그 위에 작은 집이 있어.
B: And there are some trees too. 그리고 나무도 좀 있어.
A: It must be nice to live there. 거기 사는 건 좋을 거야.
B: Yes, it looks very peaceful. 응, 정말 평화로워 보여.

### Challenge

I saw a little piece of land today. It was twice as big as I expected. My friend and I played there and had so much fun. 오늘 작은 땅덩어리를 보았다. 예상보다 두 배 컸다. 친구와 나는 거기서 놀며 정말 즐거운 시간을 보냈다.

## DAY 74

### Step 2

We took a tour of the city. 우리는 도시 투어를 했다.
That is my book. 저것은 내 책이다.
I like to drink tea. 나는 차 마시는 것을 좋아한다.
I'm tired because I didn't sleep well. 나는 잘 못 자서 피곤하다.
The ant is very small. 그 개미는 매우 작다.

### Step 3

A: I want to go on a tour. 투어를 가고 싶어.
B: That sounds fun! Where to? 재미있겠네! 어디로 갈 건데?
A: Look at that big building over there. 저 큰 건물 봐.
B: I need a drink because I'm thirsty. 목이 말라서 마실 것이 필요해.
A: Be careful, there's an ant on your cup. 조심해, 네 컵에 개미가 있어.
B: Thanks, I didn't see it! 고마워, 못 봤어!

### Challenge

I went on a tour with my family. We didn't drink from that cup because there was an ant in it. It was still a fun trip! 나는 가족과 함께 투어를 갔다. 컵에 개미가 있어서 그 컵으로 마시지 않았다. 그래도 재미있는 여행이었다!

## DAY 75

### Step 2

I wake up early every day. 나는 매일 일찍 일어난다.
We need to talk. 우리는 얘기해야 해.
My dad is very strong. 우리 아빠는 정말 강하다.
The lesson was interesting. 그 수업은 재미있었다.
We will move to a new house. 우리는 새 집으로 이사 갈 것이다.

### Step 3

A: I wake up early every day. 나는 매일 일찍 일어나.
B: Me too! I like to talking with my dad in the morning. 나도! 나는 아침에 아빠랑 얘기하는 걸 좋아해.
A: Does he help you with your lessons? 아빠가 너의 수업을 도와주니?
B: Yes, he does. He's really good at math. 응, 맞아. 그는 수학을 정말 잘해.
A: Are you going to move to a new house soon? 곧 새 집으로 이사 가니?
B: Yes, we are moving next month. 응, 다음 달에 이사 갈 거야.

### Challenge

I wake up early to talk with my dad. He helps me with my lessons before school. Then we move to the kitchen for breakfast. 나는 아빠와 얘기하려고 일찍 일어난다. 그는 학교 가기 전에 내 수업을 도와주신다. 그런 다음 우리는 아침을 먹기 위해 부엌으로 이동한다.

## DAY 76

### Step 2

All of my friends are coming. 내 모든 친구들이 온다.
Use glue to stick the paper. 종이를 붙이기 위해 풀을 사용해라.
The wedding was beautiful. 그 결혼식은 아름다웠다.
You can enter the room now. 이제 방에 들어갈 수 있다.
She is very smart. 그녀는 매우 똑똑하다.

### Step 3

A: Did you invite all your friends to the wedding? 결혼식에 모든 친구들을 초대했니?
B: Yes, everyone is coming. 응, 모두 올 거야.
A: We need to glue these decorations. 이 장식들을 붙여야 해.
B: Okay, I will help with that. 좋아, 내가 도울게.
A: Can we enter the hall now? 이제 홀에 들어갈 수 있니?
B: Yes, let's go. You are so smart for planning this! 응, 가자. 이것을 계획한 너는 정말 똑똑해!

### Challenge

I went to a wedding with my family. We all had to enter the hall quietly. My cousin used glue to fix his shoe and said he felt very smart for doing it. 나는 가족과 함께 결혼식에 갔다. 우리는 모두 조용히 홀에 들어가야 했다. 내 사촌은 신발을 고치기 위해 풀을 사용했고, 그렇게 한 것이 매우 똑똑하다고 말했다.

## DAY 77

### Step 2

The crowd cheered loudly. 군중이 크게 환호했다.
The picture is above the sofa. 그림은 소파 위에 있다.
She has green eyes. 그녀는 초록색 눈을 가지고 있다.
The student is studying hard. 그 학생은 열심히 공부하고 있다.
The exit is to the left. 출구는 왼쪽에 있다.

### Step 3

A: Look at the crowd over there! 저기 군중을 봐!
B: Yes, there are so many people. 응, 정말 많은 사람들이 있어.
A: See the balloon above the crowd? 군중 위에 있는 풍선이 보여?
B: Yes, it's right above their heads. 응, 그들의 머리 바로 위에 있어.
A: I saw a student looking for the exit. 나는 출구를 찾는 학생을 봤어.
B: The exit is on the left side. 출구는 왼쪽에 있어.

### Challenge

I saw a big crowd at the fair today. A balloon floated above everyone's heads. As a student, I kept an eye on the exit in case I got lost. 오늘 박람회에서 큰 군중을 보았다. 풍선이 모든 사람의 머리 위에 떠 있었다. 학생으로서 길을 잃을 경우를 대비해 출구를 주시했다.

## DAY 78

### Step 2

I care about you. 나는 너를 신경 쓴다.
The countryside is peaceful. 시골은 평화롭다.
The glass is full of water. 유리잔에 물이 가득하다.
She won the contest. 그녀는 대회에서 우승했다.
This area is very beautiful. 이 지역은 매우 아름답다.

### Step 3

A: I went to the countryside with my family. 가족과 함께 시골에 다녀왔어.
B: That sounds fun! Was it nice there? 재미있겠다! 거기 좋았어?
A: Yes, it was full of flowers and trees. 응, 꽃과 나무가 가득했어.
B: Did you see any animals in the area? 그 지역에서 동물들 봤어?
A: Yes, lots of them. There was even a contest for the best-looking cow!
응, 많았어. 가장 멋진 소를 뽑는 대회도 있었어!
B: Wow! Did you take care of any animals? 와! 동물들을 돌봤어?
A: Not this time, but I helped my uncle with his garden. 이번엔 안 돌봤어, 하지만 삼촌의 정원을 도왔어.

### Challenge

I went to the countryside to visit my grandparents. They needed help to care for their garden, which was full of flowers. We watched a local contest in the area and had so much fun! 나는 할머니와 할아버지를 방문하러 시골에 갔다. 그들은 꽃으로 가득한 정원을 돌보는 데 도움이 필요했다. 우리는 그 지역에서 열린 대회를 보고 정말 재미있었다!

## DAY 79

### Step 2

Mark the date on your calendar. 달력에 날짜를 표시해라.

He won a prize. 그는 상을 받았다.

Write your name on the paper. 종이에 이름을 적어라.

My house is near the park. 우리 집은 공원 근처에 있다.

The car is in front of the house. 차는 집 앞에 있다.

### Step 3

A: Look at this calendar! 이 달력을 봐!

B: It shows the prize dates for the contest. 대회의 상 받는 날짜가 나와 있어

A: I need some paper to write it down. 그것을 적을 종이가 필요해.

B: There's some paper near the desk. 책상 근처에 종이가 있어.

A: Can you put it in front of me? 내 앞에 놓아줄래?

B: Sure, here you go! 물론, 여기 있어!

### Challenge

I marked a prize on my calendar today. The details were on a piece of paper near my desk. It was in the front of my notebook, so I wouldn't forget. 오늘 달력에 상을 표시했다. 세부 사항은 책상 근처의 종이에 적혀 있었다. 내 노트북 앞쪽에 있어서 잊지 않을 것이다.

## DAY 80

### Step 2

The war ended last year. 전쟁은 작년에 끝났다.

She has a pretty doll. 그녀는 예쁜 인형을 가지고 있다.

I need to wash my car. 나는 내 차를 세차해야 한다.

The band is playing music. 밴드가 음악을 연주하고 있다.

Korea is a beautiful country. 한국은 아름다운 나라다.

### Step 3

A: Did you read about the war in the book? 책에서 전쟁에 대해 읽었니?

B: Yes, it was a sad story. 응, 슬픈 이야기였어.

A: I like this doll. It's cute! 이 인형 좋아. 귀여워!

B: It looks like it could be from another country. 다른 나라에서 온 것처럼 보여.

A: Did you see the new car outside? 밖에 새 차 봤니?

B: Yes, it belongs to the band that visited. 응, 방문한 밴드의 차야.

### Challenge

I learned about a war in history class today. My friend showed me a doll from another country. On the way home, we saw a band playing music near a car. 오늘 역사 수업에서 전쟁에 대해 배웠다. 친구가 다른 나라에서 온 인형을 보여주었다. 집으로 가는 길에 차 근처에서 음악을 연주하는 밴드를 보았다.

## DAY 81

### Step 2

My shoe is too tight. 내 신발이 너무 꽉 끼어.
Open the curtain, please. 커튼을 열어 주세요.
Only you can help me. 오직 너만 나를 도울 수 있어.
The leaf fell from the tree. 잎이 나무에서 떨어졌다.
Walk along the river. 강을 따라 걸어라.

### Step 3

A: I lost my shoe. 나는 신발을 잃어버렸어.
B: Let's check behind the curtain. 커튼 뒤를 확인해 보자.
A: There it is! Only one shoe was missing. 저기 있네! 신발 하나만 없어졌었어.
B: Look, a leaf blew in through the window. 봐, 창문을 통해 잎이 날아 들어왔어.
A: It must have come from the tree along the road. 도로를 따라 있는 나무에서 온 것 같아.
B: Let's close the curtain to keep more leaves out. 더 많은 잎이 들어오지 않게 커튼을 닫자.

### Challenge

I found my lost shoe behind the curtain today. It was the only one missing. I saw a leaf blowing along the sidewalk. 오늘 커튼 뒤에서 잃어버린 신발을 찾았다. 유일하게 없어졌던 신발이었다. 인도를 따라 날아다니는 잎을 보았다.

## DAY 82

### Step 2

Knowledge is power. 지식은 힘이다.
School starts at 8 A.M. 학교는 오전 8시에 시작한다.
I like both apples and oranges. 나는 사과와 오렌지 둘 다 좋아한다.
I have a book. 나는 책을 가지고 있다.
Don't miss the bus. 버스를 놓치지 마라.

### Step 3

A: Do you have the power to lift this? 이것을 들 힘이 있니?
B: Yes, I think so. Let's both try. 응, 그런 것 같아. 우리 둘 다 해보자.
A: We can do it together! 우리 함께 할 수 있어!
B: Did you miss the bus to school today? 오늘 학교 가는 버스를 놓쳤니?
A: Yes, I missed it by a minute. 응, 1분 차이로 놓쳤어.
B: That's okay, I can give you a ride. 괜찮아, 내가 태워줄게.

### Challenge

I used all my power to run to school today. I didn't want to miss the bus. Both my friend and I had a great day learning a new lesson. 오늘 학교에 가기 위해 모든 힘을 다해 뛰었다. 버스를 놓치고 싶지 않았다. 친구와 나는 새로운 수업을 배우며 멋진 하루를 보냈다.

## DAY 83

### Step 2

Do you want tea or coffee? 차나 커피를 원하니?
She went into the house. 그녀는 집 안으로 들어갔다.
They have a big farm. 그들은 큰 농장을 가지고 있다.
He is a teacher and also a writer. 그는 선생님이자 작가이다.
Keep an open mind. 열린 마음을 유지해라.

### Step 3

A: Do you want to visit the farm or the park? 농장이나 공원을 방문하고 싶니?
B: Let's go to the farm. We can see the animals. 농장에 가자. 동물을 볼 수 있어.
A: We can also buy fresh vegetables there. 거기서 신선한 야채도 살 수 있어.
B: Yes, that sounds great. Keep that in mind! 응, 좋겠다. 기억해 둬!
A: Should we walk into the barn first? 우리 먼저 헛간으로 들어갈까?
B: Sure, let's see what's inside! 물론, 안에 뭐가 있는지 보자!

### Challenge

I went into the farm to help or just to relax. The farm work was hard, but I also enjoyed the fresh air. It cleared my mind and made me feel better. 나는 도움을 주거나 단순히 쉬기 위해 농장에 들어갔다. 농장 일은 힘들었지만 신선한 공기를 즐겼다. 그것은 내 마음을 맑게 하고 기분을 나아지게 했다.

## DAY 84

### Step 2

The plane flew over the city. 비행기가 도시 위를 날아갔다.
He is now an adult. 그는 이제 성인이다.
The air is fresh in the morning. 아침에는 공기가 신선하다.
She works in an office. 그녀는 사무실에서 일한다.
Let's divide the tasks. 일을 나누자.

### Step 3

A: Look at the bird flying over the tree! 나무 위를 나는 새를 봐!
B: Yes, it's so high in the air. 응, 정말 높이 날고 있어.
A: Are we going to the office later? 나중에 사무실에 갈 거야?
B: Yes, we need to meet the new adult team member. 응, 새로운 성인 팀원과 만나야 해.
A: How do we divide the work for the project? 프로젝트 작업을 어떻게 나눌까?
B: We will discuss that in the meeting. 그건 회의에서 논의할 거야.

### Challenge

I watched a plane fly over our house today. My mom, who is an adult, works in an office nearby. She helps divide the tasks among her team to keep the air clean and fresh.
오늘 비행기가 우리 집 위를 나는 것을 보았다. 성인인 우리 엄마는 근처 사무실에서 일하신다. 그녀는 팀원들 사이에서 일을 나누어 공기를 깨끗하고 신선하게 유지하는 데 도움을 준다.

## DAY 85

### Step 2

The river is flowing fast. 강물이 빠르게 흐르고 있다.
The cat has a long tail. 고양이는 긴 꼬리를 가지고 있습니다.
The palace is huge. 그 궁전은 거대하다.
My brother is very tall. 내 형은 키가 아주 크다.
He stood in the middle. 그는 중간에 서 있었다.

### Step 3

A: Look at the river! It's so wide. 강을 봐! 정말 넓다.
B: Yes, I see a fish with a long tail. 응, 긴 꼬리를 가진 물고기를 봐.
A: Imagine living in a palace by the river. 강 옆 궁전에 사는 것을 상상해 봐.
B: That would be amazing! My brother would love it. 정말 멋질 거야! 내 형도 좋아할 거야.
A: We could play in the middle of the big hall. 우리는 큰 홀의 중간에서 놀 수 있을 거야.
B: Yes, and explore every room in the palace. 응, 그리고 궁전의 모든 방을 탐험하자.

### Challenge

I went to the river with my brother today. We saw a fish with a long tail swimming in the middle. We pretended the river was a palace and had lots of fun. 오늘 형과 함께 강에 갔다. 긴 꼬리를 가진 물고기가 중간에서 수영하고 있었다. 우리는 강을 궁전이라고 상상하며 재미있게 놀았다.

## DAY 86

### Step 2

She is very kind. 그녀는 매우 친절하다.
This is the end of the road. 이것이 길의 끝이다.
I'm feeling fine. 나는 괜찮아.
He won the race. 그는 경주에서 이겼다.
They sell fruit at the market. 그들은 시장에서 과일을 판다.

### Step 3

A: That was a fun race! 재미있는 경주였어!
B: Yes, it was! Everyone was so kind. 응, 그랬어! 모두가 친절했어.
A: I'm glad it didn't end too quickly. 너무 빨리 끝나지 않아서 기뻐.
B: Me too. The weather was fine today. 나도 그래. 오늘 날씨도 괜찮았어.
A: Did they sell snacks at the event? 행사에서 간식을 팔았니?
B: Yes, I bought some cookies! 응, 쿠키 좀 샀어!

### Challenge

I met a kind teacher today who helped me with my homework. At the end of the day, we watched a fun race. My friend said he will sell his old toys, which are still in fine condition. 오늘 숙제를 도와주신 친절한 선생님을 만났다. 하루가 끝날 때 우리는 재미있는 경주를 보았다. 친구는 아직도 상태가 좋은 그의 오래된 장난감을 팔겠다고 말했다.

## DAY 87

### Step 2

He started a new business. 그는 새로운 사업을 시작했다.
Who is next in line? 다음 순서는 누구인가요?
Let's do this together. 함께 하자.
I want to learn a new language. 나는 새로운 언어를 배우고 싶다.
My cousin is visiting us. 내 사촌이 우리를 방문하고 있다.

### Step 3

A: My cousin started a new business. 내 사촌이 새로운 사업을 시작했어.
B: That's great! What kind of business? 정말 좋다! 무슨 사업이야?
A: It's a bakery. We can visit it next week. 빵집이야. 다음 주에 방문할 수 있어.
B: I would love to! Maybe we can learn how to bake together.
정말 좋겠다! 아마 함께 빵 굽는 법을 배울 수 있을 거야.
A: That sounds fun. I like doing things with you. 재미있겠다. 너랑 같이 하는 거 좋아.
B: Me too. We always have a good time together. 나도. 우리는 항상 즐거운 시간을 보내잖아.

### Challenge

My cousin and I plan to start a business together. We want to learn everything we can. Our first meeting is next week. 내 사촌과 나는 함께 사업을 시작할 계획이다. 우리는 할 수 있는 모든 것을 배우고 싶다. 우리의 첫 회의는 다음 주이다.

## DAY 88

### Step 2

I have a problem with my computer. 내 컴퓨터에 문제가 있다.
The bug is on the leaf. 그 벌레가 잎에 있다.
We are traveling south. 우리는 남쪽으로 여행 중이다.
The train is arriving. 기차가 도착하고 있다.
The cat is very curious. 그 고양이는 매우 호기심이 많다.

### Step 3

A: I have a problem with my homework. 내 숙제에 문제가 있어.
B: What's the problem? Maybe I can help. 무슨 문제야? 내가 도울 수 있을지도 몰라.
A: There's a bug on my paper! 내 종이에 벌레가 있어!
B: Oh no! Let's move it outside. 이런! 그것을 밖으로 옮기자.
A: Have you ever taken the train to the south? 남쪽으로 가는 기차를 타본 적 있니?
B: No, but I'm curious about what it's like. 아니, 하지만 어떤지 궁금해.

### Challenge

I had a problem with my toy train today. A bug got inside it, and I couldn't fix it. My curious brother wanted to know if it came from the south. 오늘 내 장난감 기차에 문제가 있었다. 벌레가 그 안에 들어가서 고칠 수 없었다. 호기심 많은 내 동생은 그것이 남쪽에서 왔는지 알고 싶어했다.

## DAY 89

### Step 2

This is my favorite book. 이것은 내가 가장 좋아하는 책이다.
Let's watch a movie tonight. 오늘 밤 영화를 보자.
The museum is very interesting. 그 박물관은 매우 흥미롭다.
She is an engineer. 그녀는 엔지니어다.
The TV is in the living room. TV는 거실에 있다.

### Step 3

A: Are you coming to the museum tonight? 오늘 밤 박물관에 올 거니?
B: Yes, I am! I'm excited to see everything. 응, 갈 거야! 모든 것을 보는 게 기대돼.
A: My dad, who is an engineer, will be there too. 엔지니어인 우리 아빠도 거기 있을 거야.
B: That's cool! I'd love to meet him. 멋지다! 그분을 만나보고 싶어.
A: We can talk more about this in the living room. 거실에서 더 이야기하자.
B: Sure, let's go there now! 물론, 지금 가자!

### Challenge

I am excited about visiting the museum tonight. My dad, who is an engineer, will take me there. We talked about our plans in the living room after dinner. 나는 오늘 밤 박물관 방문을 기대하고 있다. 엔지니어인 아빠가 나를 데려다 주실 것이다. 우리는 저녁 식사 후 거실에서 우리의 계획에 대해 이야기했다.

## DAY 90

### Step 2

I need to sleep early tonight. 나는 오늘 밤 일찍 자야 한다.
The telephone is ringing. 전화기가 울리고 있다.
Look in the mirror. 거울을 봐라.
The bathroom is upstairs. 화장실은 위층에 있다.
It's almost time to go. 거의 갈 시간이다.

### Step 3

A: I need to sleep soon. I'm so tired. 나는 곧 자야 해. 너무 피곤해.
B: Me too. Let's talk more tomorrow. 나도 그래. 내일 더 얘기하자.
A: Did you see the new telephone in the living room? 거실에 있는 새 전화기 봤니?
B: Yes, it looks really nice. 응, 정말 멋져 보여.
A: I almost dropped the mirror in the bathroom today. 오늘 화장실에서 거울을 거의 떨어뜨릴 뻔했어.
B: Oh no! Be careful next time. 이런! 다음엔 조심해.

### Challenge

I almost fell asleep while talking on the telephone. Before bed, I looked in the mirror in the bathroom. I had a very tiring day. 전화 통화 중에 거의 잠들 뻔했다. 자기 전에 화장실 거울을 봤다. 매우 피곤한 하루였다.

## DAY 91

### Step 2

This part is broken. 이 부분이 고장 났다.

I love solving puzzles. 나는 퍼즐 푸는 것을 좋아한다.

This is my favorite brand. 이것은 내가 가장 좋아하는 브랜드이다.

Be careful not to burn yourself. 데지 않도록 조심해라.

My family is very important to me. 내 가족은 나에게 매우 중요하다.

### Step 3

A: I finished part of the puzzle. 나는 퍼즐의 일부를 완성했어.

B: Great job! What brand is it? 잘했어! 어느 브랜드야?

A: It's from a brand called "PuzzleFun." "퍼즐펀"이라는 브랜드에서 나왔어.

B: I like their puzzles too! 나도 그들의 퍼즐을 좋아해!

A: Be careful with the candles; we don't want to burn it. 촛불을 조심해; 그것을 태우고 싶지 않아.

B: Yes, I'll keep them away. My family loves doing puzzles together.
응, 멀리 둘게. 내 가족은 퍼즐을 함께 푸는 것을 좋아해.

### Challenge

I worked on a puzzle with my family today. We finished part of it and saw the brand name on the box. My mom warned us not to burn the pieces by accident. 오늘 가족과 함께 퍼즐을 했다. 우리는 일부를 완성했고, 상자에서 브랜드 이름을 보았다. 엄마는 우리가 실수로 퍼즐 조각을 태우지 않도록 경고하셨다.

## DAY 92

### Step 2

Let's do it again. 다시 하자.

We go to church every Sunday. 우리는 매주 일요일에 교회에 간다.

This is the last piece. 이것이 마지막 조각이다.

She has long hair. 그녀는 긴 머리를 가지고 있다.

I took a picture of the sunset. 나는 일몰 사진을 찍었다.

### Step 3

A: Are you going to church again this Sunday? 이번 일요일에도 교회에 갈 거니?

B: Yes, I go every week. 응, 나는 매주 가.

A: Did you see the picture on the wall? 벽에 있는 그림 봤니?

B: Yes, it was beautiful. 응, 정말 아름다웠어.

A: It shows the last supper. 그것은 최후의 만찬을 보여줘.

B: I noticed it. The details in the hair are amazing! 알아챘어. 머리카락의 디테일이 놀라워!

### Challenge

I went to church again with my family. I saw a beautiful picture of the last supper on the wall. My mom fixed my hair before we went inside. 나는 가족과 함께 다시 교회에 갔다. 나는 벽에 걸린 아름다운 최후의 만찬 그림을 보았다. 엄마는 우리가 들어가기 전에 내 머리를 정리해 주셨다.

## DAY 93

### Step 2

That puppy is so cute. 저 강아지는 정말 귀엽다.
Fill the bottle with water. 병에 물을 채워라.
I love to cook. 나는 요리하는 것을 좋아한다.
How are you today? 오늘 어떻게 지내니?
I need to finish my homework. 나는 숙제를 끝내야 한다.

### Step 3

A: Your new puppy is so cute! 너의 새 강아지는 정말 귀엽다!
B: Thanks! He fills our home with joy. 고마워! 그는 우리 집을 기쁨으로 채워줘.
A: How do you find time to cook and do homework? 요리하고 숙제할 시간을 어떻게 찾니?
B: I cook first, then do my homework. 나는 먼저 요리하고, 그 다음에 숙제를 해.
A: That sounds like a good plan. 좋은 계획인 것 같아.
B: It works well for me! 나에게는 잘 맞아!

### Challenge

I saw a cute cat while doing my homework. To fill the time, I decided to cook something. I wondered how to make a simple dish. 숙제를 하다가 귀여운 고양이를 보았다. 시간을 채우기 위해 뭔가 요리하기로 했다. 간단한 요리를 어떻게 만드는지 궁금했다.

## DAY 94

### Step 2

Let's start the meeting. 회의를 시작하자.
It might rain later. 나중에 비가 올지도 모른다.
What is today's date? 오늘 날짜가 무엇인가요?
Korea is a beautiful nation. 한국은 아름다운 나라이다.
Take care of your body. 너의 몸을 돌봐라.

### Step 3

A: When will the game start? 게임은 언제 시작하니?
B: It might start at 5 P.M. 오후 5시에 시작할지도 몰라.
A: Do you know the date of the game? 게임 날짜를 아니?
B: Yes, it's on June 10th. 응, 6월 10일이야.
A: Which nation is hosting the event? 어느 나라가 그 행사를 주최하니?
B: Our nation is hosting it this year. 우리나라가 올해 주최해.

### Challenge

I started a new book today about different nations. It said that the date of the festival might change. I learned how each country's culture affects the body and health. 오늘 다른 나라들에 관한 새로운 책을 시작했다. 그 책은 축제 날짜가 바뀔 수도 있다고 말했다. 나는 각 나라의 문화가 몸과 건강에 어떻게 영향을 미치는지 배웠다.

## DAY 95

### Step 2

Let's discuss the plan. 계획을 논의하자.
This is a good book. 이것은 좋은 책이다.
You should act right now. 지금 바로 행동해야 해.
We are planning a trip. 우리는 여행을 계획하고 있다.
The bird is singing. 새가 노래하고 있다.

### Step 3

A: Let's discuss the new project. 새로운 프로젝트에 대해 논의하자.
B: Sure, when do you have time? This is a good idea. 물론, 언제 시간이 있니? 좋은 생각이야.
A: I agree. We need to act quickly. 동의해. 빨리 행동해야 해.
B: Yes, we do. Are you planning a trip? 응, 맞아. 여행을 계획 중이니?
A: Yes, to the mountains. Look at that bird! 응, 산으로 갈 거야. 저 새 좀 봐!
B: It's beautiful. 정말 아름답다.

### Challenge

I discussed our trip with my family today. We had a good plan for where to go. I saw a bird act funny in the park. 오늘 가족과 여행에 대해 논의했다. 어디로 갈지에 대한 좋은 계획이 있었다. 나는 공원에서 재미있게 행동하는 새를 보았다.

## DAY 96

### Step 2

The bridge is very long. 그 다리는 매우 길다.
Turn left at the corner. 코너에서 좌회전해라.
Cover the pot with a lid. 냄비에 뚜껑을 덮어라.
The car needs more oil. 차에 더 많은 기름이 필요하다.
She did a great job. 그녀는 훌륭한 일을 해냈다.

### Step 3

A: Look at that big bridge! 저 큰 다리를 봐!
B: Yes, it's on the left side of the road. 응, 도로 왼쪽에 있어.
A: The bridge is covered with lights. 다리는 불빛으로 덮여 있어.
B: That must look great at night. 밤에 멋져 보이겠다.
A: Be careful of the oil on the road. 도로 위의 기름을 조심해.
B: Thanks for telling me. I'll watch out. 알려줘서 고마워. 조심할게.

### Challenge

I walked across the bridge today. On the left side, it was covered with flowers. We had to be careful because there was some oil on the path, but the view was great. 오늘 다리를 건넜다. 왼쪽에는 꽃으로 덮여 있었다. 길에 기름이 좀 있어서 조심해야 했지만, 경치는 훌륭했다.

## DAY 97

### Step 2

This is the book of dreams. 이것은 꿈의 책이다.
My back hurts. 내 등/허리가 아프다.
We went on an adventure. 우리는 모험을 떠났다.
I had toast for breakfast. 나는 아침으로 토스트를 먹었다.
Can you carry this bag? 이 가방을 들 수 있니?

### Step 3

A: Are you ready for a day of adventure? 하루 종일 모험할 준비 되었니?
B: Yes, I just need to eat breakfast first. 응, 먼저 아침을 먹어야 해.
A: What did you have for breakfast? 아침으로 뭐 먹었니?
B: I had cereal and juice. 시리얼과 주스를 먹었어.
A: Do you want me to carry your bag? 가방 들어줄까?
B: That would be great. My back is a bit sore. 그럼 좋겠어. 내 등이 좀 아파.

### Challenge

I had a big breakfast before our adventure. We carried our backpacks full of snacks. The trail was fun, and I loved exploring the back of the forest. 모험을 떠나기 전에 푸짐한 아침을 먹었다. 우리는 간식이 가득한 배낭을 들었다. 산책로는 재미있었고, 나는 숲의 뒤쪽을 탐험하는 것이 좋았다.

## DAY 98

### Step 2

The class is starting soon. 수업이 곧 시작된다.
Wear gloves to keep your hands warm. 손을 따뜻하게 유지하려면 장갑을 끼세요.
The beauty of nature is amazing. 자연의 아름다움은 놀랍다.
My ear hurts. 내 귀가 아프다.
What are your plans for the weekend? 주말 계획은 무엇인가요?

### Step 3

A: How was your class today? 오늘 수업 어땠어?
B: It was good. We learned a lot. 좋았어. 우리는 많은 것을 배웠어.
A: Did you see my new gloves? 내 새 장갑 봤니?
B: Yes, they are beautiful! 응, 정말 예쁘다!
A: What are you doing this weekend? 이번 주말에 뭐 할 거야?
B: I'm going to the park to enjoy the beauty of nature. 나는 자연의 아름다움을 즐기러 공원에 갈 거야.

### Challenge

I had a fun class about nature today. My teacher wore gloves to show us the beauty of different plants. I can't wait to learn more this weekend; it was music to my ears! 오늘 자연에 관한 재미있는 수업을 했다. 선생님이 다양한 식물의 아름다움을 보여주시기 위해 장갑을 끼셨다. 이번 주말에 더 많은 것을 배우는 것이 기다려진다. 귀가 쫑긋하는 소식이었다!

## DAY 99

### Step 2

I like to eat pizza. 나는 피자를 먹는 것을 좋아한다.
The prince is charming. 그 왕자는 매력적이다.
Do not touch the painting. 그림을 만지지 마세요.
Please answer the question. 질문에 대답해 주세요.
Rabbits eat carrots. 토끼는 당근을 먹는다.

### Step 3

A: Did you see the prince in the movie? 영화에서 왕자 봤니?
B: Yes, he was very brave. 응, 그는 매우 용감했어.
A: What did he eat for dinner? 그는 저녁으로 무엇을 먹었니?
B: He ate a big carrot. 큰 당근을 먹었어.
A: Can I touch the book with his story? 그의 이야기가 담긴 책을 만질 수 있을까?
B: Sure, I'll answer any questions you have. 물론, 네 질문에 모두 대답해 줄게.

### Challenge

I read a story about a prince who loves to eat carrots. He let people touch his golden crown. When asked why he loves carrots, he would always answer with a smile. 나는 당근을 먹는 것을 좋아하는 왕자에 대한 이야기를 읽었다. 그는 사람들에게 그의 황금 왕관을 만지게 했다. 왜 당근을 좋아하느냐고 물으면, 항상 미소로 대답했다.

## DAY 100

### Step 2

Everything is alright now. 이제 모든 것이 괜찮다.
It's going to rain soon. 곧 비가 올 것이다.
The woman is very kind. 그 여성은 매우 친절하다.
I love balloons. 나는 풍선을 좋아한다.
This lemon is sour. 이 레몬은 시다.

### Step 3

A: Is everything alright? 모든 것이 괜찮니?
B: Yes, just enjoying the rain. 응, 그냥 비를 즐기고 있어.
A: Look at that woman with the balloons. 풍선을 가진 저 여자를 봐.
B: She looks happy. 그녀는 행복해 보인다.
A: I tasted a sour candy today. 오늘 신 사탕을 먹었어.
B: Really? I prefer sweet ones. 정말? 나는 단 것을 더 좋아해.

### Challenge

I went outside even though it was raining. A woman gave me a balloon, which made my day. I also tried a sour candy, but it was alright. 비가 오는데도 밖에 나갔다. 한 여성이 풍선을 주었고, 그것은 나의 하루를 빛나게 했다. 신 사탕도 먹어 보았지만 괜찮았다.

## DAY 101

### Step 2

They had a big fight. 그들은 큰 싸움을 했다.
The world is a big place. 세상은 큰 곳이다.
I exercise every morning. 나는 매일 아침 운동을 한다.
My heart is beating fast. 내 심장이 빨리 뛰고 있다.
The ground is wet. 땅이 젖어 있다.

### Step 3

A: Did you see the news about the fight? 싸움에 대한 뉴스를 봤니?
B: Yes, it was happening in another part of the world. 응, 세계의 다른 지역에서 일어나고 있었어.
A: It's important to exercise for a healthy heart. 건강한 심장을 위해 운동하는 것이 중요해.
B: I agree. I like to run on the ground outside. 동의해. 나는 밖에서 땅 위를 뛰는 걸 좋아해.
A: Running outside is the best! 밖에서 뛰는 게 최고야!
B: Yes, it makes my heart feel strong. 맞아, 그것이 내 심장을 강하게 느끼게 해줘.

### Challenge

I watched a movie about a fight to save the world. It reminded me to exercise and keep my heart strong. Afterward, I did push-ups on the ground. 나는 세상을 구하기 위한 싸움에 관한 영화를 보았다. 그것은 나에게 운동을 하고 내 심장을 강하게 유지하라고 상기시켜 주었다. 그 후, 나는 땅에서 팔굽혀펴기를 했다.

## DAY 102

### Step 2

What type of music do you like? 어떤 종류의 음악을 좋아하니?
The book is on the desk. 책이 책상 위에 있다.
She is a famous singer. 그녀는 유명한 가수이다.
I like to eat fruit. 나는 과일을 먹는 것을 좋아한다.
The lake is very calm. 호수가 매우 잔잔하다.

### Step 3

A: What type of fruit do you like? 어떤 종류의 과일을 좋아하니?
B: I like apples the best. 나는 사과를 가장 좋아해.
A: Have you seen that famous desk? 그 유명한 책상을 본 적 있니?
B: Yes, it's in the museum. 응, 박물관에 있어.
A: Do you like visiting the lake? 호수 방문하는 걸 좋아하니?
B: Yes, it's a great place to relax. 응, 쉬기에 좋은 곳이야.

### Challenge

I learned about different types of fruit in class today. We talked about a famous lake where special fruit grows. I sat at my desk and drew a picture of the lake. 오늘 수업에서 다양한 종류의 과일에 대해 배웠다. 우리는 특별한 과일이 자라는 유명한 호수에 대해 이야기했다. 나는 책상에 앉아 그 호수의 그림을 그렸다.

## DAY 103

### Step 2

I baked some cookies. 나는 쿠키를 구웠다.
Finish your homework before dinner. 저녁 식사 전에 숙제를 끝내라.
She is against the idea. 그녀는 그 아이디어에 반대한다.
The kitchen is clean. 주방이 깨끗하다.
Her voice is beautiful. 그녀의 목소리는 아름답다.

### Step 3

A: Did you bake cookies before dinner? 저녁 식사 전에 쿠키를 구웠니?
B: Yes, they're in the kitchen. 응, 주방에 있어.
A: I heard your voice singing while baking. 너가 쿠키를 구우면서 노래하는 소리를 들었어.
B: Yes, I love to sing when I cook. 응, 나는 요리할 때 노래하는 걸 좋아해.
A: Are you against eating cookies before dinner? 저녁 식사 전에 쿠키를 먹는 것에 반대하니?
B: No, I think it's okay to have one! 아니, 하나 먹는 건 괜찮다고 생각해!

### Challenge

I ate a cookie before dinner today. My mom was against it, but I couldn't resist. Her voice called me from the kitchen to set the table. 오늘 저녁 식사 전에 쿠키를 먹었다. 엄마는 반대했지만, 나는 참을 수 없었다. 그녀의 목소리가 주방에서 식탁을 차리라고 불렀다.

## DAY 104

### Step 2

We can leave after lunch. 점심 식사 후에 출발할 수 있다.
He is very strong. 그는 매우 강하다.
She is taller than me. 그녀는 나보다 키가 크다.
Turn right at the next street. 다음 거리에서 우회전해라.
The meeting is in an hour. 회의는 한 시간 후에 있다.

### Step 3

A: Let's go for a walk after dinner. 저녁 먹고 산책하자.
B: That sounds good. I need to get strong. 좋아. 나는 강해져야 해.
A: Walking is easier than running. 걷는 것이 달리는 것보다 쉽다.
B: Yes, and we can talk while we walk. 맞아, 그리고 걸으면서 이야기할 수 있어.
A: Should we turn right at the corner? 모퉁이에서 우회전할까?
B: Yes, and let's walk for an hour. 응, 그리고 한 시간 동안 걷자.

### Challenge

I felt stronger after my workout today. My right arm is stronger than my left. I exercised for an hour. 오늘 운동 후에 더 강해진 느낌이었다. 내 오른팔이 왼팔보다 강하다. 나는 한 시간 동안 운동했다.

## DAY 105

### Step 2

Turn off the lights. 불을 꺼라.
Humans are intelligent. 인간은 지적이다.
I need some help. 나는 도움이 필요하다.
The fox is very clever. 여우는 매우 영리하다.
My arm hurts. 내 팔이 아프다.

### Step 3

A: Turn off the TV, please. TV를 꺼줘.
B: Okay, I'll turn it off. 알았어, 내가 끌게.
A: Some humans are as smart as a fox. 몇몇 인간은 여우만큼 영리하다.
B: Yes, I heard that. 응, 들었어.
A: I saw a fox today. 오늘 여우를 봤어.
B: Wow! I hope it doesn't bite my arm! 와! 내 팔을 물지 않길 바래!

### Challenge

I saw a fox run off into the woods today. Some humans were watching it from a distance. My friend waved his arm to say goodbye to the fox. 오늘 여우가 숲으로 도망치는 것을 보았다. 몇몇 사람들이 멀리서 그것을 보고 있었다. 내 친구는 여우에게 작별 인사를 하기 위해 팔을 흔들었다.

## DAY 106

### Step 2

I love modern art. 나는 현대 미술을 사랑한다.
This year is going by fast. 올해가 빠르게 지나가고 있다.
The cat is sleeping. 고양이가 자고 있다.
The sun sets in the west. 해는 서쪽으로 진다.
The room is messy. 방이 어지럽다.

### Step 3

A: Do you like art? 예술을 좋아하니?
B: Yes, I love drawing. 응, 나는 그림 그리는 것을 좋아해.
A: I got a cat last year. 작년에 고양이를 얻었어.
B: Really? Cats are so cute. 정말? 고양이는 너무 귀여워.
A: My cat likes to sleep in my room. 내 고양이는 내 방에서 자는 걸 좋아해.
B: Mine likes to watch the sunset in the west. 내 고양이는 서쪽에서 해지는 것을 보는 걸 좋아해.

### Challenge

I made some art in my room today. It was a picture of a cat. I showed it to my friend who lives in the west part of town; we've been friends for a year. 오늘 내 방에서 예술 작품을 만들었다. 그것은 고양이 그림이었다. 나는 그것을 마을 서쪽에 사는 친구에게 보여주었다; 우리는 1년 동안 친구였다.

## DAY 107

### Step 2

Pick your favorite color. 좋아하는 색을 고르세요.
The cart is full of groceries. 카트가 식료품으로 가득 차 있다.
We need to plan ahead. 우리는 미리 계획을 세워야 한다.
Spring is my favorite season. 봄은 내가 가장 좋아하는 계절이다.
I need to go to the bank. 나는 은행에 가야 한다.

### Step 3

A: Which fruit should we pick? 어떤 과일을 고를까?
B: Let's pick apples. 사과를 고르자.
A: Do we need a cart for the apples? 사과를 위한 카트가 필요해?
B: Yes, it's just ahead. 응, 바로 앞에 있어.
A: What's your favorite season? 가장 좋아하는 계절이 뭐야?
B: I like summer because I can go to the river bank. 여름이 좋아, 강가에 갈 수 있어서.

### Challenge

I went to the store to pick some fruits today. I pushed the cart ahead of me, looking for my favorite snacks. This season, we plan to visit the river bank for a picnic. 오늘 과일을 고르러 가게에 갔다. 내가 좋아하는 간식을 찾으면서 카트를 밀었다. 이번 계절에는 강가로 소풍을 갈 계획이다.

## DAY 108

### Step 2

He has a high fever. 그는 고열이 있다.
Be careful not to fall. 넘어지지 않도록 조심해라.
Could you help me? 나를 도와줄 수 있니?
Let's go now. 지금 가자.
She went to the store. 그녀는 가게에 갔다.

### Step 3

A: Do you have a fever? 열이 있니?
B: Yes, I think so. 응, 그런 것 같아.
A: You could fall if you don't rest. 쉬지 않으면 쓰러질 수도 있어.
B: I know, I should lie down now. 알아, 이제 누워야겠어.
A: Can I get you something to drink? 마실 것 좀 가져다줄까?
B: Yes, please. That would be nice. 응, 부탁해. 그럼 좋겠어.

### Challenge

I have a fever now, so I can't go to school. My mom said I could fall if I try to move too much. I hope to feel better soon. 지금 열이 있어서 학교에 갈 수 없다. 엄마는 내가 너무 많이 움직이려 하면 넘어질 수 있다고 말했다. 빨리 나아지길 바란다.

## DAY 109

### Step 2

There are a hundred students in the school. 학교에 백 명의 학생이 있다.
I love studying science. 나는 과학 공부를 좋아한다.
The cat is hiding below the table. 고양이가 테이블 아래에 숨어 있다.
I feel a lot of stress before exams. 나는 시험 전에는 스트레스를 많이 느낀다.
I can help you with that. 나는 그것을 도와줄 수 있다.

### Step 3

A: There are a hundred stars in the sky tonight. 오늘 밤 하늘에 백 개의 별이 있어.
B: Wow, that's a lot! 와, 정말 많다!
A: Do you like science? 과학을 좋아하니?
B: Yes, I love learning about the stars. 응, 나는 별에 대해 배우는 것을 좋아해.
A: The temperature is below freezing tonight. 오늘 밤 기온이 영하야.
B: That can cause stress for some people. 그것이 어떤 사람들에게는 스트레스를 줄 수 있어.

### Challenge

I read a science book with a hundred fun facts. One fact said that being below sea level can cause stress. It was interesting to learn how deep water can affect us. 나는 백 가지 재미있는 사실이 담긴 과학 책을 읽었다. 하나의 사실은 해수면 아래에 있는 것이 스트레스를 줄 수 있다고 말했다. 깊은 물이 우리에게 어떤 영향을 미치는지 배우는 것은 흥미로웠다.

## DAY 110

### Step 2

History is my favorite subject. 역사는 내가 가장 좋아하는 과목이다.
I met her yesterday. 나는 그녀를 어제 만났다.
However, I disagree with you. 하지만, 나는 너와 동의하지 않는다.
We played in the park. 우리는 공원에서 놀았다.
She gave me a gift. 그녀는 나에게 선물을 주었다.

### Step 3

A: Did you study history yesterday? 어제 역사 공부했니?
B: Yes, I did. 응, 했어.
A: However, I still have questions. 하지만, 아직도 질문이 있어.
B: We can talk about it at the park. 공원에서 그것에 대해 이야기하자.
A: I got a gift for you! 너에게 줄 선물이 있어!
B: Thank you! I love surprises. 고마워! 나는 깜짝 선물이 좋아.

### Challenge

Yesterday, I visited a history museum. However, I also spent time in the park nearby. I bought a small gift from the museum shop to remember the day. 어제 역사 박물관을 방문했다. 하지만, 근처 공원에서도 시간을 보냈다. 그날을 기억하기 위해 박물관 가게에서 작은 선물을 샀다.

## DAY 111

### Step 2

Can I borrow your pen? 너의 펜을 빌려도 되니?
I need to study for my exam. 나는 시험 공부를 해야 한다.
She likes to be alone. 그녀는 혼자 있는 것을 좋아한다.
The fish is swimming. 물고기가 수영하고 있다.
The giraffe is very tall. 기린은 매우 키가 크다.

### Step 3

A: Can I borrow your book to study? 네 책 빌려서 공부해도 될까?
B: Sure, but why do you want to study alone? 물론이지, 그런데 왜 혼자 공부하고 싶어?
A: I focus better when I'm alone. 혼자 있을 때 더 집중이 잘 돼.
B: That makes sense. Did you know I have a pet fish? 이해돼. 나 물고기 키우는 거 알아?
A: Really? I wish I had a pet. Maybe a giraffe! 정말? 나도 애완동물이 있었으면 좋겠어. 아마도 기린!
B: A giraffe? That's funny! 기린? 그거 재밌네.

### Challenge

I borrowed a book to study alone. While reading, I saw pictures of a fish and a giraffe. It made my study time more interesting. 나는 혼자 공부하려고 책을 빌렸다. 읽는 동안 물고기와 기린의 그림을 보았다. 그것은 내 공부 시간을 더 흥미롭게 만들었다.

## DAY 112

### Step 2

The concert was amazing. 콘서트는 놀라웠다.
Let's play outside. 밖에서 놀자.
The sand is warm. 모래가 따뜻하다.
Good evening! 좋은 저녁이에요!
The car is very fast. 차가 매우 빠르다.

### Step 3

A: Are you going to the concert tonight? 오늘 밤 콘서트에 갈 거니?
B: Yes, I am! Are you going too? 응, 나도 갈 거야! 너도 가니?
A: No, I'm going to play in the sand with my brother. 아니, 나는 내 동생과 모래에서 놀 거야.
B: That sounds fun! What time are you going? 재미있겠다! 몇 시에 가니?
A: We're going in the evening, around 6 P.M. 우리는 저녁 6시쯤 갈 거야.
B: Have a great time! Time goes by so fast when you're having fun.
즐거운 시간 보내! 즐거울 때 시간은 빨리 가.

### Challenge

In the evening, I went to a concert. Afterward, I watched children play in the sand. It was a fast-paced day but very enjoyable. 저녁에 콘서트에 갔다. 그 후에 아이들이 모래에서 노는 것을 보았다. 빠르게 지나간 하루였지만 매우 즐거웠다.

## DAY 113

### Step 2

The cloud looks like a sheep. 구름이 양처럼 보인다.
We played basketball at school. 우리는 학교에서 농구를 했다.
The duck is swimming. 오리가 수영하고 있다.
The plant will die without water. 식물은 물이 없으면 죽을 것이다.
The bone is strong. 뼈는 강하다.

### Step 3

A: Look at that cloud! 저 구름을 봐!
B: It looks like a duck. 오리처럼 보여.
A: Do you want to play basketball later? 나중에 농구할래?
B: Sure, that sounds fun. 물론, 재미있겠다.
A: Did you hear about the old duck that died? 죽은 늙은 오리에 대해 들었니?
B: Yes, it was sad. Ducks have weak bones. 응, 슬펐어. 오리는 뼈가 약해.

### Challenge

I saw clouds in the sky while playing basketball. A duck was nearby, looking for food. Sadly, I found a bone, and it made me think of animals that die. 농구를 하면서 하늘에 구름을 보았다. 근처에 오리가 먹이를 찾고 있었다. 슬프게도, 나는 뼈를 발견했고, 그것은 죽는 동물들을 생각나게 했다.

## DAY 114

### Step 2

This word is difficult to spell. 이 단어는 철자가 어렵다.
The grass is green. 잔디가 녹색이다.
The pig is eating. 돼지가 먹고 있다.
The king is wise. 왕은 지혜롭다.
I wear jeans every day. 나는 매일 청바지를 입는다.

### Step 3

A: Can you spell this word? 이 단어 철자를 말할 수 있니?
B: Yes, I can spell it. 응, 말할 수 있어.
A: Look at the pig on the grass. 잔디 위의 돼지를 봐.
B: It's rolling around! 굴러다니고 있어!
A: Did you see the king in the movie? 영화에서 왕을 봤니?
B: Yes, he was wearing jeans! 응, 그는 청바지를 입고 있었어!

### Challenge

I learned a new word today: "king." We read a story about a king who loved to play on the grass. He even wore jeans while playing with his pet pig. 오늘 "king"이라는 새로운 단어를 배웠다. 우리는 잔디에서 노는 것을 좋아하는 왕에 대한 이야기를 읽었다. 그는 심지어 애완 돼지와 놀 때도 청바지를 입었다.

## DAY 115

### Step 2

I need a new pencil. 나는 새 연필이 필요하다.
What time is it? 지금 몇 시니?
This is a great memory. 이것은 멋진 기억이다.
The holiday starts tomorrow. 휴일은 내일 시작된다.
I work from home. 나는 집에서 일한다.

### Step 3

A: Do you have a pencil I can use? 내가 사용할 연필이 있니?
B: Yes, here you go. 응, 여기 있어.
A: What time is it now? 지금 몇 시니?
B: It's 3 P.M. 오후 3시야.
A: Do you have a favorite holiday memory? 가장 좋아하는 휴일 기억이 있니?
B: Yes, I remember when we didn't have to work and had fun!
응, 우리가 일하지 않고 즐거웠던 기억이 있어!

### Challenge

I used a pencil to write about my holiday memories. It took some time, but it was worth it. Now, I have a nice story to remember when I work. 나는 연필로 휴일 기억에 대해 썼다. 시간이 좀 걸렸지만 그만한 가치가 있었다. 이제, 나는 일할 때 기억할 수 있는 멋진 이야기가 있다.

## DAY 116

### Step 2

People are very kind here. 이곳 사람들은 매우 친절하다.
Don't be lazy. 게으르지 마라.
You must finish your homework. 너는 숙제를 끝내야 한다.
My aunt is visiting us. 내 이모가 우리를 방문하고 있다.
Birds can fly. 새는 날 수 있다.

### Step 3

A: Some people can be lazy. 어떤 사람들은 게으를 수 있어.
B: Yes, but we must work hard. 맞아, 하지만 우리는 열심히 일해야 해.
A: My aunt always says that. 내 이모는 항상 그렇게 말해.
B: She sounds very wise. 그녀는 매우 지혜로운 것 같아.
A: Did you see the bird fly? 새가 나는 것을 봤니?
B: Yes, it flew so high! 응, 매우 높이 날았어!

### Challenge

My aunt says that people should not be lazy. She told me we must work hard to reach our goals. She also said, "If you work hard, you can fly high like a bird!" 내 이모는 사람들이 게으르지 말아야 한다고 말한다. 그녀는 우리가 목표를 이루기 위해 열심히 일해야 한다고 말했다. 그녀는 또한 "열심히 일하면 새처럼 높이 날 수 있다!"고 말했다.

## DAY 117

### Step 2

See you tomorrow. 내일 보자.
Good night! 좋은 밤 되세요!
The sky is blue. 하늘이 파랗다.
Her birth was a blessing. 그녀의 출생은 축복이었다.
I walk every day. 나는 매일 걷는다.

### Step 3

A: What are you doing tomorrow? 내일 뭐 할 거니?
B: I'm going out at night to see the stars. 밤에 별을 보러 나갈 거야.
A: The sky will be so blue! 하늘이 아주 파랗겠구나!
B: Yes, it will be beautiful. 응, 아름다울 거야.
A: Do you know your birth date? 너의 생일을 알고 있니?
B: Yes, it's in every memory I have! 응, 내가 가진 모든 기억 속에 있어!

### Challenge

Tomorrow night, I will see the blue moon. It only happens once in a while, like a special birth. Every time it happens, it feels magical. 내일 밤, 나는 파란 달을 볼 것이다. 그것은 특별한 출생처럼 가끔만 일어난다. 그것이 일어날 때마다 마법 같아.

## DAY 118

### Step 2

Don't lie to me. 나에게 거짓말하지 마라.
She wore a diamond ring. 그녀는 다이아몬드 반지를 꼈다.
Can you push the door? 문을 밀어줄 수 있니?
Goodbye, see you soon. 안녕, 곧 보자.
The bird is in the cage. 새가 우리 안에 있다.

### Step 3

A: Did you lie about the ring? 반지에 대해 거짓말했니?
B: No, I told the truth. 아니, 진실을 말했어.
A: Can you push the door open? 문을 밀어서 열어줄 수 있니?
B: Sure, no problem. 물론, 문제없어.
A: It's time to say goodbye to the bird. 새에게 작별 인사할 시간이다.
B: Yes, let's open the cage and let it go. 응, 우리를 열고 보내주자.

### Challenge

I saw my friend lie about losing his ring. He tried to push the blame on someone else. Before saying goodbye, we let the bird out of its cage. 나는 친구가 반지를 잃어버렸다고 거짓말하는 것을 보았다. 그는 다른 사람에게 책임을 떠넘기려고 했다. 작별 인사를 하기 전에 우리는 새를 우리에서 풀어주었다.

## DAY 119

### Step 2

He is a quick learner. 그는 빠르게 배우는 사람이다.
Use tape to fix it. 그것을 고치기 위해 테이프를 사용해라.
The cat is in the box. 고양이가 상자 안에 있다.
The cow is in the field. 소가 들판에 있다.
Don't drop the glass. 유리잔을 떨어뜨리지 마라.

### Step 3

A: Can you make a quick fix with this tape? 이 테이프로 빠르게 고칠 수 있니?
B: Sure, I'll put it in place. 물론, 제자리에 놓을게.
A: Be careful not to drop it. 떨어뜨리지 않도록 조심해.
B: I got it! Did you see the cow in the field? 알겠어! 들판에 있는 소 봤니?
A: Yes, it was walking slowly. 응, 천천히 걷고 있었어.
B: It's a nice contrast to our quick work! 우리의 빠른 작업과 좋은 대조를 이루네!

### Challenge

I fixed my book with quick tape today. I saw a cow in the field while walking. I was careful not to drop my snack on the way. 오늘 빠른 테이프로 내 책을 고쳤다. 걷는 동안 들판에서 소를 보았다. 가는 도중에 간식을 떨어뜨리지 않도록 조심했다.

## DAY 120

### Step 2

The soup is very hot. 수프가 매우 뜨겁다.
People change over time. 사람들은 시간이 지남에 따라 변한다.
I want to go home. 나는 집에 가고 싶다.
He found a coin on the ground. 그는 땅에서 동전을 발견했다.
That painting is ugly. 저 그림은 못생겼다.

### Step 3

A: The weather is so hot today! 오늘 날씨가 너무 더워!
B: Yes, I wish it would change soon. 맞아, 빨리 변했으면 좋겠어.
A: Do you want to get some ice cream? 아이스크림 먹으러 갈래?
B: That sounds perfect! 좋지!
A: Look at this old coin I found. 내가 찾은 이 오래된 동전 좀 봐.
B: It's a bit ugly, but it's interesting! 좀 못생겼지만, 흥미로워!

### Challenge

It was so hot today, I wanted a cold drink. I found an old coin that changed color over time. It looked a bit ugly but still interesting. 오늘 너무 더워서 차가운 음료가 먹고 싶었다. 시간이 지남에 따라 색이 변한 오래된 동전을 발견했다. 그것은 좀 못생겼지만 여전히 흥미로웠다.

## DAY 121

### Step 2

I am not ready yet. 나는 아직 준비가 안 됐다.
The sky is grey today. 오늘 하늘이 회색이다.
The shop is open. 가게가 열려 있다.
Please sit down. 앉아 주세요.
I like strawberry ice cream. 나는 딸기 아이스크림을 좋아한다.

### Step 3

A: That's not a grey shirt, is it? 저건 회색 셔츠가 아니지, 그렇지?
B: No, it's actually blue. 아니, 사실 파란색이야.
A: Do you want to go to the shop? 가게에 가고 싶니?
B: Sure, let's sit and plan first. 물론, 먼저 앉아서 계획을 세우자.
A: I want to buy some strawberries. 딸기를 사고 싶어.
B: Sounds delicious! Let's go. 맛있겠다! 가자.

### Challenge

I did not buy the grey shirt at the shop. Instead, I sat down and enjoyed a strawberry smoothie. It was a fun day! 가게에서 회색 셔츠를 사지 않았다. 대신에 앉아서 딸기 스무디를 즐겼다. 즐거운 하루였다!

## DAY 122

### Step 2

The airplane is taking off. 비행기가 이륙하고 있다.
Do you have a map? 지도가 있니?
The cat is sitting beside me. 고양이가 내 옆에 앉아 있다.
I have a headache. 나는 두통이 있다.
The board is broken. 판자가 부서졌다.

### Step 3

A: Have you ever been on an airplane? 비행기를 타본 적 있니?
B: Yes, I have. It's so exciting! 응, 있어. 너무 신나!
A: Do you use a map when you travel? 여행할 때 지도를 사용하니?
B: Yes, I keep one beside me all the time. 응, 항상 내 옆에 둬.
A: Do you get headaches on planes? 비행기에서 두통이 있니?
B: Sometimes, but I rest and feel better. 가끔은, 하지만 쉬면 나아져.

### Challenge

I saw an airplane in the sky today. I looked at a map beside my desk to see where it was going. I got a headache, so I rested on a wooden board. 오늘 하늘에서 비행기를 보았다. 내 책상 옆에 있는 지도를 보면서 어디로 가는지 봤다. 두통이 있어서 나무 판자에 쉬었다.

## DAY 123

### Step 2

Add some sugar to the tea. 차에 설탕을 좀 넣어라.
Her dress is green. 그녀의 드레스는 녹색이다.
The weather is nice today. 오늘 날씨가 좋다.
My keys are in my pocket. 내 열쇠는 내 주머니 안에 있다.
He has a friendly face. 그는 친근한 얼굴을 가지고 있다.

### Step 3

A: Do you want some sugar in your tea? 차에 설탕을 넣을래?
B: Yes, just a little, please. 네, 조금만 넣어 주세요.
A: Look at that green tree outside. 밖의 저 녹색 나무를 봐.
B: It's so beautiful, especially in this weather. 너무 아름다워, 특히 이 날씨에.
A: Do you have any tissues in your pocket? 네 주머니에 티슈가 있니?
B: Yes, here you go. 네, 여기 있어.

### Challenge

I put some sugar in my tea today. I wore a green jacket because the weather was cool. I found a coin in my pocket and it brought a smile to my face. 오늘 차에 설탕을 넣었다. 날씨가 시원해서 녹색 재킷을 입었다. 주머니에서 동전을 발견했고, 그것은 내 얼굴에 미소를 가져왔다.

## DAY 124

### Step 2

Let's begin the meeting. 회의를 시작하자.
She is my best friend. 그녀는 내 가장 친한 친구이다.
The zoo has many animals. 동물원에는 많은 동물이 있다.
This cake is delicious. 이 케이크는 맛있다.
I wake up early every day. 나는 매일 일찍 일어난다.

### Step 3

A: When does the movie begin? 영화가 언제 시작하니?
B: It begins at 7 P.M. 오후 7시에 시작해.
A: She loves animals so much. 그녀는 동물을 정말 좋아해.
B: Yes, she always talks about them. 응, 그녀는 항상 그것들에 대해 이야기해.
A: We had a delicious meal today. 오늘 맛있는 식사를 했어.
B: That's nice! Did you eat early? 좋겠다! 일찍 먹었니?

### Challenge

I began my day early today. My grandmother made a delicious breakfast for us. After eating, we visited the zoo to see the animals. 오늘 일찍 하루를 시작했다. 할머니께서 우리를 위해 맛있는 아침을 만들어주셨다. 식사 후에 동물들을 보러 동물원을 방문했다.

## DAY 125

### Step 2

The weather is cool today. 오늘 날씨가 시원하다.
He can drive very well. 그는 운전을 매우 잘한다.
Use a clip to hold the papers together. 종이를 고정하기 위해 클립을 사용해라.
He is a teen. 그는 십대이다.
She works at a big company. 그녀는 큰 회사에서 일한다.

### Step 3

A: The weather is so cool today. 오늘 날씨가 너무 시원해.
B: Yes, it's nice and refreshing. 맞아, 기분 좋고 상쾌해.
A: Do you know how to drive? 운전할 줄 아니?
B: Not yet, but I want to learn when I'm a teen. 아직은 아니지만, 내가 십대일 때 배우고 싶어.
A: I need a clip for these papers. 이 종이들을 위한 클립이 필요해.
B: I have one from my dad's company. 아빠 회사에서 받은 클립이 있어.

### Challenge

It was a cool day today. My dad let me drive the car. As a teen, it was exciting! At home, I used a clip to hold my papers from the company. 오늘 시원한 날이었다. 아빠가 나에게 차를 운전하게 해주었다. 십대로서 그것은 신나는 일이었다! 집에서 나는 회사의 종이를 고정하기 위해 클립을 사용했다.

## DAY 126

### Step 2

Are you crazy? 너 미쳤니?
She is very shy. 그녀는 굉장히 수줍어한다.
Today is a sunny day. 오늘은 화창한 날이다.
I have an exam tomorrow. 나는 내일 시험이 있다.
Can you fix my bike? 내 자전거를 고칠 수 있니?

### Step 3

A: Today was a crazy day! 오늘은 정말 미친 날이었어!
B: Really? What happened? 정말? 무슨 일이 있었어?
A: I was so shy during my exam. 시험 동안 너무 부끄러웠어.
B: Don't worry, you did your best. 걱정 마, 최선을 다했잖아.
A: I need to fix my computer. 내 컴퓨터를 고쳐야 해.
B: Maybe we can work on it together. 우리 함께 작업할 수 있을 거야.

### Challenge

I had a crazy day today. I felt shy during the exam. After school, I helped my friend fix his bike. 오늘 정말 미친 날이었다. 시험 동안 부끄러웠다. 학교가 끝난 후, 친구의 자전거를 고치는 것을 도왔다.

## DAY 127

### Step 2

You should study more. 너는 더 공부해야 한다.
The fog is very thick. 안개가 매우 짙다.
He is my brother. 그는 내 형제다.
They want to kill the bugs. 그들은 벌레를 죽이고 싶어한다.
Let me introduce you to my friend. 내 친구를 소개할게.

### Step 3

A: Should we go outside in the fog? 안개 속에서 밖으로 나갈까?
B: No, it's too hard to see. 아니, 너무 보기 힘들어.
A: He said he will introduce his friend to us. 그가 친구를 우리에게 소개할 거라고 했어.
B: That sounds nice. 좋겠다.
A: Did you hear about the story where the hero tries to kill the dragon?
영웅이 용을 죽이려고 하는 이야기 들었니?
B: Yes, it was very exciting. 응, 정말 흥미로웠어.

### Challenge

He should be careful in the fog. He talked about a hero killing a monster. I want to introduce him to my favorite book. 그는 안개 속에서 조심해야 한다. 그는 영웅이 괴물을 죽이는 이야기를 말했다. 나는 그에게 내 가장 좋아하는 책을 소개하고 싶다.

## DAY 128

### Step 2

She loves to draw pictures. 그녀는 그림 그리는 것을 좋아한다.
He has a strong accent. 그는 강한 악센트를 가지고 있다.
I want to go home. 나는 집에 가고 싶다.
My phone's battery is low. 내 전화 배터리가 부족하다.
There are many books on the shelf. 선반에 많은 책이 있다.

### Step 3

A: Do you like to draw pictures? 그림 그리는 것을 좋아하니?
B: Yes, I draw every day. 응, 나는 매일 그려.
A: I love your accent when you speak. 네가 말할 때의 악센트를 좋아해.
B: Thank you! I learned it at home. 고마워! 나는 집에서 배웠어.
A: Do you have many batteries? 배터리가 많이 있니?
B: Yes, we have many in the drawer. 응, 서랍에 많이 있어.

### Challenge

At home, I decided to draw a picture. My friend with a strong accent called, asking if I had any extra batteries. I found many and gave them to him. 집에서 그림을 그리기로 했다. 강한 악센트를 가진 친구가 전화를 걸어 추가 배터리가 있냐고 물었다. 나는 많이 찾아서 그에게 주었다.

## DAY 129

### Step 2

Point to the picture. 그림을 가리켜라.
Is this place safe? 이곳이 안전한가요?
The soup is warm. 수프가 따뜻하다.
Put the fruits in the basket. 과일을 바구니에 넣어라.
I bought a new phone. 나는 새 전화기를 샀다.

### Step 3

A: Can you point to the new book? 새 책을 가리킬 수 있니?
B: Sure, it's right there on the table. 물론, 바로 저기 테이블 위에 있어.
A: Is your home safe? 너의 집은 안전하니?
B: Yes, it feels very safe and warm. 응, 매우 안전하고 따뜻하게 느껴져.
A: Look at the basket. It's full of fruit. 바구니를 봐. 과일이 가득해.
B: I love having fresh fruit. It's a nice new basket. 나는 신선한 과일을 좋아해. 멋진 새 바구니야.

### Challenge

I pointed to the new basket on the shelf. It looked safe and strong. I felt warm inside when I held it.
나는 선반 위의 새 바구니를 가리켰다. 그것은 안전하고 튼튼해 보였다. 내가 그것을 들었을 때 마음이 따뜻해졌다.

## DAY 130

### Step 2

She has short hair. 그녀는 짧은 머리를 가지고 있다.
The room is very dark. 방이 매우 어둡다.
The table is too low. 테이블이 너무 낮다.
I had an egg for breakfast. 나는 아침으로 계란을 먹었다.
Let's go for a walk. 산책하러 가자.

### Step 3

A: I took a short walk today. 오늘 짧은 산책을 했어.
B: Was it nice outside? 밖이 좋았니?
A: Yes, but it got dark quickly. 응, 하지만 빨리 어두워졌어.
B: Did you see anything interesting? 흥미로운 것을 봤니?
A: I saw a nest with low branches and eggs. 낮은 가지와 알이 있는 둥지를 봤어.
B: That sounds lovely! I love nature. 멋지다! 나는 자연을 좋아해.

### Challenge

I took a short walk today. The sky was dark, and the sun was low. I found an egg on the ground.
오늘 짧은 산책을 했다. 하늘은 어두웠고, 해는 낮았다. 땅에서 계란을 발견했다.

## DAY 131

### Step 2

She looked very sad. 그녀는 매우 슬퍼 보였다.
I have a test tomorrow. 나는 내일 시험이 있다.
The store is closed. 가게가 닫혀 있다.
Can you guess the answer? 답을 추측할 수 있겠니?
The elephant is very big. 코끼리는 매우 크다.

### Step 3

A: I feel sad today. 오늘 슬퍼.
B: Why? Did something happen? 왜? 무슨 일 있었어?
A: I didn't do well on the test. 시험을 잘 못 봤어.
B: I'm sorry to hear that. Want to go to the store? 그거 유감이야. 가게에 갈래?
A: Sure, that might cheer me up. 그래, 그게 날 기분 좋게 할지도 몰라.
B: Guess what? I saw a toy elephant there! 맞춰봐! 거기서 장난감 코끼리를 봤어!

### Challenge

I felt sad after the test today. I went to the store to feel better. I guess I saw a toy elephant there.
오늘 시험 후에 슬펐다. 기분이 나아지기 위해 가게에 갔다. 거기서 장난감 코끼리를 본 것 같다.

## DAY 132

### Step 2

The roof needs repairing. 지붕은 수리가 필요하다.
What do you want to do? 무엇을 하고 싶니?
This bag is very heavy. 이 가방은 매우 무겁다.
Can you come to my party? 내 파티에 올 수 있니?
The button is missing. 단추가 없어졌다.

### Step 3

A: What should we do today? 오늘 뭐 할까?
B: Let's fix the roof. It's leaking. 지붕을 고치자. 물이 새고 있어.
A: That sounds like a heavy job. 그거 힘든 일 같다.
B: Yes, but we can do it together. 응, 하지만 함께 할 수 있어.
A: Did you see the new button on my coat? 내 코트에 새 단추 봤어?
B: Yes, it looks nice. Where did you get it? 응, 좋아 보여. 어디서 샀어?

### Challenge

I saw a worker on the roof today. He had to do a heavy job. My mom asked him to come inside to fix a button on her coat. 오늘 지붕 위에서 일하는 사람을 봤다. 그는 무거운 일을 해야 했다. 엄마가 그에게 안으로 들어와 코트의 단추를 고쳐달라고 부탁했다.

## DAY 133

### Step 2

The dialogue in the movie was great. 영화 속 대화는 훌륭했다.
It's important to exercise. 운동하는 것은 중요하다.
We are going to the cinema. 우리는 영화관에 갈 것이다.
They will build a new school. 그들은 새 학교를 지을 것이다.
The file is on my desk. 파일은 내 책상 위에 있다.

### Step 3

A: The dialogue was so funny. 대화가 너무 웃겼어.
B: Yes, I loved it. Exercise is very important. 응, 나도 좋았어. 운동은 매우 중요해.
A: I agree. Let's go to the cinema tonight. 동의해. 오늘 밤 영화관에 가자.
B: Sure, what time? They're building a new park. 그래, 몇 시에? 그들은 새 공원을 짓고 있어.
A: That's great. I need to find my file. 그거 좋다. 내 파일을 찾아야 해.
B: It's on your desk. 네 책상 위에 있어.

### Challenge

I had an important dialogue with my friend today. We talked about the new cinema they built. I saved our conversation in a file. 오늘 친구와 중요한 대화를 나눴다. 우리는 그들이 지은 새 영화관에 대해 이야기했다. 나는 우리의 대화를 파일에 저장했다.

## DAY 134

### Step 2

There's nothing in the fridge. 냉장고 안에 아무것도 없다.
Do you know her? 그녀를 아니?
Let's make a cake. 케이크를 만들자.
I'm late for the meeting. 회의에 늦었어.
Wash the dishes, please. 설거지 좀 해줘.

### Step 3

A: What are you doing today? 오늘 뭐 해?
B: Nothing much. You? 별거 없어. 너는?
A: I know how to make a great dish. 나 맛있는 요리 만드는 법 알아.
B: Really? Can you teach me? 정말? 나 좀 가르쳐 줄 수 있어?
A: Sure, but don't be late. 물론이지, 하지만 늦지 마.
B: I won't be! I want to learn. 안 늦을게! 배우고 싶어.

### Challenge

I know I should not make noise at night. Last night, I made a dish in the kitchen. Now it's late, so I will do nothing and rest. 밤에 소음을 내면 안 된다는 것을 알고 있다. 어젯밤에 부엌에서 요리를 했다. 지금은 늦었으니 아무것도 하지 않고 쉴 것이다.

## DAY 135

### Step 2

The forest is very dense. 숲은 매우 울창하다.
The store is on the corner. 가게는 모퉁이에 있다.
We need to get to the airport early. 우리는 일찍 공항에 가야 한다.
I can't decide what to wear. 무엇을 입을지 결정할 수가 없다.
The flag is waving in the wind. 깃발이 바람에 펄럭이고 있다.

### Step 3

A: Have you ever been to the forest near the corner? 모퉁이 근처 숲에 가본 적 있어?
B: Yes, it's very peaceful there. 응, 거기 아주 평화로워.
A: We need to go to the airport soon. 곧 공항에 가야 해.
B: Did you decide what time we should leave? 언제 출발할지 정했어?
A: Yes, we should leave when the flag is lowered. 응, 깃발이 내려갈 때 출발해야 해.
B: Okay, I'll be ready by then. 알겠어, 그때까지 준비할게.

### Challenge

I went for a walk in the forest. At the corner, I saw a flag. My family decided to visit the airport next.
나는 숲에서 산책을 했다. 모퉁이에서 깃발을 보았다. 우리 가족은 다음에 공항을 방문하기로 결정했다.

## DAY 136

### Step 2

It is very cold today. 오늘은 매우 춥다.
The lake is very deep. 호수는 매우 깊다.
My parents are kind. 우리 부모님은 친절하시다.
She is very clever. 그녀는 매우 영리하다.
Her skin is soft. 그녀의 피부는 부드럽다.

### Step 3

A: I saw a cartoon movie yesterday. 어제 만화 영화를 봤어.
B: What was it about? 그거 어떤 내용이었어?
A: It was about a clever dolphin living in the deep sea.
깊은 바다에 사는 영리한 돌고래에 관한 이야기였어.
B: That sounds exciting! Did your parents watch it with you? 정말 흥미롭네! 부모님도 같이 보셨어?
A: Yes, they did. The dolphin had shiny, smooth skin.
응, 같이 봤어. 돌고래는 반짝반짝하고 매끈한 피부를 가지고 있었어.
B: Wow, that's amazing! 와, 정말 놀랍다!

### Challenge

I found a deep hole in the yard. My parent said to be careful. They are always so clever about keeping our skin safe. 마당에서 깊은 구멍을 발견했다. 우리 부모님이 조심하라고 하셨다. 그들은 항상 우리 피부를 안전하게 지키는 데 매우 영리하시다.

## DAY 137

### Step 2

If it rains, we will stay inside. 비가 오면 우리는 안에 있을 것이다.
Where is the restroom? 화장실이 어디에 있니?
I hurt my finger. 손가락을 다쳤다.
The tree is very tall. 나무가 매우 크다.
The fruit is fresh. 과일이 신선하다.

### Step 3

A: If you need to go, the restroom is over there. 가야 한다면 화장실은 저기에 있어.
B: Thanks! I'll go in a minute. 고마워! 곧 갈게.
A: Look at this tree. It's so big! 이 나무 좀 봐. 정말 커!
B: Yes, and the air here feels fresh. 응, 그리고 여기 공기가 신선해.
A: Ouch, I hurt my finger. 아야, 손가락을 다쳤어.
B: Be careful next time! 다음 번엔 조심해!

### Challenge

If you need the restroom, it's near the tree. I hurt my finger climbing it. The air feels so fresh today.
화장실이 필요하면 나무 근처에 있어. 나무를 오르다가 손가락을 다쳤어. 오늘 공기가 정말 신선하게 느껴진다.

## DAY 138

### Step 2

He is very tall. 그는 매우 키가 크다.
Her husband is a chef. 그녀의 남편은 요리사이다.
I need to get a new phone. 나는 새 전화기를 사야 한다.
These pants are too tight. 이 바지는 너무 꽉 낀다.
She loves to teach. 그녀는 가르치는 것을 좋아한다.

### Step 3

A: Your husband is very tall! 네 남편 정말 키가 크다!
B: Yes, he is. He plays basketball. 응, 맞아. 그는 농구를 해.
A: Where did he get those pants? 그는 그 바지를 어디서 샀어?
B: He got them from the store downtown. 시내 가게에서 샀어.
A: Does he teach basketball? 그는 농구를 가르치니?
B: Yes, he loves to teach kids. 응, 그는 아이들을 가르치는 걸 좋아해.

### Challenge

My dad is very tall. He bought new pants today. He will teach me how to play basketball.
내 아빠는 매우 키가 크다. 오늘 새 바지를 사셨다. 그는 나에게 농구하는 법을 가르쳐줄 것이다.

## DAY 139

### Step 2

The book is on the table. 책이 탁자 위에 있다.
Hold my hand. 내 손을 잡아.
The floor is wet. 바닥이 젖어 있다.
Stand in line. 줄을 서.
I ride my bicycle to school. 나는 자전거를 타고 학교에 간다.

### Step 3

A: Can you put the book on the table? 책을 탁자 위에 올려줄래?
B: Sure, I'll do that now. 물론, 지금 할게.
A: Hold on, is the table wet? 잠깐만, 탁자가 젖어 있니?
B: Yes, it is. Let me dry it first. 응, 그래. 먼저 닦을게.
A: Do you see the line of bicycles outside? 밖에 자전거 줄 보이니?
B: Yes, they're all parked in a row. 응, 줄 지어 주차되어 있어.

### Challenge

I saw a bicycle on the sidewalk. I tried to hold it, but the seat was wet. There was a long line of bikes next to it. 보도에서 자전거를 봤다. 자전거를 잡아보려 했지만, 시트가 젖어 있었다. 그 옆에 자전거들이 길게 줄지어 있었다.

## DAY 140

### Step 2

The family is very poor. 그 가족은 매우 가난하다.
The wall needs painting. 벽은 페인트칠이 필요하다.
Did you pass the test? 시험에 합격했니?
The king wore a crown. 왕은 왕관을 썼다.
Be aware of the danger. 위험을 조심해.

### Step 3

A: The family in the story is very poor. 이야기 속 가족은 매우 가난해.
B: Yes, it made me sad to read about them. 응, 그들 이야기를 읽으니 슬펐어.
A: Did you see the crown on the wall? 벽에 있는 왕관 봤어?
B: Yes, it looks so shiny and bright. 응, 정말 반짝이고 밝아 보여.
A: They had to pass through many dangers to get it. 그들은 그것을 얻기 위해 많은 위험을 겪어야 했어.
B: Yes, the adventure was full of danger! 응, 모험은 위험으로 가득했어!

### Challenge

I read a story about a poor boy. He found a crown behind a wall. He had to pass through danger to get it. 가난한 소년에 대한 이야기를 읽었다. 그는 벽 뒤에서 왕관을 발견했다. 그는 그것을 얻기 위해 위험을 지나야 했다.

## DAY 141

### Step 2

The sun is shining. 태양이 빛나고 있다.
My foot hurts. 발이 아프다.
We need to save money. 우리는 돈을 절약해야 한다.
Ask me anything. 무엇이든 물어봐.
Her dress is red. 그녀의 드레스는 빨간색이다.

### Step 3

A: The sun is very bright today. 오늘 태양이 매우 밝다.
B: Yes, it's a beautiful day. My foot is sore. 응, 아름다운 날이야. 발이 아파.
A: You should rest it. We need to save more money. 쉬어야 해. 우리는 더 많은 돈을 절약해야 해.
B: I agree. Can I ask you a question? 동의해. 질문해도 돼?
A: Sure, go ahead. 물론, 해봐.
B: Where did you buy your red shoes? 빨간 신발 어디서 샀어?

### Challenge

I played outside in the sun today. I hurt my foot and needed help. My friend asked, "Is your foot red?" before helping me. 오늘 햇빛 아래서 놀았다. 발을 다쳐서 도움이 필요했다. 친구가 "발이 빨간색이니?"라고 묻고 나서 도와줬다.

## DAY 142

### Step 2

The door is open. 문이 열려 있다.
I will never forget you. 나는 결코 너를 잊지 않을 것이다.
This is the way home. 이것이 집으로 가는 길이다.
She works at a hospital. 그녀는 병원에서 일한다.
Please close the window. 창문을 닫아주세요.

### Step 3

A: Can you close the door, please? 문을 닫아줄래?
B: Sure, I'll do it now. 물론, 지금 할게.
A: I hope we never have to go to the hospital again. 다시는 병원에 가지 않기를 바라.
B: Yes, I agree. It was a scary experience. 응, 동의해. 무서운 경험이었어.
A: Do you know the way to the park? 공원으로 가는 길 알아?
B: Yes, I can guide you there. 응, 내가 안내할게.

### Challenge

I went to the hospital today. The doctor said never to close the door completely. It must stay open for safety. 오늘 병원에 갔다. 의사가 문을 완전히 닫지 말라고 했다. 안전을 위해 문이 열려 있어야 한다고 하셨다.

## DAY 143

### Step 2

You can stay here. 여기 머물러도 돼.
Pizza is my favorite food. 피자는 내가 가장 좋아하는 음식이다.
They went to hunt in the forest. 그들은 숲에서 사냥을 갔다.
He has a good sense of humor. 그는 유머 감각이 좋다.
I need the scissors. 나는 가위가 필요하다.

### Step 3

A: I had to stay home today. 오늘 집에 있어야 했어.
B: Really? What did you do at home? 정말? 집에서 뭐 했어?
A: I watched my favorite show. It was about a treasure hunt.
내가 좋아하는 쇼를 봤어. 보물찾기에 관한 내용이었어.
B: That sounds fun! Did it have a lot of humor? 재미있겠다! 유머도 많았어?
A: Yes, it was very funny. One character even tried to cut a rope with scissors.
응, 정말 웃겼어. 한 캐릭터가 가위로 밧줄을 자르려고 했어.
B: That sounds interesting. 흥미롭게 들리네.

### Challenge

I stayed at my friend's house today. We watched my favorite show about a lion who likes to hunt. The humor was funny, and we used scissors to make paper animals. 오늘 친구 집에서 머물렀다. 우리는 사냥을 좋아하는 사자에 관한 내가 가장 좋아하는 프로그램을 보았다. 유머가 재미있었고, 가위를 사용해 종이 동물을 만들었다.

## DAY 144

### Step 2

The cat is hiding behind the curtain. 고양이는 커튼 뒤에 숨고 있다.
Please sit on this side. 이쪽에 앉아주세요.
He is at the store. 그는 가게에 있다.
She has a beautiful smile. 그녀는 아름다운 미소를 가지고 있다.
I like this song. 나는 이 노래를 좋아한다.

### Step 3

A: Look behind the curtain. 커튼 뒤를 봐.
B: There's nothing there. It's just a wall. 거기 아무것도 없어. 그냥 벽이야.
A: Did you check the other side? 다른 쪽 확인해봤어?
B: Yes, I looked at both sides. 응, 양쪽 다 봤어.
A: Can you smile for the picture? 사진 찍을 때 미소 지어줄래?
B: Sure! What song should we play while we take the picture? 물론! 찍는 동안 무슨 노래 틀까?

### Challenge

I found my book behind the chair. It was at the side of the room. I smiled when I heard my favorite song playing. 의자 뒤에서 책을 찾았다. 방 한쪽에 있었다. 내가 가장 좋아하는 노래가 나올 때 미소 지었다.

## DAY 145

### Step 2

Please stand up. 일어나 주세요.
The park is across the street. 공원은 길 건너편에 있다.
I'm glad you came. 네가 와서 기뻐.
Today is my birthday. 오늘은 내 생일이다.
The price is double. 가격이 두 배이다.

### Step 3

A: Can you stand here for a moment? 잠시 여기 서줄래?
B: Sure, what do you need? 물론, 뭐 필요한 거 있어?
A: Look across the street. Do you see that sign? 길 건너편 봐봐. 저 표지판 보이니?
B: Yes, I see it. What does it say? 응, 보여. 뭐라고 쓰여 있어?
A: I'm so glad you're here for my birthday. 네가 내 생일에 와서 정말 기뻐.
B: Me too! Let's have double the fun today! 나도! 오늘 두 배로 즐기자!

### Challenge

Today was my birthday, and I was very glad. I got a double scoop of ice cream. My friend and I stood across from each other, eating ice cream. 오늘은 내 생일이어서 정말 기뻤다. 아이스크림 두 스쿱을 받았다. 친구와 나는 서로 마주 보고 서서 아이스크림을 먹었다.

## DAY 146

### Step 2

I'm very tired. 나는 매우 피곤하다.
We went for a cycle ride. 우리는 자전거를 타러 갔다.
The classroom is clean. 교실은 깨끗하다.
I love the sea. 나는 바다를 사랑한다.
He is a hero. 그는 영웅이다.

### Step 3

A: The sea is very calm today. 오늘 바다가 매우 잔잔하다.
B: Yes, it's perfect for sailing. 응, 항해하기에 완벽해.
A: Did you finish the cycling race? 자전거 경주를 끝냈니?
B: Yes, it was very challenging. 응, 매우 도전적이었어.
A: Who is your favorite hero? 네가 가장 좋아하는 영웅은 누구야?
B: I like the one who saved the classroom from the fire. 나는 교실을 불에서 구한 사람을 좋아해.

### Challenge

I was very happy in the classroom today. We learned about the sea and its creatures. My hero is a diver who explores the ocean. 오늘 교실에서 매우 행복했다. 우리는 바다와 그 생물들에 대해 배웠다. 나의 영웅은 바다를 탐험하는 잠수부다.

## DAY 147

### Step 2

I like apples, but I don't like bananas. 나는 사과를 좋아하지만, 바나나는 좋아하지 않는다.
Her story is true. 그녀의 이야기는 사실이다.
Can you speak louder? 좀 더 크게 말해줄래?
We had supper at 7 P.M. 우리는 저녁을 7시에 먹었다.
The house is big. 그 집은 크다.

### Step 3

A: Is it true that you speak three languages? 너가 세 개 언어를 말한다는 게 사실이야?
B: Yes, it is, but I'm still learning. 응, 사실이야, 하지만 아직 배우고 있어.
A: Are you coming for supper tonight? 오늘 밤 저녁 먹으러 올 거야?
B: I'd love to, but I have to help at home. 그러고 싶지만, 집에서 도와야 해.
A: Can I visit your house this weekend? 이번 주말에 네 집에 가도 될까?
B: Sure, that sounds great! 물론이지, 좋아!

### Challenge

I wanted to play outside, but I had to do homework. It is true that I love to speak with my friends. After supper, I stayed at my house. 나는 밖에서 놀고 싶었지만, 숙제를 해야 했다. 친구들과 이야기하는 것을 좋아한다는 것은 사실이다. 저녁 식사 후에 집에 머물렀다.

## DAY 148

### Step 2

The cat is sleeping on the bed. 고양이가 침대 위에서 자고 있다.
I will fry the chicken. 나는 닭고기를 튀길 것이다.
I enjoy reading books. 나는 책 읽는 것을 즐긴다.
She likes to paint. 그녀는 그림 그리기를 좋아한다.
Our team will win. 우리 팀이 이길 것이다.

### Step 3

A: The bed is too soft. 침대가 너무 부드러워.
B: I like it that way. Are you going to fry the fish? 나는 그게 좋아. 생선을 튀길 거야?
A: Yes, it tastes better that way. Do you enjoy movies? 응, 그렇게 하면 더 맛있어. 영화 보는 거 좋아해?
B: Yes, especially comedies. She loves to paint. 응, 특히 코미디. 그녀는 그림 그리기를 좋아해.
A: She's very talented. I hope we win the game. 그녀는 매우 재능이 있어. 우리가 경기를 이겼으면 좋겠어.
B: Me too. 나도 그래.

### Challenge

I jumped on my bed this morning. My mom fried some eggs, and I enjoyed breakfast. Later, I painted a picture and won a small prize at school. 오늘 아침 침대에서 뛰어놀았다. 엄마가 계란을 튀겨주셨고, 나는 아침을 즐겼다. 나중에 그림을 그리고 학교에서 작은 상을 받았다.

## DAY 149

### Step 2

She wore a red skirt. 그녀는 빨간 치마를 입었다.
The instructions are clear. 지침이 명확하다.
How are you today? 오늘 어때?
I don't eat much meat. 나는 고기를 많이 먹지 않는다.
The bedroom is upstairs. 침실은 위층에 있다.

### Step 3

A: Do you like my new skirt? 내 새 치마 어때?
B: Yes, it's very pretty on you. 응, 너한테 잘 어울려.
A: Thank you! Are you cooking meat for dinner? 고마워! 저녁으로 고기를 요리할 거야?
B: Yes, we're having steak tonight. 응, 오늘 저녁에 스테이크를 먹을 거야.
A: Can you help me clear the table? 식탁 좀 치우는 것 도와줄래?
B: Sure, then I'll go to my bedroom to rest. 물론, 그리고 나서 내 침실로 가서 쉴게.

### Challenge

I wore my favorite skirt today. It's clear that you like it too. We talked about our favorite meat dishes in my bedroom. 오늘 내가 가장 좋아하는 치마를 입었다. 너도 그걸 좋아한다는 게 명확하다. 우리는 내 침실에서 가장 좋아하는 고기 요리에 대해 이야기했다.

## DAY 150

### Step 2

I live in Seoul. 나는 서울에 산다.
This game is fun. 이 게임은 재미있다.
The helicopter is flying overhead. 헬리콥터가 머리 위로 날고 있다.
I'm very hungry. 나는 매우 배고프다.
She is in elementary school. 그녀는 초등학교에 다닌다.

### Step 3

A: Do you live near the park? 공원 근처에 사니?
B: Yes, it's a fun place to visit. 응, 방문하기 재미있는 곳이야.
A: Have you ever seen a helicopter up close? 가까이서 헬리콥터 본 적 있어?
B: No, but I think it would be exciting. 아니, 하지만 흥미로울 것 같아.
A: Are you hungry? Let's eat something. 배고프니? 뭐 좀 먹자.
B: Yes, I'm so hungry. What's for dinner? 응, 너무 배고파. 저녁은 뭐야?

### Challenge

I live in a fun neighborhood. Today, I saw a helicopter flying overhead. After that, I felt hungry and ate lunch at my elementary school. 나는 재미있는 동네에 산다. 오늘 헬리콥터가 머리 위로 나는 것을 보았다. 그 후, 배고파서 초등학교에서 점심을 먹었다.

## DAY 151

### Step 2

Can you tell me a story? 이야기 하나 해줄래?
My hand is cold. 내 손이 차가워.
Add some salt to the soup. 수프에 소금을 좀 넣어.
I need some money. 나는 돈이 좀 필요해.
The car is in good condition. 차 상태가 좋다.

### Step 3

A: Can you tell me what happened? 무슨 일이 있었는지 말해줄래?
B: Sure, I'll explain everything. 물론, 다 설명해줄게.
A: Do you need a hand with that? 그거 도와줄까?
B: Yes, please. Can you pass the salt? 응, 부탁해. 소금 좀 건네줄래?
A: Here you go. Do you have enough money for lunch? 여기 있어. 점심 살 돈 있어?
B: Yes, I do. Thanks for asking. 응, 있어. 물어봐줘서 고마워.

### Challenge

My mom told me to wash my hands before dinner. She asked for salt to add to the soup. I saved my money under the condition that I could buy a toy later. 엄마가 저녁 먹기 전에 손을 씻으라고 하셨다. 엄마는 수프에 넣을 소금을 요청하셨다. 나는 나중에 장난감을 살 수 있다는 조건으로 돈을 저축했다.

## DAY 152

### Step 2

The sun is very bright. 태양이 매우 밝다.
This is a nice place. 여기는 좋은 장소이다.
The dolphin is swimming. 돌고래가 헤엄치고 있다.
I love watching snow fall. 나는 눈이 내리는 것을 보는 것을 좋아한다.
The street is busy. 거리는 분주하다.

### Step 3

A: The sun is so bright today. 오늘 태양이 정말 밝다.
B: Yes, it's a perfect day to go to the beach. 응, 해변에 가기 완벽한 날이야.
A: I love that place where we can see dolphins. 나는 우리가 돌고래를 볼 수 있는 그곳이 좋아.
B: Me too! They are so playful. 나도! 그들은 정말 장난꾸러기야.
A: Did you see the snow last night? 어젯밤에 눈 봤어?
B: Yes, it covered the entire street. 응, 온 거리를 덮었어.

### Challenge

I visited a bright place today near the beach. I saw a dolphin jumping out of the water. On the way home, snow started to fall on the street. 오늘 해변 근처의 밝은 곳을 방문했다. 물 밖으로 뛰어오르는 돌고래를 보았다. 집에 가는 길에 눈이 거리에 내리기 시작했다.

## DAY 153

### Step 2

They will arrive soon. 그들은 곧 도착할 것이다.
I have a thirst for knowledge. 나는 지식에 대한 갈증이 있다.
Here is a present for you. 여기에 너를 위한 선물이 있다.
Don't break the glass. 유리잔을 깨뜨리지 마.
The baby is sleeping. 아기가 자고 있다.

### Step 3

A: What time will you arrive? 몇 시에 도착할 거야?
B: I'll arrive at 3 P.M. 오후 3시에 도착할 거야.
A: I feel a strong thirst for coffee right now. 지금 커피가 너무 마시고 싶어.
B: No problem! I will get some on the way. 문제 없어! 가는 길에 사올게.
A: Did you get the present for the baby? 아기 선물 샀어?
B: Yes, I hope it doesn't break. 응, 깨지지 않길 바라.

### Challenge

I arrived at the party and felt a thirst. I gave a present to the baby. Be careful not to break it.
파티에 도착해서 목이 말랐다. 아기에게 선물을 주었다. 그것을 깨지 않도록 조심해.

## DAY 154

### Step 2

The clothes are dry. 옷이 말랐다.
She is very pretty. 그녀는 매우 예쁘다.
What is your age? 나이가 몇 살이에요?
Hello, how are you? 안녕하세요, 잘 지내세요?
I like to read books. 나는 책 읽는 것을 좋아한다.

### Step 3

A: Hello! How are you today? 안녕! 오늘 어때?
B: Hi! I'm good, thank you. 안녕! 좋아, 고마워.
A: Have you read this book? 이 책 읽어봤어?
B: Yes, it's pretty interesting. 응, 꽤 흥미로워.
A: Your skin looks dry. Do you need lotion? 네 피부가 건조해 보여. 로션 필요해?
B: No, thanks. At my age, it's normal. 아니, 고마워. 내 나이에는 정상이에요.

### Challenge

Hello! Today, I read a pretty storybook. Even at my age, I still enjoy it. The pages were dry and crisp.
안녕! 오늘 나는 예쁜 동화책을 읽었다. 내 나이에도 여전히 그것을 즐긴다. 페이지는 건조하고 바삭했다.

## DAY 155

### Step 2

Can you help me find my keys? 내 열쇠 찾는 것 좀 도와줄래?
The table is set. 식탁이 차려졌다.
She works as a teacher. 그녀는 교사로 일한다.
Plants grow with sunlight. 식물은 햇빛으로 자란다.
Open your mouth wide. 입을 크게 벌려.

### Step 3

A: Did you find your book? 책 찾았어?
B: Yes, it was on the table. 응, 탁자 위에 있었어.
A: Great! You read as much as you can. 잘했어! 최대한 많이 읽어.
B: Yes, I want to grow smarter. 응, 더 똑똑해지고 싶어.
A: Look at that plant! It grew so tall. 저 식물 좀 봐! 정말 많이 자랐어.
B: Wow! It almost reaches my mouth. 와! 거의 내 입까지 닿겠어.

### Challenge

I found my book on the table. As I grow older, I read more and more. The story made my mouth smile.
탁자 위에서 책을 찾았다. 나이가 들수록, 더 많이 읽는다. 그 이야기는 내 입에 미소를 짓게 했다.

## DAY 156

### Step 2

Hang your coat here. 코트를 여기 걸어.
Please wait for me. 제발 나를 기다려줘.
How do you use this? 이것을 어떻게 사용하니?
Which airline are you flying with? 어느 항공사를 이용하니?
Something is wrong. 뭔가 잘못됐다.

### Step 3

A: Can you hang up your coat? 코트 걸어줄래?
B: Sure, I'll do it now. 물론, 지금 할게.
A: We need to wait for the next bus. 다음 버스를 기다려야 해.
B: Okay, I can wait a bit longer. 알겠어, 좀 더 기다릴 수 있어.
A: Which airline did you use for your trip? 여행에 어느 항공사를 이용했어?
B: I used SkyAir, but they got my luggage wrong. SkyAir를 이용했는데, 짐을 잘못 보냈어.

### Challenge

I hang my coat by the door. We had to wait for our flight because the airline had the wrong time. I used my phone to check for updates. 문 옆에 코트를 걸었다. 항공사가 시간을 잘못 알려줘서 비행기를 기다려야 했다. 업데이트를 확인하려고 전화기를 사용했다.

## DAY 157

### Step 2

I like to write stories. 나는 이야기를 쓰는 것을 좋아한다.

Do you have a pen? 펜 있어?

The baby is crying. 아기가 울고 있다.

The kid is playing outside. 아이가 밖에서 놀고 있다.

The mountain is very high. 산이 매우 높다.

### Step 3

A: Did you write your homework? 숙제 썼어?

B: Yes, I finished it yesterday. 응, 어제 끝냈어.

A: Do you have any plans for today? 오늘 계획 있어?

B: I have to watch my little brother. 내 동생을 봐야 해.

A: Why is that kid crying? 저 아이는 왜 울고 있어?

B: I think he lost his toy. He was so high up on the slide.

아마도 장난감을 잃어버린 것 같아. 그는 미끄럼틀 위에서 너무 높이 올라갔어.

### Challenge

I wrote a story about a kid today. He lost his toy and began to cry. His dad picked him up high to make him feel better. 오늘 아이에 대한 이야기를 썼다. 그는 장난감을 잃어버리고 울기 시작했다. 그의 아빠가 기분을 나아지게 하기 위해 높이 들어 올렸다.

## DAY 158

### Step 2

It may rain tomorrow. 내일 비가 올지도 모른다.

Let's go out. 나가자.

I am very busy today. 나는 오늘 매우 바쁘다.

Come here, please. 여기로 와주세요.

Choose your favorite color. 좋아하는 색을 고르세요.

### Step 3

A: You may want to go out for a walk. 산책하러 나가고 싶을지도 몰라.

B: I might, but I'm very busy today. 그럴지도 모르지만, 오늘은 매우 바빠.

A: If you finish early, come here. 일찍 끝나면 여기로 와.

B: Okay, I'll try my best. 알겠어, 최선을 다할게.

A: What do you want for lunch? You can choose. 점심 뭐 먹고 싶어? 고를 수 있어.

B: I may choose a sandwich. 샌드위치를 고를지도 몰라.

### Challenge

I may go out to play later. I am busy with homework right now. When I'm done, I will choose a game to play here. 나중에 나가서 놀지도 몰라. 지금은 숙제로 바빠. 끝나면 여기서 할 게임을 고를 거야.

## DAY 159

### Step 2

They are my friends. 그들은 내 친구들이다.
She is always happy. 그녀는 항상 행복하다.
Do you have a question? 질문 있니?
Let me show you something. 내가 뭔가를 보여줄게.
Thank you for your help. 도와줘서 고마워.

### Step 3

A: They always have good ideas. 그들은 항상 좋은 아이디어를 가지고 있어.
B: Yes, I learn a lot from them. 응, 나는 그들에게서 많은 것을 배워.
A: Did they ask you a question today? 오늘 그들이 너에게 질문했니?
B: Yes, they asked me to show my project. 응, 그들이 내 프로젝트를 보여달라고 했어.
A: That sounds interesting! How did it go? 흥미롭게 들리네! 어떻게 됐어?
B: It went well. They thanked me for my work. 잘 됐어. 그들이 내 일을 고마워했어.

### Challenge

They always ask good questions in class. The teacher likes to show them the answers. I want to thank them for being helpful. 그들은 항상 수업에서 좋은 질문을 한다. 선생님은 그들에게 답을 보여주기를 좋아하신다. 그들이 도움이 되어 고맙다.

## DAY 160

### Step 2

Please focus on your work. 당신의 일에 집중하세요.
I like to take a bath. 나는 목욕하는 것을 좋아한다.
I received a letter. 나는 편지를 받았다.
The movie was exciting. 그 영화는 흥미로웠다.
My uncle is very funny. 내 삼촌은 매우 재미있다.

### Step 3

A: Can you focus on your homework now? 지금 숙제에 집중할 수 있니?
B: Yes, I'll start in a minute. 응, 곧 시작할게.
A: Did you take a bath today? 오늘 목욕했니?
B: Yes, I did. It was very relaxing. 응, 했어. 매우 편안했어.
A: Have you written a letter to your uncle? 삼촌에게 편지를 썼니?
B: Not yet, but I'll do it after watching a movie. 아직, 하지만 영화를 보고 나서 쓸 거야.

### Challenge

I need to focus on my homework. Afterward, I will take a bath. My uncle sent me a letter about a new movie we can watch together. 나는 숙제에 집중해야 한다. 그 후에 목욕을 할 것이다. 삼촌이 우리가 함께 볼 수 있는 새 영화에 대해 편지를 보내셨다.

# 진짜 영어실력을 위한 초등 VOCA800

©정승익

초판 1쇄 인쇄 | 2024년 7월 8일

지은이 | 정승익
편집인 | 김진호
디자인 | 김다현
마케팅 | 네버기브업

펴낸곳 | 네버기브업
ISBN | 979-11-987748-0-4

이메일 | nevernevergiveup2024@gmail.com